I0069996

Takaful and Mutual Insurance

Takaful and Mutual Insurance

Alternative Approaches to Managing Risks

Serap O. Gönülal, Editor

THE WORLD BANK
Washington, D.C.

© 2013 International Bank for Reconstruction and Development / The World Bank
1818 H Street NW
Washington DC 20433
Telephone: 202-473-1000
Internet: www.worldbank.org

Some rights reserved

1 2 3 4   15 14 13 12

This work is a product of the staff of The World Bank with external contributions. Note that The World Bank does not necessarily own each component of the content included in the work. The World Bank therefore does not warrant that the use of the content contained in the work will not infringe on the rights of third parties. The risk of claims resulting from such infringement rests solely with you.

The findings, interpretations, and conclusions expressed in this work do not necessarily reflect the views of The World Bank, its Board of Executive Directors, or the governments they represent. The World Bank does not guarantee the accuracy of the data included in this work. The boundaries, colors, denominations, and other information shown on any map in this work do not imply any judgment on the part of The World Bank concerning the legal status of any territory or the endorsement or acceptance of such boundaries.

Nothing herein shall constitute or be considered to be a limitation upon or waiver of the privileges and immunities of The World Bank, all of which are specifically reserved.

Rights and Permissions

This work is available under the Creative Commons Attribution 3.0 Unported license (CC BY 3.0) http://creativecommons.org/licenses/by/3.0. Under the Creative Commons Attribution license, you are free to copy, distribute, transmit, and adapt this work, including for commercial purposes, under the following conditions:

Attribution—Please cite the work as follows: Gönülal, Serap O. 2013. *Takaful and Mutual Insurance: Alternative Approaches to Managing Risks.* Washington, DC: World Bank. DOI 10.1596/978-0-8213-9724-4. License: Creative Commons Attribution CC BY 3.0

Translations—If you create a translation of this work, please add the following disclaimer along with the attribution: *This translation was not created by The World Bank and should not be considered an official World Bank translation. The World Bank shall not be liable for any content or error in this translation.*

All queries on rights and licenses should be addressed to the Office of the Publisher, The World Bank, 1818 H Street NW, Washington, DC 20433, USA; fax: 202-522-2625; e-mail: pubrights@worldbank.org.

ISBN (paper): 978-0-8213-9724-4
ISBN (electronic): 978-0-8213-9725-1
DOI: 10.1596/978-0-8213-9724-4

Cover photo: © Curt Carnemark/World Bank.
Library of Congress Cataloging-in-Publication Data has been requested.

Contents

Box

Figures

Tables

Foreword

Access to insurance, as part of a broad range of essential financial services, is especially important for poor households in order to smooth consumption, build assets, absorb shocks, and manage risks associated with irregular and unpredictable income. Without access to good formal insurance services, the poor depend on less reliable and often far more expensive informal sector mechanisms.

Yet, in many majority Islamic countries, accessing and using insurance products has been quite limited, as many Muslims avoid such services over concerns about *riba* (interest), *gharar* (uncertainty and ambiguity in contracts), and *maysir* (speculative risk), among other factors. Takaful insurance products are emerging as a central part of the Shariah-compliant family of financial services, helping meet insurance needs in ways that are consistent with the local norms and beliefs of many majority Islamic countries.

Takaful has been developing steadily since the first Shariah-compliant insurer was founded in 1979, based on a Shariah-compliant cooperative model resembling mutual insurance. This is based on a group of participants donating funds into a pool that members can then use in the event of specified unfavorable contingencies. While practitioners have applied varying business models and standardization remains a challenge, many policy makers recognize the potential of takaful to expand financial inclusion and have aimed to promote the industry with supportive legislation and effective regulation. The response has been strong, with premiums growing about 30 percent (inflation adjusted) annually between 2007 and 2010, reaching US$8.3 billion. This robust performance is expected to continue, based on substantial latent demand in Muslim majority countries and improvements in the industry, including better distribution capabilities.

In support of continued progress in the takaful market, the World Bank's Non-Banking Financial Institutions Group is launching the Takaful Development Program. The initiative aims to facilitate capacity building and knowledge sharing, as well as promote sound regulation, financial literacy, and financial inclusion. We hope that this book will move the takaful agenda forward, fostering wide-ranging discussions on the challenges and opportunities in developing takaful, and highlighting examples of what has worked and what has not. Concerted effort by all stakeholders will be needed to expand access and develop takaful further, improving the ability of many poor households to cope with adversity and enhancing well-being.

Mahmoud Mohieldin
Managing Director
The World Bank

Acknowledgments

This book sheds light on a particular segment of the insurance industry that has strong potential to reach individuals who have little awareness of the benefits of traditional insurance and corners of the world where new forms of insurance may improve the quality of life and economic well-being of many people.

This has been an exceedingly interesting experience in which I learned to develop takaful structures using the existing models prevalent around the world, while simultaneously keeping the sharia rules. Based on these fundamentals, I have searched for ways to expand the boundaries of insurance for people with little awareness of insurance concepts. If a system compatible with their culture is introduced, the potential benefits are enormous.

I owe a lot to my director and my previous manager, Loic Chiquier, who encouraged me to undertake comprehensive work on this issue and to turn that work into a book. I was hesitant at the start, as the task of developing tools that could reach unpenetrated segments of the global population loomed so large. I was uncomfortable with the belief that there are either old or bold pilots, but there are rarely old *and* bold pilots—a golden rule of bureaucracy.

However, emboldened by their encouragement and feeling the excitement of exploring uncharted territory, I embarked on this journey accompanied by a highly competent crew who provided valuable guidance. Building a dedicated team was essential to achieving a meaningful outcome, and I owe many thanks to the authors who provided their generous support to the project. In particular, the assistance of Zainal Abidin Mohd Kassim and Hassan Scott Odierno is gratefully acknowledged. Without their support, this rather challenging, if not turbulent, journey might have lacked both substance and spirit. In addition, I would like to thank the meritorious deans of the insurance world, Dawood Yousef Taylor and Rodney Lester, who provided excellent finishing touches in the review process. In particular, Rodney improved the writing style of the book and eliminated obscure structures, making the writing more fluid. Finally, Nick Goulder merits special thanks for his splendid work, expertise, and command of both the conventional and unconventional sides of the insurance realm. He was the one who helped to clarify and summarize the ideas.

Specific debt is owed to my manager, Michel Noel, who gave me every possible support and removed every obstacle to finalizing the book, particularly when we were working around the clock.

Uloaku Oyewole deserves special mention, as without her support this time-consuming job would have much more difficult; her dedication and friendship were encouraging throughout the process. I thank Elizabeth Forsyth for her excellent editing of the final manuscript; her efforts turned the book into a crystal clear gem. And I especially thank my dear spouse, Ali Umit Gönülal, who has always encouraged me by telling me that all people would choose to cover their property and life if suitable insurance tools were made available for them and that this would enhance the quality of their lives.

In sum, I acknowledge a debt of gratitude that can never be repaid to all those people who shared their knowledge and wisdom with me. I hope this book will convey their dedication and passion and open a new chapter of discussion and understanding that will contribute to the insurance world, leading, eventually, to positive outcomes.

About the Authors

Alberto G. Brugnoni, a former director with Merrill Lynch Bank, is an independent Islamic finance adviser. In the mid-1980s, he pioneered some of the first Islamic transactions in Europe, and in September 1986, he attended the conference launching Islamic finance in the United States, hosted by the State Department in Washington, DC. The conference was attended by Ahmed al-Naggar and moderated by Ibrahim Shihata, Chief Counsel of the World Bank. In 1997, he released "Pilot Project Genoardo," a seminal study for the establishment of a Mediterranean Development Bank based on sharia-compliant principles. This was followed in 2006 by the first real estate sharia-compliant transaction in Italy and a project for the rehabilitation of Syrian landfills using Islamic finance instruments. In September 2011, he successfully structured the first syndicated Islamic facility in the Russian Federation for Ak Bars Bank. The transaction was named "Europe Deal of the Year" by the *Islamic Finance News* and was the cover story of the March 2012 edition of *Business Islamica* magazine. At present, he is based in Kabul with the remit to launching Takaful in Afghanistan.

Brugnoni is the founder and managing director of ASSAIF (www .assaif.org), which is possibly the oldest Islamic finance consultancy in Europe that provides strategic institutional advisory services worldwide to governments, central banks, public and semi-public institutions, and regional and local authorities. Brugnoni regularly chairs some of the major Islamic finance forums worldwide and gives presentations in Arabic, English, French, and Italian. He is president of the Advisory Council of the World Congress of Muslim Philanthropists.

Serap O. Gönülal has 28 years of experience in insurance and reinsurance market development, regulation, and supervision. Before joining the World Bank in 2000, she worked in the Turkish Treasury in the Insurance Regulatory and Supervisory Body, dealing directly with regulating and supervising insurance companies, reinsurance companies, and intermediaries. She was the project coordinator and implementer for the standardization and development of the actuarial profession in Turkey and set up the Turkish Catastrophic Insurance Pool after the earthquake of 1999.

She has written numerous reports and papers on the subject of insurance regulation and supervision with the World Bank and is currently promoting motor third-party liability insurance, risk-based supervision, Solvency II, bancassurance, and takaful/Islamic insurance in developing countries and emerging economies. She has conducted financial sector assessments in many countries as part of the World Bank–International Monetary Fund Financial Sector Assessment Program. Before 2000, she represented the Turkish Treasury on several committees of the International Association of Insurance Supervisors.

Gönülal has written numerous reports and technical papers on the subject of insurance regulation. She coauthored *Earthquake Insurance in Turkey*, published by the World Bank in 2006. She contributed to *Protecting the Poor: A Micro Insurance Compendium*, published by the Consultative Group to Assist the Poor and the International Labour Organisation in 2008. She wrote several chapters and edited *Motor Third-Party Liability Insurance*, published by the World Bank in 2009.

Zainal Abidin Mohd Kassim is senior partner at Actuarial Partners Consulting Sdn Bhd, an actuarial consulting company based in Kuala Lumpur, Malaysia. He has been a consulting actuary with the company since 1982. Prior to joining the company, he worked at Prudential in the London office. His 30 years of consulting experience span the full spectrum of actuarial services, including life and casualty insurance, family and casualty takaful, retirement benefits, and investment consulting.

In 1985, he was appointed as actuary to the first takaful operator in Malaysia. He has written many articles and spoken at numerous conferences globally on his experience with the development of takaful. He has also been involved in strategic analysis and setup of takaful and retakaful operators in Africa, Asia, and Europe. As one of the first actuaries working in takaful and retakaful, he has been on the forefront of the technical development of various takaful contracts and has interacted with many sharia scholars on the practice of takaful.

Kassim is a fellow of the Institute of Actuaries of the United Kingdom and an associate of the Society of Actuaries in the United States. He graduated in 1978 from City University in London with a First Class Honors degree in actuarial science. He is a past president of the Actuarial Society of Malaysia.

Ismail Mahbob joined MNRB Retakaful Berhad—the first Malaysian retakaful company—in 2007 as president and chief executive officer. He entered the industry in 1977 as an insurance broker. Since then, he has held senior management positions in various insurance and reinsurance companies. Prior to MNRB Retakaful, he was senior vice president with Labuan Reinsurance (L) Ltd. with responsibilities in three main areas: (a) underwriting markets in Indonesia, the Indian subcontinent, the Middle East, and Africa; (b) overseeing the company's business involvement at Lloyd's; and (c) heading the Retakaful Division (window).

Mahbob is active in industry associations and activities and spearheads many of their initiatives. He is also a frequent speaker at conferences and forums and contributes articles to industry trade magazines.

Hassan Scott Odierno has been a partner with Actuarial Partners Consulting in Malaysia and been involved in takaful since 1996, specializing in life and takaful consulting. He is the appointed actuary for both takaful operators and conventional insurers, extending from Malaysia to Mauritius and Kenya to Hong Kong SAR, China. He has helped local and multinational companies to set up takaful operations, including feasibility studies, product and model development, and business projections in countries such as Bahrain, Indonesia, Malaysia, and Saudi Arabia. He has been involved in merger and acquisition exercises for insurers in economies such as Bahrain; Malaysia; Singapore; Thailand; and Taiwan, China. Odierno is the coauthor of a takaful book, a contributing author to another book, and a frequent author of articles and presentations on takaful. He also advises two universities in Malaysia with regard to their risk management and actuarial science programs.

Sabbir Patel is senior vice president and chief financial officer of the International Cooperative and Mutual Insurance Federation (ICMIF). He joined ICMIF in 1996 and qualified as a chartered certified account (FCCA) in 2001. In 2002, he completed his master's degree at the Institute of Development and Policy Management and holds a Chartered Insurance Institute diploma. In addition to heading the Finance Department, he works closely with new and emerging member organizations.

As vice president and treasurer of Allnations Inc. (www.allnations .coop), he has overseen the restructuring of the organization since 2004 and provided capital support to members in Ecuador, Ghana, and Uruguay.

In addition, Patel has been spearheading ICMIF support to the takaful sector since 2001, including setting up the ICMIF takaful website (www .takaful.coop), issuing the takaful newsletter, coordinating an annual workshop, and assisting the establishment of cooperative-based takaful schemes in developing and developed insurance markets. As a result of these efforts, ICMIF now has 21 takaful operators as member organizations.

Abbreviations

3BL	triple bottom line
AAOIFI	Accounting and Auditing Organization for Islamic Financial Institutions
ICA	International Cooperative Alliance
ICMIF	International Cooperative and Mutual Insurance Federation
IFSB	Islamic Financial Services Board
ILO	International Labour Organisation
IMFI	Islamic microfinance institution
MACIF	Mutuelle Assurance des Commerçants et Industriels de France
MAIF	Mutuelle d'Assurance des Instituteurs de France
MRTT	mortgage-reducing term takaful
NGO	nongovernmental organization
SAB	sharia advisory board
SGAM	Société de Groupe d'Assurance Mutuelle
STM	Syarikat Takaful Malaysia
UN	United Nations

Overview

The joint stock model and the mutual or cooperative model have been the traditional ways of delivering insurance. The takaful model has now emerged as the third leading structure.

Takaful has grown nearly 30 percent annually (2007–10), with premiums in 2010 reaching US$8.3 billion and expected to reach US$12.0 billion in 2012. Strong growth is anticipated to continue. Since insurance itself is a dynamic factor in strengthening stable economic development and since takaful coverage is acceptable to many where traditional insurance products are not, this book explains what takaful is, how it differs from the traditional insurance models, and why fostering it is a worthwhile endeavor.

The book begins by analyzing the main distinctions between the joint stock model and the mutual model:

- Policyholders own the mutual; this is rarely the case for joint stock companies.
- Mutuals mainly write only low-volatility insurance risks; joint stock companies cover the full range of insurance products. There are some exceptions, such as specialist professional indemnity mutuals.
- The joint stock company provides full risk transfer (as long as the company is solvent); the mutual essentially is a risk-sharing mechanism.

- There is some alignment of interest between the mutual and its policy-holders. This is very weak where joint stock companies are concerned.
- Shareholders of joint stock companies look after their own interests when managing their managers. This can be a problem for the policy-holders of a mutual.
- Mutuals do not pay dividends and so in principle should be able to charge lower premiums than joint stock insurers.

Sharia objects to conventional insurance in three key areas:

- *Uncertainty* (gharar). *Gharar* is involved in the lack of transparency as to what portion of the premium is for management expenses, what portion is for claims payments, and what portion is for shareholder or policyholder returns. *Gharar* is exemplified by the Islamic prohibition of the sale of "tomorrow's daily catch" of a fisherman, whose size is uncertain and possibly even zero.
- *Speculative risk* (maysir). Joint stock insurance is speculative, with insurers seeking to profit from the risk that an indeterminate event will occur.
- *Unacceptable investment instruments*. Sharia prohibits the use of interest-based instruments (*riba*) and certain types of equity companies.

Some critical differences separate takaful from conventional insurance models. The takaful company administers a risk-sharing pool but, unlike a conventional insurance company, does not accept the related risk, is based on Islamic contracts, (usually) has a sharia advisory board that approves practice and development, and conducts an annual sharia audit.

Thus the takaful company operates two distinct sets of assets and accounts: one for its shareholders and one for its policyholders. The risks inherent in insurance are then (usually) divided as follows:

- Expenses of running the enterprise fall to the shareholders and not the policyholders.
- Operational risks likewise fall to the shareholders.
- Underwriting risks fall to the policyholders on a mutualized basis.
- Each set of assets retains its own investment risks.

Underwriting surpluses are normally fed back into lower future pric-ing. In the event of underwriting losses, shareholders lend assets (without interest) to the policyholder pool until underwriting surpluses can repay those loans. Underwriting surpluses need to be supervised by appropriate corporate governance.

Sharia scholars vary in their interpretation of the *muamalat* (law governing business transactions). Differences can arise in the following areas: Should shareholders share in underwriting profits? How should any surplus be allocated in the event of a winding up? Should risk premiums be paid into a *waqf* or trust fund?

Finally, religion is not a prerequisite for participation: it is not necessary for a takaful policyholder to be a Muslim.

The book then surveys the range of mutual structures. Cooperatives and mutuals hold some 24 percent of the global insurance market (2009 data). This varies considerably by country (2009 data), with mutuals holding 44 percent of the German market, 41 percent of the French, 40 percent of the Japanese, 34 percent of both the U.S. and the Dutch, 16 percent of the Canadian, 15 percent of the Italian, 9 percent of the Korean, 6 percent of the U.K., and 0.5 percent of the Chinese markets.

Cooperatives are better defined than mutuals. They embrace the values of self-help, self-responsibility, democracy, equity and solidarity, and ethical attributes such as honesty, openness, social responsibility, and caring for others. These values are reflected in the seven principles of the international cooperative movement: voluntary and open membership; democratic member control; member economic participation; autonomy and independence; education, training, and information; cooperation among cooperatives; and concern for the community.

Cooperatives have a proven record of creating and sustaining employment, providing more than 100 million jobs today. The international cooperative movement started in Rochdale, United Kingdom, in 1844. The Cooperative Insurance Company in the United Kingdom was founded in 1867, and the International Cooperative Alliance was founded in 1895 at a meeting of delegates from a dozen countries stretching from Argentina to Australia. The movement is truly global, with huge cooperatives in many countries, including Japan, where Zenkyoren, founded in 1951, now has assets of half a trillion dollars and annual premium income of US$60 billion.

The vision of mutuals is more loosely defined than the principles of the cooperative movement, but there are many parallels. Typically, mutuals have been founded to respond to the needs of particular occupational groups—examples include MAIF in France (education), HUK-Coburg in Germany (public sector workers), NFU Mutual in the United Kingdom (farmers), and the Professional Provident Society in South Africa (dentists). Recently, both the management and members of mutuals have been attracted by the allure of demutualization. This process, more or less irreversible, has dissipated the original vision and purpose of many mutuals.

The prospects for mutuals and cooperatives are bright with regard to the basic sustainability of the business franchise, but there are threats from Solvency II. In Europe, for example, more than two-thirds of the European Community's 5,000 insurers are mutuals, who accept about a quarter of the market's premiums. So, there are very many small mutual insurers whose capital position is threatened by the broad capital pressures of Solvency II. A.M. Best employs a distinct methodology when rating mutuals, and it is hoped that the European Community will recognize the need to treat mutuals differently than joint stock companies.

There is scope for takaful providers to learn from the cooperative and mutual sector. First, is the objective to reach size or maximize profitability? Members usually want the cheapest product, but managers are often interested in maximizing their own profit. Second, governance at mutuals is sometimes weak. The failure of U.K. Equitable Life is one example among many. The International Cooperative and Mutual Insurer Federation has been keen to promote best governance practice, giving rise to the release in the United Kingdom in 2005 of an Annotated Combined Code of good practice.

Two examples of the energy and vision created by successful mutuals are Folksam in Sweden and Macif in France. Folksam, founded in 1908, has taken a strong lead in improving road safety and being socially responsible in its investment strategy and environmental practices. It is dynamic in promoting gender and racial equality, and its vision has stretched to working with the Cooperative Insurance Group in Kenya to launch a microinsurance product for uninsured Kenyans. Macif was established much more recently in 1960 as a mutual for merchants and manufacturers. Its ethical foundations are built on three mutualist principles of the company being nonprofit, the collective policyholder being the insurer, and one member having one vote. Macif mirrors many Folksam initiatives, with an emphasis on sustainability. It funds the Macif Foundation, which promotes social innovation. It also joined forces with two other major French mutuals to form a second-tier mutual. This model may provide ideas about how to strengthen the cooperative and mutual movement.

The book then examines faith-based risk-sharing structures, including, in addition to takaful,

- *Christian health-sharing arrangements.* Operating since the 1980s, these are noncontractual and suffer from weak governance and almost no regulation.
- *Christian associations.* A subset of the wider cooperative movement, these focus on support for orphans, bereavement, educational scholarships, and joint purchasing discounts, among others.
- *Christian mutual insurers.* There are many of these, both in the United States and elsewhere, offering standard insurance products for church-related risks using the mutual model.
- *Jewish insurance.* Like takaful, Jewish insurance is sensitive to the avoidance of abuse of any interest component and the appropriate sharing of any surplus.

The book also considers hybrid insurance structures, including, in addition to takaful,

- *Reciprocal inter-insurance exchanges.* These unincorporated entities aim to satisfy special insurance needs of professionals (such as doctors), local authorities, and universities. They sometimes meet insurance-regulatory standards and sometimes do not. When extra-regulatory, they usually offer noncontractual benefits and suffer from weak governance. When well managed—the Farmers Insurance Exchange is an admirable model—they can be very effective.

- *Discretionary mutuals.* Typically, the board can decide whether to accept an application for membership, what level of protection to offer, and whether to make payments upon receipt of a claim. Often the "discretionary" status avoids the need for regulatory supervision, which can give rise to weak capital positions and sometimes also weak loss reserves. The Capricorn Mutual in Australia is a dynamic example.

The takaful models have evolved relatively quickly since the first takaful—the Islamic Insurance Company—was founded in 1979. The Islamic Fiqh Academy clarified the basis for takaful in 1985 following the Organization of the Islamic Conference in Jeddah, issuing three key statements:

- Sharia prohibits commercial insurance.
- Cooperative insurance founded on charity is acceptable.
- Muslim countries should work to establish cooperative insurance institutions.

However, the academy did not clarify the following:

- How should insurance risk be separated so that it only falls on members?
- Which sharia-based contract and which takaful model should be used, and how should profits be distributed—from investment surplus, underwriting surplus, or both?
- Is a sharia advisory board required?

The first of these principles—ensuring that the takaful operator does not accept any part of the underwriting risk—has become a widely accepted part of the takaful structure. The second principle has given rise to a plethora of variants, with four main operational models:

- *Mudharaba*, whereby the operator enjoys a (possibly different) share in both investment surplus and underwriting surplus from which actual management expenses are deducted.
- *Wakala*, whereby the ultimate investment and underwriting surpluses are fully returnable to members, but the operator takes a fixed fee, usually both directly from the base contributions and additionally from the individual member's account.
- *Wakala* with *mudharaba*, whereby the operator not only takes the fixed fees in *wakala* but also enjoys a share of the investment (but usually not underwriting) surplus. Separate contracts are required for each element.
- The pure cooperative model in which all profit belongs to the participants.

The range of these four models is considerable, with conflicts of interest giving rise to potential problems:

- The *wakala* model, where fees are a fixed percentage of contributions, tends to sell only larger policies, making it difficult to promote takaful to smaller customers.
- If the operator shares in underwriting surplus (which many interpret goes against the *maysir* principle, where the surplus is used to service shareholders capital and, in return, the shareholders capital is used to cover underwriting losses, either as a loan to participants or as outright transfers, as in Saudi Arabia for those companies that operate under the cooperative law), there is an inclination to price products conservatively to maximize the operator's return. Many interpret the sharing of underwriting surplus as going against the *maysir* principle.

- If the operator does not share in underwriting surplus and there is less incentive to produce underwriting surplus, the pressure to underprice can create solvency concerns. This pressure is familiar to commercial motor insurers, where the agent (in takaful, the "agent" is the operator) is interested in high turnover, while the insurer (in takaful, the "insurer" is the risk pool) requires price integrity.

The question of whether a sharia council is required gives rise to a further way to categorize takaful risk pools:

- Companies only selling takaful with a sharia council
- Companies only selling takaful without a sharia council
- Companies selling a mixed group of both takaful and traditional products (known as "takaful windows"). This last group includes many mainstream stock insurers who have recognized the opportunities of takaful but do not wish to establish a separate corporate entity. Some doubts have been expressed about whether "takaful windows" are truly sharia compliant.

A further issue relates to the contingency of a takaful underwriting deficit. The operator in such a situation has a natural interest in supporting the underwriting risk pool and often does so by means of advancing a *qard* or a loan that is interest free. Jurisdictions with takaful-specific regulations usually make transparent provision for the use of *qard*. However, in some cases, *qard* has been used to fund statutory deficits (which are subsequently treated as impaired and thus are written off), which does not align with the sharia principle that debts should be repaid.

Countries differ widely concerning their regulatory responsiveness to takaful:

- Malaysia is a leading regulator of takaful insurance, with guidelines covering capital adequacy, financial reporting, anti-money-laundering, and prudential limits and standards.
- Bahrain's regulatory framework sets out explicitly the need to use the *wakala* model for underwriting and the *mudharaba* model for investment returns. This gives rise to a transparent market, but may stifle innovation.
- Countries such as Singapore and the United Kingdom have no takaful-specific regulation, but host takaful entities. This lack of specific regulation makes the development of takaful more difficult.

Allied with a sound regulatory framework, takaful can learn valuable lessons from the cooperative and mutual movement:

- Ensure good governance and transparency.
- Recognize that, as takaful businesses grow, members will base decisions more on price than on ethics and values, unless these principles are constantly emphasized and communicated.
- Ensure that all employees embrace takaful principles and embed them in the corporate strategy.
- Support community project work, which will enhance the value of the takaful risk pool in the community.
- Emphasize cooperation between takaful operators to the benefit of all.

It is important to understand the nature of the principal-agent relationship in takaful. First, in the mutual model, the policyholder is also an enterprise owner; in takaful, the policyholder delegates all matters to the takaful operator, whose shareholders own all the equity in the business. Second, the provision of insurance contravenes the basic sharia principle of *gharar* or uncertainty. This cannot be fully eradicated, but it is possible to use a specific type of unilateral contract to forgive the *gharar*. This is achieved by the use of a *tabarru'* (translated as "donation") to pay what in commercial insurance is known as the premium toward the risk pool. Third, the *wakala* structure essentially creates an agency agreement, whereby the principal (the policyholder) pays the agent (the takaful operator) a fee for operating the takaful.

Hence, a key aspect of running a takaful risk pool is the principle of dividing the contribution (the premium) into the part that constitutes the agency fee and the part that finances the risk pool. We have already noted the inherent conflict between the interest of the agent (in takaful, the operator) in volume growth and the need for price integrity in the risk pool. We have yet to see takaful structures that would allow the principal to terminate the services of an agent who has not been running the business prudently. Specifically, the risk pool's loss reserves are a matter of judgment. The operator sets them, but a conflict of interest may well provide for diminished loss reserves following (for example) a period of unsustainable deductions from the premium for agency fees. In some cases, there is scope for the sharia council within the takaful to exercise its powers to achieve good corporate governance, balancing the interest of the operator with that of the participants, but technical skills within such councils are often not at optimal levels.

Disputes have arisen between sharia scholars who approve of the takaful operator sharing in underwriting profits and those who do not. The matter has not been resolved. To an extent, it is academic because, by raising the fee element of the contribution and reducing the risk pool contribution, the takaful operator can effectively allocate more funds to one account than to the other.

The book then considers investments in takaful. Takaful products range from savings products to risk-coverage products. The savings products have long-term investment objectives such as retirement and education. Risk-coverage products with significant investment objectives include mortgage-reducing term takaful to cover Islamic loans. Takaful risk pools need to have a strong investment strategy for longer-term risk pool funds.

The types of investments that are available vary by country, and the selection is evolving, but they generally include equities, *sukuks* (Islamic bonds), Islamic investments, and property investments.

Equities are allowed, with the exception of industries producing alcohol, pork products, entertainment, tobacco, weapons, and defense as well as businesses failing a financial leverage limit test.

Most *sukuk* arrangements originate in Malaysia, where RM 300 billion (US$100 billion) in *sukuk* instruments were outstanding in 2011. Some scholars do not consider *sukuks* to be sharia compliant. In 2007 the president of the Sharia Council of the Accounting and Auditing Organization for Islamic Financial Institutions estimated that 85 percent of all *sukuks* in issuance were noncompliant. As a result, efforts have been made to ensure that subsequent issues of *sukuks* are more sharia compliant. The rules for sharia compliance make *sukuks* similar to equities: for both, commitments to return the original principal to policyholders are prohibited. This, of course, makes it difficult for investments looking for the equivalent of a bond, that is, investments requiring a guaranteed return of the principal.

Various types of *sukuks* exist. These include *musharaka, diminishing musharaka* (both having equity elements), *mudaraba* (a kind of delegated investment partnership), *murabaha* (a commodity-based contract), *ijara* (a lease), *salam* (advanced purchase), and *istisna'* (an order to make a commodity).

Not all *sukuks* have unblemished records. The Dubai World developer, Nakheel Holdings, sold leasehold rights to Nakheel SPV, which in turn issued US$4 billion in *sukuks* to finance the purchase. In November 2009, it became clear that these assets were highly likely to fail. Fortunately, a loan from the Abu Dhabi government to Dubai World enabled the *sukuks* to be redeemed.

Other issues with *sukuks* include the short tenor or time horizon, which is usually limited to five years, and the limited volume of trading in secondary markets, which reduces transparency with regard to market value.

Islamic deposits are also generally in accounts with short tenors of up to five years. The vast majority of takaful operators' deposits are in *mudharaba* general investment accounts, which in Malaysia formed 33 percent of Islamic deposits at the end of 2010.

Finally, property investments confront the issue of sharia compliance with regard to the occupation of leaseholders. For example, receiving rent income from an alcohol producer is not acceptable. Takaful operators normally avoid this type of investment.

The pressure to conform to sharia compliance requirements thus creates additional costs for all types of investments.

Takaful providers have major investment strategy challenges, particularly with regard to products such as mortgage-reducing term takaful, where consistent and predetermined investment returns are needed to achieve a specific 20-year target benefit. This creates real problems when the *sukuk* options are limited. This, in turn, creates a challenge for risk-based capital because the inability to position investments in commitment-matching instruments raises the risk charge against the exposure. In the future, the risks of a mismatch and the costs of an implicit guarantee will become a growing concern for takaful operators.

Next, the book considers the enterprise risks inherent in takaful operations. Because two balance sheets are involved—that of the risk pool and that of the operator—an analysis of enterprise risks needs to take both into account:

- *Expense risk* falls on the takaful operator in all cases (other than for pure cooperatives and for the *mudharaba* investment model as practiced in Sudan).
- *Underwriting risk*, in principle, falls on the policyholders. If early pricing is too low, or if early loss incidence is very heavy, the risk pool may need a *qard* or loan from the operator to survive. This becomes a business decision for the operator. In models that permit the operator to share in underwriting surplus (notably in Saudi Arabia, but also elsewhere), underwriting risk has contingent exposures for the operator.
- *Investment risk* is borne by both the operator and the risk pool. Mortgage-reducing term takaful creates problems for the operator if the investments do not perform as advertised.

- *Operational risks* include mispricing, misselling (a significant issue in takaful), inappropriate distributions of funds, and sharia noncompliance. These all fall on the operator, except in the pure cooperative model.

The question of fund distribution is growing in importance. When should the operator distribute underwriting surplus and to whom? How much should be retained as operating risk capital?

After assessing these various enterprise risks, both the risk pool and the operator are going to need appropriate levels of risk-based capital. On both sides, the regulatory framework has yet to mature in most countries.

Questions of corporate governance and regulation are also becoming more important. Policyholders are rarely represented on takaful boards, while sharia supervisors are often unfamiliar with technical insurance issues. Who protects the interests of policyholders? Regulators need to take as strong a position as possible because the current framework does not protect policyholders sufficiently.

Further business challenges include the need to have suitable investment opportunities (the success of takafuls is likely to be materially dependent on having good access to a wide range of *sukuk* bonds) and the need to achieve customer loyalty. Takaful promotes the prospect of surplus sharing, but where *qard* needs to be repaid there is a risk that customers will become dissatisfied.

The book then considers regulatory policy issues. To succeed, takaful has to keep insolvencies to a minimum by setting and maintaining capital adequacy standards, checking the adequacy of loss reserves, checking and maintaining the quality of assets, and monitoring and managing enterprise risk.

The policyholder often is not financially aware, which makes misselling a major hazard. For this reason, monitoring and supervisory standards are advisable.

Takaful contracts need to be simple and transparent. In most countries, there is no standardized policy form.

The relationship between policyholder and the takaful should be clear, with regulations requiring open declaration of (a) the operator's fee (particularly any sharing in profits) and (b) the takaful's policy (and perhaps history) regarding payment of surpluses to policyholders. Malaysia and Saudi Arabia regulate to limit intermediary commissions, but many countries do not.

Companies should be required to treat customers fairly. Most countries have some regulation in this respect.

The various levels of corporate governance should be regulated, including the responsibilities of the board of directors, the responsibilities of the sharia advisory board, and the role of actuaries, who have a key responsibility for setting both loss reserves and pricing.

Most countries require sharia certification, which undoubtedly promotes good practice.

The approach to solvency standards is evolving. While takaful may develop for a period, with policyholders trusting the promise of surplus sharing, the likely path will be of diminishing sharing and increasing price competition. So, capital requirements need to be set with this in mind.

Thus far, the book has looked across the development of takaful without considering the type of product or its customer. While a tiny minority of Muslims live in extraordinary wealth, the great majority live in low-income or lower-middle income countries where the incidence of poverty is high. One important goal is to reach this huge group of people. A key means to do this is through microtakaful products. Here the statistics are telling:

- Microcredit has 77 million clients worldwide (about 3 percent of the world's poor).
- 380,000 of those—under half of 1 percent—buy Islamic microfinance products.
- 80 percent live in just three countries—Afghanistan, Bangladesh, and Indonesia.
- 300,000 are reached by 126 institutions operating in 14 countries; the other 80,000 are reached by Indonesian cooperatives.

A critical challenge is that the target policyholder is accustomed to addressing risk only after the loss occurs. By contrast, the mainstream buyers of takaful are keen to manage risk before the loss occurs. Therefore, a sound distribution channel is critical. Options include the following:

- A normal takaful operator
- A partnership between a takaful operator and an Islamic microfinance institution
- A community-based model
- A provider model (that is, via a hospital, clinic, or other cooperative)
- A social protection model.

Vital to many successful microtakaful distribution arrangements has been the use of *zakat*. The fourth pillar of Islam, *zakat* is neither a tax nor a charity, but rather a devotional obligation. When channeled appropriately, it funds some of the most successful forms of microtakaful distribution.

Keys to success here are achieving distributional cost-efficiencies, providing education (a vital challenge), choosing products appropriate to the customer (that is, mainly life risks and not savings products), working with the distributor, avoiding all commissions, and streamlining claims settlements. Nevertheless, a wide range of microinsurance products has been delivered effectively, including life, health, crop, property, livestock, funeral, flood, personal accident, and even unemployment. Many of these have been tailored to regional needs.

The book then moves from considering the range of potential takaful customers to looking at the means to strengthen the takaful market in terms of the balance sheet. Diversifying and managing risk within the risk pool is subject to some complexity. As with commercial insurers who buy reinsurance, takaful risk pools can buy retakaful. Note that it is the risk pool, not the takaful operator, that purchases retakaful.

Retakaful is subject to sharia constraints similar to those of direct takaful insurance. The first fully dedicated retakaful operator was founded in 1997. Since 2005, at least seven retakaful operators have been founded, including subsidiaries of three of the world's top five reinsurers. The ownership structures (heavily the *wakala* model) and management issues discussed for takaful providers are equally relevant to retakaful operators. The consensus is that retakaful operators should only work with takaful customers to ensure that every transaction is *halal*, or permissible.

The careful adherence to sharia principles makes for some difficulties within a retakaful business. With a collection of facultative acceptances, sufficient parallels exist with the direct takaful risk pool approach that concerns need not arise. However, with excess of loss treaty business, the nature of the risk transfer arrangement—and the accumulative nature of such risks across a direct market—gives rise to important questions of sharia principle. Such treaties are efficient, dynamic forces for effective growth, and the absence of clear agreement regarding the permissibility of such arrangements is holding back the development of takaful.

The final arena addressed is that of regulating takaful. It would be a gross error to assume that regulating takaful is the same as regulating commercial insurers. On the contrary, takaful is a hybrid structure that presents unique challenges to regulators:

- There are two "regulators"—the need to conform to sharia principles while also conforming to financial constraints.

- There are even two boards—the sharia advisory board and the board of directors. Do auditors sign off on sharia compliance?
- Reimbursing policyholders with surplus is much more complex than paying dividends to shareholders (different policy years may develop surpluses at different times in their development).
- Questions of "substance over form" regarding the admissibility of "takaful windows" need careful consideration. It is not acceptable for a commercial operator to sell products under a takaful branding if the products are not truly takaful in nature.
- Solvency standards are a unique challenge because of the difficulty of evaluating the value of the policyholders' commitments to continue paying contributions.
- The validity of the investment instruments is a continuing concern, both as to whether certain types of *sukuks* are admissible and whether they have good credit standing.
- The need to generate capital within the takaful risk pool is always going to conflict with the need to show policyholders a healthy surplus return.
- The need for the operator's shareholders to see returns and the policyholders to enjoy the surplus is another source of tension.
- Treatment of *qard* is a continuing matter for debate.

Other ancillary issues relate to taxation obligations and the appropriateness or otherwise of investments in equities for risk protection products.

Thus far, the range of takaful regulation in practice is very wide. Malaysia is often considered to have the most takaful-supportive regime. In contrast, Bahrain's approach is very rules based. Some countries with large Muslim populations have been slow to recognize the importance of takaful. There is much to be achieved by taking a constructive approach to regulation.

In summary, takaful insurance has enormous potential to enhance the lives of Muslims throughout the world. It can cover life, health, property, motor, and liability risks and also reach the smallest families and the poorest communities through microtakaful. Takaful also has enormous potential to enhance the economic development of the Muslim world.

The path is not without challenges. Whether these are on the investment front, the operational management front, the educational front, the distributional front, or the regulatory front, there are dynamic concerns on all sides. But in each case, good solutions are possible. What is required is for these challenges and the possible solutions to be more widely known and appreciated and for debate to flow freely so that takaful can develop in as efficient a manner as possible.

CHAPTER 1

Introduction

Serap O. Gönülal

The uncertainty of life has always been an enigma. A "throw of the dice" seems to decide whether someone is born into a life of luxury or poverty. Out of a craving for certainty, the concept of insurance was born. In return for a premium, an insurance policy pays out a specified sum assured on the occurrence of a contingent event. How this arrangement works in practice can vary, but the intention is the same: to indemnify the insured should an insured event result in injury or a loss of property or life.

Historically, there have been three basic corporate models for delivering this service: the incorporated mutual or cooperative, the stock company, and the less significant exchange (typified by unincorporated North American reciprocal exchanges). In recent years, a fourth model has emerged: a hybrid approach known as takaful—an Arab word for cooperative. Hybrid here means that takaful has some of the characteristics of a reciprocal or mutual and some of those of a stock company with mutual protection of participants. Ownership of the takaful management company is legally with the stockholders, but insurance risks are shared exclusively among policyholders (technically "contributors"). The differences among the mainstream models in operation today and how they allocate and manage risks are the subject of chapter 2.

Takaful markets span much of the globe, with a particular concentration in underpenetrated Islamic markets, the largest being Malaysia. Growth and general awareness have improved significantly since 2000, as interest in Islamic finance has grown, particularly during the recent fiscal crisis. Despite the global financial crisis and the slowdown in growth in the conventional insurance sector, takaful grew at an average annual rate of nearly 30 percent (inflation adjusted) between 2007 and 2010 (Swiss Re 2011). Takaful contributions (premiums) reached US$8.3 billion in 2010 and are expected to reach US$12.0 billion in 2012 (Ernst & Young 2011). Strong growth is likely to continue in key markets.

The development of takaful likely will be driven by the desire of Muslims to join world markets in a controlled and acceptable manner. In this sense, takaful could be considered a middle ground between stock insurers and mutual operations. Both mutual-cooperative and takaful operations have significant variations in their approach and practices. There is no one single definition of exactly what a takaful operation is, just as there is no one standard definition of exactly how a mutual operates. Regulations have played a key role in the form of development for both takaful and mutual operations and will likely continue to do so in the future. Both depend on a proper understanding by regulators of the risks inherent in their structures and the nuances required for their operations to flourish and develop.

Before looking more deeply at how takaful develops, it is worth reviewing the cooperative and mutual sector to consider examples of good practice from which takaful insurers may be able to learn. While the legal structures and ownership models of cooperatives and mutual insurers are important, what is potentially of even more relevance to takaful is the way in which these points of differentiation from proprietary insurers are reflected in actual *practice*. It is time to look in more detail at some examples of how "the cooperative and mutual difference," as it is sometimes called, is manifested in the day-to-day operations of the business. This is done in chapter 3, where we focus on the legal and corporate governance of cooperative and mutual insurers and analyze the experiences of several insurers that have stressed their mutuality.

In chapter 4, we focus on certain risk-sharing arrangements emerging specifically from the Abrahamic religious traditions. We describe these in detail and discuss their implications for some current challenges facing takaful.

In chapter 5, we review the hybrid structures, making the link between mutual insurance and hybrid structures containing elements of both mutuality and shareholder capitalism. On the surface, takaful appears to be similar to conventional mutual insurance. In some respects, it is even more similar to reciprocal structures. However, the vast majority of takaful companies today operate as stock companies. Unlike traditional mutual companies, takaful companies are oriented toward making a profit and are capitalized like any other ordinary stock company. Those that are not profit oriented are almost identical to the original concept of reciprocal exchanges. The key differences are that takaful companies must have a sharia supervisory board, they cannot earn or charge interest on loans, and they largely avoid investing in non-sharia-compliant industries. Takaful industry practice is gradually converging toward a hybrid business model, which combines a fixed-fee model for underwriting (*wakala*) with profit sharing for investment activities (*mudaraba*).

In chapter 6, we provide a more in-depth comparison of the mutual and takaful approaches, exploring lessons that could ideally be transferred to takaful and contrasting these with the reality of modern takaful structures.

Takaful, like Islamic finance, is guided by the sharia law of *muamalat* (commercial law) and is therefore separate from the sharia law of *ibada* (laws governing belief and the worship of God). Thus, a belief in the religion of Islam is not a precondition for participation in Islamic finance and takaful. Nor are the principles underlying Islamic finance and takaful proprietary to Muslims. Indeed, takaful shares many of the same principles that have made mutual insurance a success around the world. In addition to these shared principles, the *muamalat* prohibits the taking of interest income. Further, to ensure complete transparency in any bilateral transaction, *muamalat* prohibits contracts based on uncertainty. Adapting takaful to modern regulations (particularly capital requirements) has required departures from the true mutual model. These are explained in chapter 7, which describes takaful as an integrated approach to potentially conflicting requirements.

Chapter 8 discusses the issue of investments in takaful, beginning with the investment needs of takaful, the types of products being sold, and the models being used. We then explain the main assets used in takaful, along with the criteria for selecting assets. Risk-based capital is highlighted and linked to the choice of investment strategy as well as the selection of strategies for structuring assets to match liabilities.

We focus on corporate governance in depth in chapter 9. If we consider a stock company, the loyalties are clear: the management works for the shareholders, while the board of directors ensures that management performs to the shareholders' expectations. In regulated industries, such as banking and insurance, another layer of responsibilities involves ensuring that the company adheres to the stringent operating standards imposed by the regulator. Then there is the relationship between the stock insurer (a company capitalized by stockholders' capital) and the policyholders. In most cases, there is only one balance sheet and one profit and loss account, so the policyholder transfers risk to the insurer's balance sheet through the payment of a premium. The insurance contract clearly sets out the legal basis of the exchange, and the insurer is obliged to pay out the loss if the insured event transpires. The profits of the insurance company are tightly linked to underwriting performance of the insurance business and the returns earned from investing the assets of the company. The insurer keeps the regulator comfortable by (among other obligations) maintaining adequate capital and surplus at all times to ensure a high probability that claims will be paid. Naturally, as far as the insurer is concerned, the less capital is required the better, while the regulator will usually seek to ensure an adequate margin of safety.

The unique characteristics of takaful make its success somewhat dependent on a supportive regulatory environment. The hybrid nature of its setup (management company combined with mutual risk pool) makes it difficult for takaful to thrive in an environment that promotes only stock companies or only mutuals. The regulatory approach in countries where takaful coexists with conventional insurance has been to encourage takaful, but not to favor one above the other. The exception is Saudi Arabia, which has closed down all takaful operations, demanding that all insurance companies adhere strictly to the cooperative insurance regulations, which have still to be ratified as sharia compliant. In chapter 10, we focus on specific takaful issues such as governance and the solvency regulatory environment. We also summarize how takaful is governed in particular countries—Bahrain, Indonesia, Malaysia, Saudi Arabia, Sudan, and the United Arab Emirates.

In chapter 11, we analyze the developing world of microtakaful. The sort of empowerment provided by microinsurance can lift people, whatever their religion or race, out of poverty by giving them some security and a real hope of becoming financially self-sustaining. Many Muslims are found among the working poor, particularly in countries where significant proportions of the population still live in rural areas, and takaful is ideally suited to these often conservative populations.

Reinsurance under the takaful model is called retakaful. It is structured similarly to takaful except that the participants are primary takaful risk pools. In fact, there is no such word as "retakaful" in either Arabic or English. The term was coined by the takaful and insurance fraternity in their efforts to Islamicise or Arabicise terminology for components of the industry's sharia-compliant supply chain. Replicating the concept of rein-surance as being "insurance for insurance companies," retakaful is thus viewed as "takaful for takaful companies." In chapter 12, we focus on the role of retakaful in the growth and development of the takaful industry.

As Malaysia's and Bahrain's takaful regulations are perceived as the most advanced, we analyze the regulatory architecture of these two coun-tries. Malaysia has certain measures in place that favor takaful, such as tax incentives, while Bahrain fosters takaful growth through harmonization and standardization. In the United Arab Emirates, specific regulation has been introduced only recently. Opposition to the hybrid business model, or adherence to the wave of standardization, not only adds to the confusion of policyholders and consumers but also hinders growth of the industry. To avoid confusion and remove the barriers, consensus is needed among sharia scholars in each country as to how takaful should be imple-mented. The regulatory architecture is a vital tool in this effort. While in some countries the government has to decide what "sharia-compliant" means, in other jurisdictions this may not be possible, and an early consensus among local scholars on how takaful is structured becomes important. We discuss these issues in chapter 13.

Our endeavor in this book is to bring a broad understanding of the background of mutual insurance structures and more specifically the rapidly developing hybrid takaful sector. We believe that demand for takaful insurance will continue to grow vigorously. It has a very important role to play in providing economic stability and empowering individuals across many nations. We trust that this book will encourage regulators to provide supportive regulatory frameworks, encourage capital providers to invest in takaful structures, and encourage businesses and consumers to use takaful products.

References

Ernst & Young. 2011. *The World Takaful Report: Transforming Operating Performance*. Dubai: Ernst & Young.

Swiss Re. 2011. *Sigma*. Zurich Swiss Reinsurance Company.

CHAPTER 2

The Primary Insurance Models

Zainal Abidin Mohd Kassim

We start by considering the mutuals and how they manage risks. The micro model for the mutual is the family unit itself. Indeed, in many societies the individual turns to the family for assistance in times of need. The problem with such arrangements is that, while the monetary loss of the individual can be compensated by assistance from other members of the family, the family as a whole remains in a position of monetary loss. Assuming that the financial loss will be spread equally among all individuals in the family, the monetary loss per family member is smaller the larger the family. If the family consists of just five individuals, the loss spread over five individuals is greater per individual than if the same loss is spread over 50 individuals. For this reason, the concept of organized mutual assistance funds grew among affinity groups, such as people in the same profession or of the same religious belief—the predecessors to mutual insurers and friendly societies. This commonality in profession and religion added a degree of trust in the stewardship of the mutual or friendly society, which was often managed by the senior members of the affinity group itself.

Profit making was not the target of mutual insurers. Rather, service and affordability were the main concerns. By definition, a mutual organization is one in which the customers are also the owners of the organization. Financial benefits among the policyholders within a mutual can be derived from lower premiums overall, as there is no shareholder capital to service: all surplus arising accrues to members.

The history of modern life insurance can be traced to two Church of Scotland ministers in 1744, when for the first time the "art" of insurance moved into the "science" of actuarial principles. The typical insurance arrangements that existed prior to this date were more akin to gambling, with zero reserves and claims made on a pay-as-you-go basis. Under this new arrangement (set up for widows and orphans of the ministers of the Church), a fund was set up to receive premiums at the start of the year. Claims were paid using those prepaid premiums and the income earned on the investment of those premiums. This marked a radical shift from the previous pay-as-you-go arrangements.

The role of mutuals was pivotal in the growth of modern insurance, as is apparent in the earliest definition of modern insurance (in 1906, by Dr. Alfred Manes, a German insurance expert, quoted in Richmond 1943, 183):

> Insurance is an economic institution resting on the principle of mutuality, established for the purpose of supplying a fund; the need arises from a chance occurring whose probability can be estimated.

The earliest form of insurance (the pay-as-you-go variety) arose as a result of the needs of mercantile trade. Loans made to shippers included a margin (in the form of higher interest rates) to cover the possibility that a ship would not complete its journey due to specified hazards.

Modern insurance has evolved from mutual insurers to stock companies financed by stockholder capital. This is as a result of a need to prefund potential loss in modern insurance; stockholder capital is put to work to increase the probability that claims will be paid. In return for this guarantee, the stockholders exact a return financed from the surpluses expected from underwriting the risk. This surplus arises from the excess of risk premiums over and above the claim payouts (including specific loadings) and from any expense profits or investment margins on assets covering insurance liabilities.

What Are the Differences between Stock Insurance Companies and Mutuals?

The obvious difference between mutual and stock insurers is the ownership of the profits and losses of the insurance fund. In a mutual, these profits and losses (which are a natural consequence of premiums being paid in advance and the uncertainty arising from the investment of these premiums) are for the account of the policyholders. In a stock company, they accrue to the shareholders in total or in part, depending on contractual terms. In addition to this obvious difference, there are differences in the type of risks they tend to write. Generally, stock insurers tend to write the riskier lines of business. This is because stock insurers can absorb a higher variance of loss ratios due to their ability to tap the capital markets. Mutuals tend to thrive where claims are more predictable (as in life insurance) and thus where the demand for capital (which for a mutual takes the form of retained surpluses) is less. There is also the perception that the demand placed on the management team of stock companies is much more than the demand placed on the management team of mutuals. This is probably due to the fragmented form of shareholding in mutuals (many small equity holders who are generally less organized); in stock companies, the shareholders are more demanding with regard to financial results.

Another difference lies in the cost of insurance. Due to the ownership structure, while policyholders of stock companies know the cost of their cover for certain (the premiums paid), the net price of a mutual policy is not known until ex post dividends are paid. This makes comparison of premium rates between mutuals and stock companies difficult. Table 2.1 summarizes the differences between stock companies and mutuals.

The difference between stock and mutual operations can also extend to how the insurance funds are invested. Some mutuals are "owned" or managed by affinity groups who subscribe to a certain investment philosophy. For example, the premiums paid into the faith-based Mutual Aid eXchange (MAX) in the United States ultimately serve and stay in the

Table 2.1   Principal Differences between Stock Companies and Mutual Companies

Indicator	Stock company	Mutual company
Equity structure	Stockholders	Owned by policyholders
Risks underwritten	Full spectrum	Typically restricted to low-volatility risk
Risk mitigation basis	Risk transfer, need for capital to guarantee claim payouts	Risk sharing, available capital limited generally to retained surpluses
Alignment of stockholder interest	Weak between stockholders and policyholders	Policyholders are also stockholders; managing the managers can be an issue
Cost of coverage	Need to service capital from surpluses	All things being the same, cheaper, because no stockholder capital to service

churches covered (Quakers, Mennonites, and others) and the community groups they serve. All funds from the transaction of insurance are invested in accordance with the teachings of the churches.

In contrast, stock companies manage investments to maximize total returns and underwriting profits, taking into account the amount of capital employed. While risk management is an integral part of the investment decisions made for funds managed by a stock company, constraints are not necessarily placed on how funds are invested or how they are used to generate returns other than those placed by the company's own risk appetite and the law of the land.

Is Takaful a Mutual?

One of the challenges facing any insurance start-up is the need to attain critical size as soon as possible. This has to do with the high costs associated with running an insurance operation and the need to generate a sufficiently large portfolio to have a statistically credible claims experience. Regulators require such operations to conform to stringent minimum standards under the headings of "fit and proper" management, systems, initial capital, and ongoing solvency margin. The key to success for any insurance operation is to attain critical size within a short period of time. One measure of critical size is when the expense loadings in the premiums collected are sufficient to meet the costs of running the insurance operation. Regulators impose minimum capital requirements to ensure that companies can meet initial expense overruns and impose solvency capital requirements to ensure that they can pay claims in most circumstances. A start-up mutual rarely can meet such capital requirements.

For these reasons, the takaful companies that operate in most countries around the world while professing to embrace the risk-sharing principles of mutual insurers do involve shareholder capital. How can this be? To understand this, we first need to consider why conventional insurance is not acceptable to the majority of Muslims.

The key objections of sharia (Islamic jurisprudence) to conventional insurance can be summarized as follows:

- *Lack of transparency (that is, uncertainty or gharar).* For example, it is not clear what portion of the premium is used to meet management expenses, how much is set aside to pay claims, and what return, if any, the policyholder will receive. Both takaful and conventional contracts have elements of uncertainty as far as what return the policyholder will receive, but takaful contracts use *tabarru'* (treating "premiums" as donations) to forgive, but not remove, the *gharar.*

- *Speculative risk (that is, involving gambling or* maysir). Although insurance has evolved from an approach akin to gambling to one based on the science of probabilities, the concept remains one of speculative capital seeking profit from the uncertainty or indeterminacy of the insured events. In takaful, as there is risk sharing rather than risk transfer, this dependence on speculative capital is reduced, if not entirely eliminated. This uncertainty is effectively forgiven (but does not disappear), as premiums may be characterized as a charitable donation in a takaful fund.

- *Restrictions placed on investments.* Sharia restricts what investments are permissible, including a prohibition on investments that are deemed harmful to human well-being (for example, tobacco- and alcohol-based investments) and interest-based instruments (known as *riba*). The former category of investments is similar to socially responsible investments. There is no requirement, however, that investments can only benefit Muslims or Islam.

In addition to these objections to conventional insurance, there are several other major differences of importance between insurance and takaful:

- No insurance risk is transferred to the takaful company. Insurance risk is shared by the participants.
- Islamic contracts must underpin the takaful operation, such as *wakala* (agency) or *mudaraba* (investment) contracts.
- A sharia advisory board must approve the process and issue a fatwa claiming adherence to sharia standards for the operation.
- An annual sharia review or audit of the operation must take place to ensure that the sharia-compliant structure agreed within the original fatwa is still operational.

These objections can be met by ensuring sufficient transparency in the premiums, sharing underwriting risks among the insured rather than transferring risks from the insured to the insurer, and managing the investment of the funds of the insurance pool appropriately. Taking into account the difficulties of setting up a mutual in a heavily regulated industry, the modern setup of takaful is essentially that of (a) a stock company responsible for managing the business and initial regulatory capital and (b) a separate takaful pool or pools where the participants (that is, policyholders) share the contingent risks. This legal separation of assets (separate balance sheets) and profits (separate profit and loss accounts) is possible only in jurisdictions that provide for a separate set of special regulations (for example, Bahrain and Malaysia). In other jurisdictions (for example, Indonesia, but this is expected to change), provisions are made for "takaful windows." The issue for such windows is whether the assets of participants can be "ring fenced" from those of stockholders, as the assets of the participants are not available to meet the liabilities of the stockholders.

Allocation of Risks

So how are risks allocated in takaful companies, and how does this differ from the risk allocation of mutuals? We now consider the various risks inherent in insurance and how they are managed.

Expense Risk

The transparency in takaful can be seen in the need for the fees and income of the operator from the takaful operation to be clearly specified in the takaful contract. These fees or income form the basis from which the takaful company meets its expenses and pays dividends to its stockholders. In a takaful setup where the stockholders' profits and losses are separate from the participants' profits and losses, the expense risk is clearly borne by stockholders. In a mutual, the expense risk is borne by policyholders and affects the dividends (profits) distributed to the policyholders.

Operational Risk

As the management is employed by the stockholders and therefore responsible for the proper running of the business, operational risk is also the responsibility of the stockholders. The fees (income) received from the participants for running the business should therefore compensate the operator for carrying this risk. Here again, maintaining separate balance sheets for stockholders and participants allows this risk to be quantified and appropriate capital maintained. In a mutual, operational risk is the responsibility of all participating policyholders. Given the fragmented equity structure, effective management can be an issue in a mutual and give rise to higher operational risk.

Underwriting Risk

Conventional stock companies are not sharia compliant because of the method by which they manage insurance risks. In return for a premium, the stock company pays claims as and when they occur. This clearly transfers risk from the policyholders to the insurer when the insurer undertakes a speculative venture that will make either a profitable gain or a financial loss for its capital base. In a mutual, the insurance risks are shared among the policyholders, who manage real risks (a loss can only transpire when an insured contingent event occurs) by agreeing to indemnify each other through the premiums paid. This is also the basis for managing insured risks in takaful.

However, there is one important difference in how claims are managed in a mutual and in a takaful company, and it has to do with how deficits (when claims liabilities exceed free assets in the risk pool) are managed. In takaful, the stockholders are obliged to provide an interest-free loan to the takaful risk pool to cover such temporary deficits. This loan is subsequently repaid from future surpluses in the risk pool. Obviously, such a facility is lacking in a mutual, as there are no stockholders. In theory, a mutual could raise funds externally through appropriately structured debt instruments, but this would come at a cost and have no certainty of success.

Also, a major conflict of interest is inherent in a process where the operator manages the risk on behalf of the participants, may enjoy a share of the surplus depending on the arrangements agreed, but never shares in any deficits generated (other than an interest-free loan, *qard al hasan*, that is repaid to the operator). Corporate governance must be brought into play to ensure that the operator does not use this process to its advantage.

Investment Risk

In a mutual, investment risks are for the account of the policyholders. In a takaful, they are for the account of participants in the takaful pools and for the account of stockholders for assets in the stockholders' fund. In this regard, a third pool needs to be created when a life or family operation is involved. The risks for this pool are borne by the participants in a unit-linked setup.

The investments of a takaful operation (including the takaful pools) have to be sharia compliant. While some mutuals based on religious affinity do restrict where their funds can be invested, in most mutuals such restrictions do not arise.

Other Differences

The wave of demutualization in the years preceding the financial crisis of 2008 was driven partly by policyholders of mutuals cashing out on the value of the business of the mutual. This value consists of the orphan estate in the mutual (orphan because the surpluses were generated by previous policyholders and theoretically cannot be distributed to existing policyholders unless the operation is demutualized) and the ongoing value of the mutual as a business (so-called structural value). In takaful, participants do not own the estate (takaful is relatively new, so no estate exists in most takaful operations), as there is a sharia requirement (as yet untested) to give to charity any unallocated surplus in a winding up, but no requirement to distribute surplus while the operation is ongoing. The ongoing value of takaful as a business is owned by the stockholders because they funded the infrastructure of the business and control the distribution of the products.

The other obvious difference between a mutual and a takaful operation is the need for the takaful company to maintain a sharia advisory board, which is responsible for ensuring that the operation itself is sharia compliant at all times. The board reviews not only the investments of the takaful operation but also the operational aspects of the business. It is not responsible for setting the level of fees that the operator charges participants (other than ensuring that these fees are made transparent to participants), for managing the business, or for selecting managers and vendors, as these are deemed purely business decisions.

Due to the structure of the modern takaful operation, a question that frequently arises is who is responsible for managing the conflicts of interest that can arise between the stockholders (who manage the business) and the participants (who bear the underwriting risk). This is indeed a difficult conflict to manage, and the question remains unanswered at this time.

Growing Pains

The need for takaful to adhere to sharia law (specifically the law governing business transactions, termed *muamalat*) and the current lack of a global standard as to how these laws should apply to takaful mean that practices vary between jurisdictions and sometimes even within a jurisdiction. The business laws that apply in most Muslim countries are not based wholly on sharia, and in the end how takaful is conducted is driven primarily by the rules and regulations applicable in the jurisdiction concerned. The sharia itself is flexible, leading to even more scope for variations in the implementation of takaful.

For example, sharia scholars may differ in opinion on the following:

- Whether the takaful shareholders are entitled to a share of any underwriting profits
- How any surplus on a winding up of a takaful fund(s) should be allocated
- Whether the *tabarru'* (risk premiums) should be paid into a *waqf* (trust fund).

What is important is that Muslims in a particular jurisdiction should broadly agree on the application of sharia law to takaful in that jurisdiction.

In addition to sharia issues, there is the difficulty of aligning the interests of stakeholders in takaful. Unless appropriate regulations and adequate corporate governance are in place, management has incentives to prioritize profit to shareholders and to relegate policyholders' interests to a secondary issue. This agent-principal conundrum has yet to be resolved in takaful.

Conclusion

There are obvious differences between a stock insurer, a mutual, and a takaful operation. Table 2.2 summarizes these differences by how risks are allocated.

Takaful is not only for Muslims. It complies with sharia principles related to how business should be conducted, but it does not compel the buyer of a takaful policy to subscribe to the other sharia principles that together make up the religion of Islam—that is, how to worship God,

Table 2.2   Allocation of Risk, by Type of Operation

Setup	Underwriting risk	Expense risk	Operational risk	Investment risk
Stock company	Stockholders	Stockholders	Stockholders	Stockholders
Mutual	Policyholders	Policyholders	Policyholders	Policyholders
Takaful	Participants	Stockholders	Stockholders	Stockholders for the operator's fund and participants for the participants' funds

sharia criminal law, and sharia family law. Indeed, in many countries where takaful has been established, there continues to be significant non-Muslim participation in takaful. Insurance generally is not easily understood, and takaful, which requires increased product transparency in its structure and social responsibility when investing funds, can only expand the choices available to consumers.

Reference

Richmond, G. W. 1943. "Insurance Tendencies in England." *Annals of the American Academy of Political and Social Science* 161 (May): 183–93.

CHAPTER 3

Overview of Mutual Structures

Sabbir Patel

The concepts of cooperation and mutuality have long been at the heart of insurance. Indeed, the story can be traced back to the earliest of times. As Bernstein (1996) notes, "Occupational guilds in both Greece and Rome maintained cooperatives whose members paid money into a pool that would take care of a family if the head of the household met with premature death." A similar principle operated in medieval times, when members of particular crafts created their own guilds.

According to the cooperative historian Jim Kennedy, cooperation and insurance are closely connected in many parts of the world: "There have been many basic cooperatives around the world providing security. The tontines in Africa and the thrift societies of South Africa and the Caribbean combined insurance and credit. There are still ancient friendly societies in Southeast Asia, which help in cases of sickness, accident, and death. There were health and fire mutuals in Austria and Italy whose members pledged to bear losses jointly" (Kennedy 1999).

The transformation of these self-help ventures into a modern insurance *industry* came with the development of international trade and commerce,

The author would like to acknowledge the contributions of Andrew Bibby (ICMIF), Charlotte Köhler Lindahl (Folksam, Sweden), and Sebastien Chauve (MACIF, France) to this chapter.

particularly as a result of the hazards and high costs involved in merchant shipping. In the late seventeenth century, the primary naval powers were the Dutch and the English, with fleets of ships circling the globe and bringing goods to Europe. The story of what became an insurance institution, Lloyd's of London, is well known: it emerged from the informal meetings of merchants and seafarers in the London coffee shop opened by Edward Lloyd in about 1687, where risks were discussed and underwritten. Almost a century later, in 1771, 79 underwriters formally subscribed £100 each to create the Society of Lloyd's, an unincorporated group of individuals operating under their own self-regulated code of behavior (Bernstein 1996).

Given this background, it is not surprising that mutuals and cooperatives still play a significant role in the global insurance industry. Each year the International Cooperative and Mutual Insurance Federation (ICMIF) conducts a mutual market share survey, analyzing data from 70 countries representing 99.2 percent of the world's insurance market. The latest survey, based on 2009 data, found that mutuals and cooperatives together hold more than 24 percent of the total global insurance market (ICMIF 2011b; table 3.1).

The mutual sector significantly outperformed the market in four of the five regions in 2009, as it did in 2008. As with the global market, the developing continents saw positive growth in premiums, while the developed continents, Europe and North America, experienced small reductions in premiums overall (table 3.2). Over the past two years, the mutual market significantly outperformed the market, reflecting the fact that values-based insurers are attracting more customers than are shareholder insurers.

Table 3.1   Mutual Market Share, by Region, 2008–09

Region	Mutual market (% of total market)		% change in mutual market share	Swiss Re (% of global market)
	2008	2009		
North America	30.2	32.4	+7.3	30.5
Europe	24.7	25.5	+3.2	39.4
Asia and Oceania	20.2	21.2	+5.0	26.2
Latin America	9.6	9.5	−1.0	2.7
Africa	1.3	1.5	+15.4	1.2
Total	24.8	25.9	+4.3	100.0

Sources: ICMIF and Swiss Re 2010.

Table 3.2   Mutual-Cooperative Market Share and Growth in Premiums, by Region, 2007–09

Region	Premiums (US$ millions)			% change in premiums, 2008–09	% change in market
	2007	2008	2009		
North America	370,225	406,061	405,340	−0.2	−7.1
Europe	370,295	417,617	410,759	−1.6	−4.9
Asia and Oceania	176,184	201,963	224,770	+11.3	+6.1
Latin America	7,916	9,717	9,869	+1.6	+2.8
Africa	514	623	653	+4.8	−5.9
Total	925,134	1,035,981	1,051,391	+1.5	−2.8

Source: Swiss Re 2010.

Mutual Market Share in the 10 Largest Insurance Markets

The largest insurance market, with 28 percent of the world insurance premiums, is the United States, where the mutual-cooperative market share is more than 30 percent. Mutuals also have more than a third of the market in four other leading insurance markets, notably Japan, France, Germany, and the Netherlands (the second, fourth, fifth, and eighth largest insurance markets, respectively).

As we shall see, the mutual and cooperative insurers surveyed by ICMIF have differing ownership structures and corporate governance arrangements. What unites most of them is what they are *not*: they are not conventionally structured proprietary companies where directors have the responsibility of operating their business in order to provide returns for the shareholder owners. Table 3.3 shows the mutual market share in 2008 and 2009 for the 10 largest insurance markets, which together represent 76.6 percent of the global insurance market.

In eight out of the 10 largest insurance markets, the mutual sector increased its market share. The United Kingdom had the second smallest mutual market share of all and yet saw the biggest increase in market share—an increase of 9.4 percent to reach 5.8 percent—which occurred on the back of a 25.6 percent increase the previous year. This was primarily due to the whole sector producing excellent growth: 55 of the 60 mutuals all outperformed the industry. In the United Kingdom in recent years, mutuals have sought to raise awareness among consumers of the difference between mutuals and stock companies; with stock companies being at the center of the global recession, many customers have looked for alternative suppliers for financial services products. Arguably, these factors have contributed to the mutuals' business growth.

Table 3.3   Mutual-Cooperative Market Share in 10 Largest Insurance Markets, 2008–09

	Country	Mutual market (% of total market)		% change, 2008–09	Swiss Re (% of global market)
		2008	2009		
1	United States	31.5	33.9	+7.6	28.0
2	Japan	38.1	39.8	+1.7	12.6
3	United Kingdom	5.3	5.8	+9.4	7.6
4	France	40.5	41.3	+2.0	6.9
5	Germany	44.1	44.3	+0.5	5.9
6	Italy	16.0	14.7	−8.1	4.1
7	China	0.5	0.5	+0.0	4.0
8	Netherlands	33.2	33.6	+1.2	2.6
9	Canada	15.3	16.0	+4.6	2.5
10	Korea, Rep.	9.0	8.8	−2.2	2.4
	Total	n.a.	n.a.	n.a.	76.6

Source: ICMIF and Swiss Re 2010.
Note: n.a. = not applicable.

The United States continues to experience excellent growth, with market share increasing 7.6 percent in 2009 to reach 33.9 percent, with both life and non-life showing strong growth. This continues the strong growth seen in 2008 of 9.8 percent. Life market share grew from 21.9 percent in 2007 to 29.5 percent in just two years. While the U.S. life market contracted 13.3 percent over these two years, combined premiums in the mutual market grew 16.5 percent, a remarkable achievement in any market.

The only negative performance was in Japan, where the mutual-cooperative sector lost 9.4 percent of its market share, due largely to the entry of Japan Post into the market and the subsequent accounting changes. In addition, the mutual sector lost some goodwill and hence business as a result of nonpayment scandals that affected the whole sector. Nonetheless, the figures for 2006 for mutual market share in Japan were 37.9 percent, so the figures for 2007 (41.7 percent) may be extraordinary, particularly when compared to trend of the mutual market share that has been noted each year since 2005, when it was 36.1 percent.

This distinction has been emphasized strongly by the ICMIF and by some of its member companies, in particular since the 2007–08 global financial crash, which saw strong public distrust of and distaste for the excesses of many conventional financial institutions.

Cooperative and Mutual Structures

Having looked at what cooperative and mutual insurers are *not*, we should, perhaps, look more closely at how they are structured. The first point to bear in mind is that there can be differences between countries. These can be the result of differences both in the historical paths taken by national cooperative, labor, and social movements and in the enabling legislation provided for insurance operators by states.

Cooperatives

Of the two types of business, cooperatives are the more rigorously defined. Cooperative businesses are expected to operate under a set of cooperative principles and values, developed under the auspices of the International Cooperative Alliance (ICA) and last revised in 1995. The ICA defines a cooperative as "an autonomous association of persons united voluntarily to meet their common economic, social, and cultural needs and aspirations through a jointly owned and democratically controlled enterprise."

Cooperative values, again as defined by the ICA, are "the values of self-help, self-responsibility, democracy, equality, equity, and solidarity." The ICA adds, "In the tradition of their founders, cooperative members believe in the ethical values of honesty, openness, social responsibility, and caring for others."

Finally, the ICA has set out seven principles by which cooperatives put their values into practice (box 3.1). The "one member, one vote" principle is clearly at the heart of cooperative governance, as is the importance of member autonomy (some so-called cooperatives—in reality, state-run ventures—were created in the 1970s and 1980s, particularly in developing countries, and gave legitimate cooperatives an undeservedly poor reputation). The seventh principle states that cooperatives must have wider objectives beyond profit maximization.[1]

Cooperatives have been formally recognized by the United Nations (UN), which since 1992 has declared the first Saturday in July as International Day of Cooperatives (taking over a tradition previously organized by the cooperative movement itself). The UN has also declared 2012 as the International Year of Cooperatives. The resolution adopted by the UN General Assembly commends the fact that "cooperatives, in all their various forms, promote the fullest possible participation in the economic and social development of all people, ... are becoming a major factor of economic and social development, and contribute to the eradication of poverty."[2]

Box 3.1

Seven Principles of Cooperatives

1. *Voluntary and open membership.* Cooperatives are voluntary organizations, open to all persons able to use their services and willing to accept the responsibilities of membership, without gender, social, racial, political, or religious discrimination.

2. *Democratic member control.* Cooperatives are democratic organizations controlled by their members, who actively participate in setting their policies and making decisions. Men and women serving as elected representatives are accountable to the membership. In primary cooperatives, members have equal voting rights (one member, one vote) and cooperatives at other levels are also organized in a democratic manner.

3. *Member economic participation.* Members contribute equitably to, and democratically control, the capital of their cooperative. At least part of that capital is usually the common property of the cooperative. Members receive limited compensation, if any, on capital subscribed as a condition of membership. Members allocate surpluses for any or all of the following purposes: developing their cooperative, possibly by setting up reserves, part of which at least would be indivisible; benefiting members in proportion to their transactions with the cooperative; and supporting other activities approved by the membership.

4. *Autonomy and independence.* Cooperatives are autonomous, self-help organizations controlled by their members. If they enter into agreements with other organizations, including governments, or raise capital from external sources, they do so on terms that ensure democratic control by their members and maintain their cooperative autonomy.

5. *Education, training, and information.* Cooperatives provide education and training for their members, elected representatives, managers, and employees so they can contribute effectively to the development of their cooperatives. They inform the general public—particularly young people and opinion leaders—about the nature and benefits of cooperation.

6. *Cooperation among cooperatives.* Cooperatives serve their members most effectively and strengthen the cooperative movement by working together through local, national, regional, and international structures.

7. *Concern for community.* Cooperatives work for the sustainable development of their communities through policies approved by their members.

Cooperatives have also been formally recognized by the International Labour Organization (ILO), most recently in the ILO Promotion of Cooperatives Recommendation, 2002 (Recommendation 193). The ILO states that cooperatives are "important in improving the living and working conditions of women and men globally as well as making essential infrastructure and services available even in areas neglected by the state and investor-driven enterprises. Cooperatives have a proven record of creating and sustaining employment—they provide over 100 million jobs today; they advance the ILO's Global Employment Agenda and contribute to promoting decent work."[3]

The international cooperative movement looks back to an iconic event in the northern English industrial town of Rochdale in 1844 as representing the start of the modern movement. This was the decision by 28 Rochdale working men to create their own cooperative grocery shop. The move, which aimed to provide good-quality food at fair prices, was taken at a time of rapid industrialization, when workers in the growing towns and cities often found it difficult to buy unadulterated food at prices they could afford. The so-called Rochdale Pioneers drew up nine founding principles, which included gender equality and one member, one vote.

The International Cooperative Alliance itself was founded in 1895, and the first meeting drew delegates from cooperative movements in Argentina, Australia, Belgium, Denmark, France, Germany, India, Italy, the Netherlands, Serbia, Switzerland, and the United States, as well as the host country Britain. Cooperatives developed in different ways in different industrial countries: for example, while the consumer cooperative movement developed from its Rochdale roots to become historically the strongest element of the cooperative scene in Britain, other countries have seen more agricultural cooperatives (where agricultural producers are the co-op members) and producer cooperatives (where the workers are the co-op members). In Germany, the influence of Franz Hermann Schulze-Delitzsch (1808–83) and his contemporary Friedrich Wilhelm Raiffeisen (1818–88) led to the early development of financial cooperatives, including cooperative loan societies and credit banks.

Among those members of the ICMIF that declare themselves as cooperatives are some that are structured with individual policyholders as the co-op members, responsible collectively for choosing management and benefiting collectively from trading surpluses. Numerous cooperative insurers are also structured as "second-level" cooperatives, where the members are "primary" cooperatives rather than individuals. This is perhaps the most common route, since the impetus behind the creation of cooperative insurance operations in many countries has been a desire by existing cooperatives to manage their insurance requirements together and to benefit from keeping any profits from insurance within the cooperative economy.

For example, the Cooperative Insurance Company (later the Cooperative Insurance Society) was formed in this way in Britain in 1867, following efforts by several consumer cooperative societies, including the Rochdale Pioneers, which now—as part of the giant Cooperative Group—has a hybrid structure in which individuals and cooperative societies share ultimate ownership. The Canadian cooperative insurer known simply as The Co-operators is another example of a second-level cooperative. It is owned by 45 member cooperatives and credit union federations.

Cooperative insurers of this kind are particularly significant in Japan, which is home to the giant Zenkyoren, the world's largest cooperative insurer, with assets of around US$500 billion and annual premium income of about US$60 billion. Zenkyoren, established in 1951, focuses primarily on insuring Japan's large agriculture sector. Zenrosai, founded in 1957, is another major insurance cooperative, in this instance serving worker and consumer cooperatives. Other significant Japanese cooperative insurers include Kyosuiren, the national insurance federation of fishery cooperatives.

In several countries, cooperative insurers have traditionally had strong connections with the trade union movement. Trade unions participate formally in the membership and corporate governance of some of these insurers. A notable example is the very successful insurance cooperative in Singapore, NTUC Income, which was established in 1970 by the trade union federation National Trades Union Conference (NTUC).

Most states have legislation for cooperatives that is separate and distinct from that applying to other incorporated businesses. The European Union created the European Cooperative Society, a Europe-wide legal vehicle for incorporating cooperatives operating transnationally. Introduced in 2003, the European Cooperative Society matches the equivalent European Company (Societas Europaea) legislation for conventional share-ownership companies and has been used by a small number of cooperative societies operating in more than one European Union member state. In recent years, there has been international recognition that—in some countries at least—cooperative legislation may be outdated and in need of reform.

Some businesses that are generally regarded as cooperatively run are incorporated in ways other than conventional cooperative legislation. For example, some insurance companies with share capital and publicly traded shares nevertheless are considered to be part of the cooperative family, because cooperative organizations hold a majority shareholding in the business.

One particularly striking example is Unipol (Unica Polizza), Italy's third largest insurance group. Unipol began life back in 1962–63, as a result of an initiative by a group of cooperatives in the Bologna area that wanted to pool their insurance interests. In 1972, Unipol widened its reach to bring in the three main Italian trade union federations as co-owners. A few years later, it widened its base further to include unions and associations representing agricultural workers, artisans, and retailers. Then in 1986, it took the unusual step of raising equity capital on the Italian stock exchange. Currently just under 50 percent of its ordinary share capital is freely traded, as is 100 percent of its preference shares. The majority (50.2 percent) voting stake in the group, however, is held by Finsoe, a company that is majority owned by cooperatives. Unipol's access to equity capital means that the company has access to resources for building the business through acquisitions.

Another example of cooperatives choosing to access equity capital is MCIS Zurich, originally the Malaysian Cooperative Insurance Society (MCIS), which changed its statutes to become a public company in 1998 and four years later merged with the local subsidiary of the giant Zurich Insurance Group. Zurich is a minority shareholder in the venture.

Mutuals

There is no internationally agreed definition of a mutually owned business equivalent to the ICA's 1995 statement of values and principles for cooperatives. Nevertheless, in practice the two terms and concepts are somewhat fluid: because of particular national traditions and legislative models, businesses that in one country would be structured as cooperatives may very likely be created as mutuals elsewhere.

This was tacitly acknowledged when, in 1993, what had been the International Cooperative Insurance Federation changed its name to include mutuals and relaunched itself as ICMIF. The change was debated at considerable length, but in the end the organization "came down firmly in favour of admitting members from the *economie sociale*, the term coined by the French cooperative theorist Charles Gide to embrace those organizations which belonged neither to the state sector nor the private corporate ownership sector but which 'had a community focus and roots'" (Kennedy 1999). ICMIF is the only sectoral organization of the ICA to have made this change, although the ICA itself is discussing ways of deepening its relationship with mutual insurers and other social enterprises.

Mutual insurers (including some types of friendly society) typically have been created to provide protection for particular occupational groups, often professional workers. For example, the French mutual MAIF (Mutuelle d'Assurance des Instituteurs de France) was originally set up to provide insurance for primary school teachers, and it remains strongly oriented to the educational world. Another French mutual MACIF (Mutuelle Assurance des Commerçants et Industriels de France), created in 1960 with MAIF's help, was originally for shopkeepers and industrialists.

There are many other examples: in South Africa, the Professional Provident Society was set up by eight dentists in 1941, and although it has extended its scope to graduates and other professionals, it remains dedicated to this niche market.

In Germany, the leading insurer HUK-COBURG has, since 1977, made its products available to all, although organizationally it remains a mutual dedicated to civil servants and other public sector workers, who make up the organization's membership. Its chief executive, Wolfgang Weiler, sees its mutual status as very important: "We feel committed to the principle of mutuality, which governs our corporate activities. As a mutual insurer our company is not owned by investors whose expectations on financial performance and yield we would otherwise have to consider" (ICMIF 2011c).

In the United Kingdom, NFU Mutual is the market leader in insurance for farmers. Created by eight farmers in 1910, about half of the business is linked to agriculture and remains closely linked with the National Farmers Union (an association rather than a trade union), to which it makes annual financial contributions.

In both the United States and Canada, mutual insurers (often based in small geographic areas) continue to have a major role, particularly in delivering non-life general insurance. The U.S. National Association of Mutual Insurance Companies (NAMIC) is a venerable institution with a history going back to 1895 that links more than 1,400 U.S. mutual companies in the property and accident insurance market, ranging from major national insurers such as Farm Mutual and Nationwide to very small agriculturally based businesses, the county and farm mutuals.

CAMIC, the Canadian Association of Mutual Insurance Companies, links 91 of the 106 property and casualty mutuals across Canada, many established by farmers more than a century ago.

Like cooperatives, mutuals are controlled by their members, who are generally the insurance company's policyholders. Indeed, mutuals may be closer to their policyholders in terms of their corporate governance than are second-level cooperatives, which represent individual members at one remove.

Not every mutual has all of its policyholders as members, however. As we have seen, HUK-COBURG offers insurance products to everyone, but limits its membership to public workers. Elsewhere, the divide between mutual membership and customers has widened much more markedly. In Canada, a historical quirk related to Canadian provincial regulations (removed more than 70 years ago) meant that some policyholders were not able to become members. The vast majority of Canada's mutual insurers have rectified this, but four mutuals consider it administratively easier to maintain a very low membership base. One of these is now subject to moves toward demutualization (ICMIF 2011a).

The atrophying of the mutual principle in some insurers—to the extent that, for the vast majority of policyholders, there might be no perceived difference between mutuals and proprietary insurers—led to a wave of demutualization in several countries, with the collective assets of the mutuals partly passed out to members in the form of shares. In the United Kingdom, the largest mutual, Standard Life, demutualized in 2006; other major U.K. mutuals, including Norwich Union (now Aviva) and Friends Provident, also demutualized around the same period.

Even where insurers remain legally constituted as mutuals, low engagement of membership can raise concerns about corporate governance. ICMIF has taken a strong lead in encouraging the cooperative and mutual insurance sector to develop very high levels of corporate governance, stressing the reputational and business benefits that can follow from having a base of engaged members. A seminar on corporate governance was held by ICMIF for the first time in 2008, in Toronto. However, a significant minority of mutual insurers choose not to work with other mutuals in ICMIF or in regional mutual organizations such as Amice (Europe), Asia and Oceania Association (Asia-Oceania), and ICMIF/Americas.

In the United Kingdom, mutual insurers and friendly societies have jointly developed an annotated combined code for corporate governance, which is seen as a model for use elsewhere in the world. U.K.

mutuals have also discussed the development of a "mutual brand" to highlight their difference from conventionally structured insurers (AMI/AFS 2008).

Mutual insurers, particularly the smaller ones, have been concerned in recent years that insurance regulators and supervisory authorities are insufficiently briefed on mutual and cooperative forms of business and are imposing regulatory requirements that are inappropriate for the sector. This is a particular concern in Europe in relation to the capital requirements specified in the Solvency II Directive. The French mutual insurance federation ROAM (Réunion des Organismes d'Assurance Mutuelle), with 46 member firms, has taken a lead in campaigning against this aspect of Solvency II and has launched a website in four languages, www.stopsolvabilite2.com. ROAM fears that hundreds of smaller mutuals across Europe could vanish.

Mutual organizations such as ROAM have called on the European Union to create an approved European Mutual Society legal structure, analogous to the European Cooperative Society model. French law already assists mutual insurers wanting to develop their business through the SGAM (Société de Groupe d'Assurance Mutuelle), a legal vehicle that creates a kind of second-level holding group for mutuals. The legislation has been used successfully, most recently by MACIF, MAIF, and a third mutual, Matmut, which have created a joint holding group (ICMIF 2009a).

Another interesting development in recent years has been the creation of a new wave of small mutuals, generally focused on particular occupational groups. One example is Capricorn Mutual, based in Australia and set up in 2003 to provide a commercially feasible alternative to conventional insurance for small businesses engaged in car repair and servicing work. To be eligible, businesses have to be members of the 10,000-strong Capricorn Cooperative Society.

A similar model has been chosen by the National Federation of Retail Newsagents (NFRN), a trade association in the United Kingdom, which in 1999 decided to create NFRN Mutual. The venture now has more than 3,000 members. Also in the United Kingdom is Marathon Mutual, which provides cover for care homes. These three ventures, and other "modern mutuals," have used the services of an intermediary facilitation company for help in becoming established and for their operational needs. Technically, firms such as these are usually set up as *discretionary mutuals* rather than as insurers, a process that avoids the requirements imposed on insurance providers. This means that the mutual's members pay contributions in exchange for protection against risks rather than paying premiums for insurance. Claims are assessed by the mutual's board, and the board has discretion in whether or not to pay out. Nevertheless, since the board is democratically elected by the mutual's members, in practice it is highly unlikely that legitimate claims will be denied (ICMIF 2008a).

The Prospects for Cooperative and Mutual Insurers

As ICMIF's annual mutual market share surveys show, the cooperative and mutual insurance industry continues to hold a significant minority share of the global insurance market, with particularly strong representation in some key countries. The market share is tending to grow slightly relative to stock insurers.

There is no doubt that demutualization (a particular phenomenon in some countries in the years prior to the 2007 global financial crisis) did weaken the sector, notably in the United Kingdom, but also in Australia. Demutualization was often proposed as a way of accessing new sources of capital, although cynics would note that the process was usually initiated by senior managers, who identified an opportunity to increase their prestige and remuneration. Historically, demutualization tended to attract member support, with members benefiting individually from the distribution of previously accumulated surplus, normally in the form of shares.

Although demutualization remains a live issue in some countries (for example, Canada), it has become a much less significant phenomenon in the past few years. Its legacy has been mixed, however, not least because the process is a "one-way street" (once floated, the option to remutualize is generally lost forever). Furthermore, the big demutualization drives of the 1990s and 2000s left some parts of the cooperative and mutual movement feeling defensive and unsure of their legitimacy.

As mentioned, some cooperative and mutual insurers consider the regulatory requirements being introduced through the Solvency II initiative as posing a potential threat. The process for developing a new European risk-based regulatory system started in 2002 and is likely to be fully implemented by 2014. It was the first European directive to use the Lamfalussy principles to develop European directives in conjunction with the industry, but not the first to be completed due to the complexity and diversity of the insurance industry. All insurers, as defined by the directive, are subject to Solvency II. There is no differentiation or special dispensation for mutual, cooperative, or member-owned organizations.

However, it is expected that certain dispensations will be given to smaller insurers based on "proportionality" principles. Of the more than 5,000 regulated insurers in Europe, two thirds are mutual, and mutuals represent 25 percent of the European market by premiums; therefore, the majority of smaller insurers undoubtedly will be mutuals. The current definition of small insurer, termed "non-directive insurers," is an insurer with premiums below €5 million.

The European Commission, which is leading the development of Solvency II, is yet to decide what exclusions will be given under the proportionality principle, but it is hoped that exclusions will be given in the area of reporting, governance, and capital. The costs to implement a complex new regulatory system are far greater for smaller organizations in proportion to their total costs than they are for large organizations. It is hoped, therefore, that the proportionality principles of Solvency II will avoid the "law of unintended consequences," which could result in the disappearance of small mutuals and the loss of market diversification that they bring.

Lessons for Takaful from Mutual Structures

In recent years, ICMIF has undertaken considerable work around takaful development, including the production of a regular takaful newsletter, the creation of a takaful network with a conference held annually, and the establishment of a dedicated website, www.takaful.coop. One of ICMIF's senior vice presidents has produced a brief to extend ICMIF's work in this area. The organization has also created a takaful class of membership, and several takaful organizations participated in ICMIF's most recent world conference, held in Manchester, United Kingdom, in late 2011.

It is worth looking at the cooperative and mutual sector to consider examples of good practice from which takaful insurers may be able to learn. While legal structures and ownership models of cooperatives and mutuals are important, what is potentially even more relevant to takaful is the way in which these points of difference from proprietary insurers are reflected in actual *practice*. It is time to look in more detail at some examples of how "the cooperative and mutual difference," as it is sometimes called, is manifested in the day-to-day operations of the business.

It is appropriate to begin with first principles and to ask what constitutes success for a cooperative or mutual. For conventional businesses, the

answer is easy: a successful company is one that ends the year with sufficient profit to satisfy shareholders. For member-owned businesses, however, this is not necessarily the case. For example, a mutual may be
deliberately aiming for lower profits compared to its share-based com-
petitors, in order to provide low-cost cover or higher levels of customer
service. Low profits in this context represent a competitive advantage,
leading to greater market penetration, not a weakness.

Other implications for insurers are not driven by the imperative to
maximize returns to their investors. Mutuals and cooperatives are better
able to take a longer-term perspective when setting their business strategy
than are companies seeking to maximize dividends. Certainly, this argument was advanced in the immediate aftermath of the 2007–08 global
financial crisis, which left mutuals and cooperatives relatively unscathed.

A study by U.S. economist Robert Hartwig offers some support for
this argument. Hartwig looked at more than 280 insurance companies
that were still trading after 100 years and found that 62 percent of them
were structured as mutuals. He argued that longevity was attributable
partly to an approach in which management acted as stewards of the
business, with the objective of passing on a healthy firm safely to the
next generation of managers and policyholders. Long-lasting firms also
tended to set management remuneration at a less-inflated level relative to average employee wages and to have a strong customer focus
(ICMIF 2010).

The significant difference in aim and purpose between mutuals and
proprietary insurers has been recognized by the rating agency A.M.
Best, which operates a distinctive methodology when rating a mutual or
cooperative. As A.M. Best puts it, "The lack of traditional shareholder
ownership means that most mutual insurers tend to focus mainly on
serving their selected market segments. Typically, any profits are either
retained or distributed to policyholders as policy dividends or reduced
premiums. Indeed, profitability targets and expectations of mutuals
tend to be lower than those of competing proprietary companies" (A.M.
Best 2007).

A.M. Best adds that using return achieved on capital as a rating assessment tool can also be problematic, given that mutuals and cooperatives
do not generally have access to equity capital: "Mutual companies have …
traditionally maintained higher capital ratios than their peers. Thus, given
the higher capitalisation levels, mutuals have generally reported lower
returns on capital than stock companies. However, the efficient use of the

excess capital to generate business growth, maintain competitive business profiles, and provide market-rate operating returns on their business are viewed as key areas of strength for higher rated entities over the long term" (A.M. Best 2007).

Through its specialist methodological approach, A.M. Best is attempting to compare like with like, to distinguish strong mutuals and cooperatives from their more poorly performing colleagues. This is valuable, not least because the fact that an insurer is structured as a cooperative or mutual does not in itself mean that the business is well managed or able to meet its own criteria of success. Indeed, the absence of shareholder investors and the professional scrutiny and analysis that the presence of investment capital attracts can mean that mutuals and cooperatives with poor management and poor corporate governance can avoid criticism. Historically, some senior managers in mutual insurers were not subject to adequate oversight by those appointed to protect member interests. The spectacular problems of the venerable U.K. mutual Equitable Life in 2000 constitute one high-profile example.

Partly in response to cases like Equitable Life, ICMIF has taken a keen interest in developing models of good corporate governance practice for the cooperative and mutual sector. This work has perhaps been most advanced in the United Kingdom, where mutual insurers and friendly societies in 2005 agreed to adopt an annotated combined code of good practice for the sector. The code, part of a broader initiative in the United Kingdom to improve corporate governance standards, is based on 25 indicators grouped in 5 sections, which cover the workings of the board and its directors, arrangements for directors' remuneration, financial reporting and auditing, and relations with members and stakeholders.

The code is subject to self-assessment each year by each company, which is required to report publicly its level of compliance in its annual report. Some elements of the code are also reviewed as part of the audit process (ICMIF 2008b).

Initiatives like these are strengthened by the growing desire of some cooperatives and mutuals to promote much more strongly their difference from proprietary insurers. They are aware that their ownership structures can be embraced as a competitive advantage to attract customers disenchanted with conventional financial big business. The more that policyholders in cooperatives and mutuals understand the governance structures of their insurer—in particular, the idea that the business is in some sense "theirs"—the more they are likely to participate and provide the necessary oversight of the work of the board of directors and the more likely they are to stay as customers.

Folksam

The Swedish insurer Folksam has stressed its mutuality for very many years. As its website puts it, "Folksam is a mutual company, meaning our customers are also our owners. The profit doesn't go to shareholders, it stays within the company and benefits us all … Our vision [is] that 'People should feel secure in a sustainable world.'"[4]

Folksam's emphasis on its ownership structure was reinforced in 2010 with a rebranding exercise that created the new slogan *Engagerade för dig* (Committed to you). Its 2010 annual report points out the commercial benefits that it gains from this approach: "It is of great importance to all types of companies to have satisfied customers and satisfied owners, and for Folksam it is a significant advantage that these groups coincide" (Folksam 2010).

Folksam is a major player in the Swedish insurance market, with a total market share in non-life insurance of more than 15 percent and a particularly strong position in the country's household and motor insurance market. It claims about 4 million customers, almost half the total Swedish population. It has about SKr 300 billion (US$40 billion) in assets under management.

Folksam was founded in 1908, in its own words, as "a response to great injustices"—the inability of ordinary people on low incomes to be able to obtain the sort of insurance protection relevant for them. It developed out of the country's social democratic movement, in particular, the trade union movement, and Sweden's trade unions continue to have close links with the insurer (including access to group insurance policies for union members). However, Folksam interprets its social remit very broadly.

For example, it has taken a very strong lead for more than 30 years in efforts to improve road safety. It has a sophisticated road safety research operation, which, among other things, analyzes the causes of road accidents and identifies poor safety features in models of cars on the market. It also aims to promote a greater understanding of road safety issues among policy makers and the general public as well as car manufacturers. As it points out, road accidents entail heavy losses for public health and the national economy, but above all for the individuals affected. Of course, this initiative is a particularly appropriate intervention for an insurer to take. Folksam undertakes similar work to try to reduce other types of accidents and ill health. The research Folksam conducts on road safety is unique, as it looks at real-life data collected from black boxes that register crash impulses.

Folksam publishes an analytical report based on its traffic research ("Safe and Environmental-friendly"), which is based on in-depths studies from the data collected and also looks at the carbon dioxide emissions. Customers who own the most safe and environmentally friendly cars pay lower premiums.

Folksam's strong sense of social responsibility is reflected in its investment policy. Folksam played a key role in development of the global Principles for Responsible Investment, an initiative set up by the UN Secretary General and launched in 2006, and it applies a set of formal socially responsible investment policies for all assets under management. These address issues related to corporate environmental practice, human rights, and corruption. Exclusion criteria are applied to cluster ammunition and tobacco.

Folksam's socially responsible investment policies are based on a principle of engagement with the companies whose shares it holds. Folksam uses its shareholder rights actively by voting at annual general meetings and aims to raise public awareness, for example, by publishing league tables ranking companies by their performance in terms of responsible business and action on climate change. It monitors between 2,000 and 3,000 companies a year and (particularly in relation to human rights and environmental concerns) raises issues directly with the companies' senior management, where appropriate. Several companies have introduced guidelines and targets for their environmental work following dialogue with Folksam (Folksam 2010).[5]

Folksam also scrutinizes companies' remuneration policies for directors and senior staff and presses for a more equal gender distribution on company boards. Its stance on equality and diversity is driven by ethical considerations but also has a business dimension, as it explains: "Keeping competent men and women out of the boardrooms on the grounds of gender, age, nationality, or belonging to the 'wrong' network is detrimental to the prospects of long-term profitability. Increased gender equality on boards would lead to greater skills and expertise ... which in turn results in companies that are more efficient and thus enjoy higher profits in the long term" (Folksam 2010).

Folksam is a pioneer in environmental practices, and each year it publishes an audited sustainability report. Several aspects of its business, including its practice on motor and building claims, are environmentally certified under ISO 14001. It switched to an environmentally friendlier standard of electricity 10 years ago and in 2008 began to use solely wind power of specified origin. It has operated on a climate-neutral basis since 2006, offsetting the company's annual carbon dioxide emissions by supporting agroforestry initiatives in Mexico and Uganda.

Sweden is an increasingly multiethnic country, and Folksam has sought to ensure that the insurance needs of immigrant communities are adequately served. Its multilingual call center in Malmö handles calls from customers and potential customers in languages other than Swedish (about 18 languages of the most common immigrant communities, including Somali, Kurdish, Arabic, and Polish). In 2009, Folksam launched a sharia-compliant savings product tailored specifically for the country's half a million Muslims.

Folksam is, as of this moment, the first insurance company in the world to offer insurance products (non-life) that are certified with an eco-label—the world's toughest eco-label, "Good Environmental Choice."

As part of its corporate social responsibility work, Folksam has fostered a strong relationship with CIC (Cooperative Insurance Company) Group in Kenya. Together with the Swedish Cooperative Centre, Folksam and CIC Group launched an innovative pilot project in 2008 that was founded by the ILO and the Bill and Melinda Gates Foundation for low-income people in Kenya. The project devised a package of microinsurance products aimed at reaching uninsured Kenyans. Folksam also plays an advisory role with CIC Group, seeking to inspire and develop the company's perspective.

Folksam's influence is significant within the community of mutual and cooperative insurers, and it has played a key role in recent work by ICMIF in relation to both socially responsible investing and sustainability. For its chief executive officer Anders Sundström, its structure as a mutual is particularly appropriate: "Mutuality is long term and is therefore a good match for insurance activity, which is also long term" (Folksam 2010).

The MACIF Group

MACIF was established in 1960 as a mutual for merchants and manufacturers. Today it is the largest French insurer by number of policies in family and motor insurance, with 5.7 million vehicles covered (as of December 31, 2010). It offers a wide range of insurance products to its 4.8 million members.

Like Folksam, it strongly promotes its differentiation from conventional insurers: it is collective, socially inclusive, and democratic. The MACIF Group holds three mutualist principles:

- *Nonprofit.* Surpluses are not distributed to shareholders in the form of dividends, but rather are reinvested in order to guarantee the best quality and prices to its members.
- *The policyholder as insurer.* Members are individually insured and act collectively as the insurer. This circle of solidarity reinforces the responsibility of each member.
- *One member, one vote.* The golden rule of transparent governance is that all members are equal. Policyholders elect some 2,000 regional delegates, who elect some 150 national delegates to the General Assembly, who in turn elect the 24 members of the board of directors. These delegates directly influence how the insurer undertakes its work. One example is the initiative launched at the delegates' request to provide insurance products and customer services specifically targeted at the deaf and hard of hearing.

The MACIF Group also works with organizations, including retail associations, professional bodies, trade unions, and nongovernmental organizations, that play a direct part in the corporate governance of the MACIF Group through the Association of Delegates from the Social Economy.

Many of the initiatives mentioned in relation to Folksam are also undertaken by the MACIF Group. For example, MACIF takes an active interest in issues of sustainability and, among other things, offers insurance premium discounts to motorists with environmentally friendly vehicles. It has recently joined forces with the French Consumer Safety Commission and the National Consumer Institute in a joint campaign to reduce everyday accidents. This campaign aims to improve safety awareness among older people, who suffer two thirds of the deaths in France from accidents in and around the home. For children between the ages of about five and 10, it has produced a series of entertaining online games drawing attention to potential hazards in the home.

The MACIF Group funds the not-for-profit MACIF Foundation to promote social innovation in order to identify new responses to the major challenges of society. It supports projects based on two principles: co-construction and multiple partnerships. In recent years, about € 3.7 million has been distributed in grants to around 150 projects, mainly focused on housing, environment, food supply, and mobility projects.

The MACIF Group is a strong advocate of cooperation between mutuals and cooperatives and provides institutional representation with international organizations. It was one of the founding members in 1990 of Euresa, a European economic interest group that unites the insurance mutual companies and cooperatives of the social economy sector in different European countries and promotes cooperation in order to improve the offer of quality products and services.

Equally interesting has been the decision by the MACIF Group to join forces with two other large French mutuals to create a second-tier mutual known as Sferen, which is an SGAM. Sferen is not a traditional merger, but rather a formalized alliance between companies that keep their individual sovereignty and governance arrangements, while instituting the principle of financial solidarity among them (ICMIF 2009a).

The SGAM model has wider significance in that it is a determinedly mutual solution to the business imperative of achieving growth and economies of scale that, for conventionally structured businesses, often lead to mergers and acquisitions. It reflects a form of capital that distinguishes mutual and cooperative societies from proprietary insurers, and it also respects the element of member control implicit in the mutual and cooperative model. If vehicles such as the French SGAM were to be developed internationally, it could transform the ability of mutual and cooperative businesses to develop real global reach.

The MACIF Group's participation in Sferen is directly in line with one of the central principles of the international cooperative movement, that of collaboration and inter-trading within other businesses in the social economy (as noted in this chapter, the International Cooperative Alliance's sixth principle pertains to cooperation among cooperatives). There are numerous other examples from within the ICMIF member network: one particularly successful initiative is that of mutuals and cooperatives in South America who are combining to organize their reinsurance needs through the Latin American Reinsurance Group.

Notes

1. International Cooperative Alliance, www.ica.coop.
2. United Nations, General Assembly Resolution 62/128, December 18, 2009. See UN (2009).

3. International Labour Organisation, http://www.ilo.org/empent/units/cooperatives/lang-en/index.htm.

4. Folksam, http://www.folksam.se/English.

5. Folksam, http://www.folksam.se/English; also see ICMIF 2009b.

References

A.M. Best. 2007. "Rating European Mutual Insurers: Best's Rating Methodology." A.M. Best, September 3.

AMI/AFS (Association of Mutual Insurers/Association of Friendly Societies). 2008. "The Combined Code on Corporate Governance." AMI, Cheshire, U.K.

Bernstein, Peter L. 1996. *Against All Odds*. New York: John Wiley.

Folksam. 2010. *Annual Review 2010*. Stockholm: Folksam.

ICMIF (International Cooperative and Mutual Insurance Federation). 2008a. "UK Mutuals Adopt Code of Governance." *Voice* 60 (January).

———. 2008b. "UK Mutual Insurers." *Voice* 61 (April).

———. 2009a. "Mutuals Combine Forces." *Voice* 65 (July).

———. 2009b. "Taking a Stand for Socially Responsible Investment." *Voice* 65 (July).

———. 2010. "How to Live to a Hundred, Insurance Style." *Voice* 69 (October).

———. 2011a. "Canadian Mutuals Fight Demutualisation Danger." *Voice* 71 (July).

———. 2011b. "Mutual Market Share 2009."

———. 2011c. "Putting Customers at the Heart of the Business." *Voice* 72 (October).

Kennedy, Jim. 1999. *Not by Chance*. Manchester, U.K.: Holyoake Books.

Swiss Re. 2010. "Statistical Appendix." In *World Insurance in 2009: Premiums Dipped, but Industry Capital Improved*, 27–40. Sigma no. 2/2010. Zurich: Swiss Reinsurance Company, December.

UN (United Nations). 2009. *Cooperatives and Social Development*. New York: UN General Assembly.

CHAPTER 4

Faith-Based Risk-Sharing Structures

Hassan Scott Odierno

This chapter describes certain risk-sharing arrangements emerging from the Abrahamic religious traditions and discusses their implications for some current challenges facing takaful.

Faith-Based Insurance

The vast majority of faith-based insurance is either Islamic (takaful) or Christian (mainly Roman Catholic). Faith-based insurance can be broadly categorized as the following:

- Christian health-sharing arrangements
- Christian associations
- Christian mutual insurers
- Takaful
- Jewish insurance.

Christian Health-Sharing Arrangements

Christian health-sharing arrangements consist of people grouping together to assist each other in paying their major health care costs. They began in the 1980s and have become an alternative to the formal health insurance system for an estimated 100,000 Americans. Such groups range from small community-based arrangements to multistate organizations such as Samaritan Ministries International and Medi-Share, which each month direct the flow of millions of dollars of benefits from individuals to members with eligible health care expenses. Such arrangements have been gaining mainstream recognition, receiving exemption from the recent health care bill passed in the United States (Sullivan 2010).

The general process for such an arrangement is that every month each member is assigned a share in the medical needs of another member. The process for the Samaritan Ministries is shown in figure 4.1:

Figure 4.1   Process for Samaritan Ministries

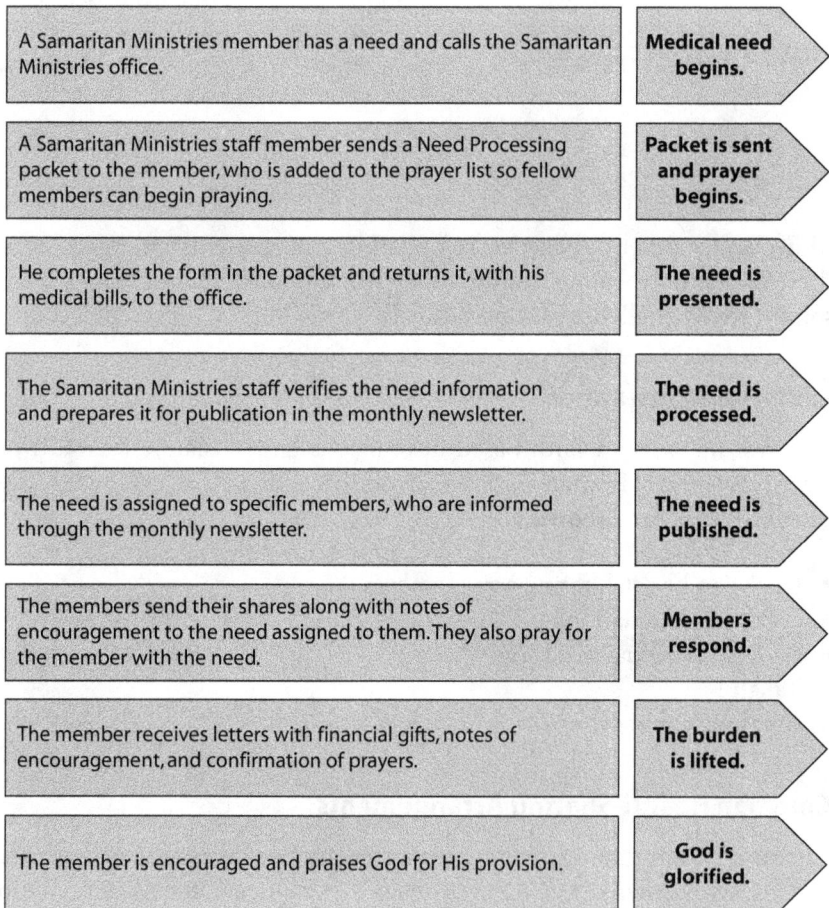

A Samaritan Ministries member has a need and calls the Samaritan Ministries office.	**Medical need begins.**
A Samaritan Ministries staff member sends a Need Processing packet to the member, who is added to the prayer list so fellow members can begin praying.	**Packet is sent and prayer begins.**
He completes the form in the packet and returns it, with his medical bills, to the office.	**The need is presented.**
The Samaritan Ministries staff verifies the need information and prepares it for publication in the monthly newsletter.	**The need is processed.**
The need is assigned to specific members, who are informed through the monthly newsletter.	**The need is published.**
The members send their shares along with notes of encouragement to the need assigned to them. They also pray for the member with the need.	**Members respond.**
The member receives letters with financial gifts, notes of encouragement, and confirmation of prayers.	**The burden is lifted.**
The member is encouraged and praises God for His provision.	**God is glorified.**

Source: Samaritan Ministries International, http://www.samaritanministries.org/works/index.php.

Samaritan Ministries is not Christian health insurance, as insurance implies a contract where one party agrees to be responsible for another party's risk of loss in exchange for a premium. In this arrangement, Christians assist one another with medical expenses through voluntary giving. This is similar to the takaful concept of paying contributions. In reality, should a member not voluntarily give as requested, he or she will not remain a part of the group, again similar to takaful. Here it is made very clear that, should there be insufficient funds, shares will be combined for several months, if possible, and, if required, all claims will be scaled down accordingly. This need to avoid guaranteed payments is one reason why these sharing arrangements have not ventured too far beyond health coverage, where contributions (shares) can be modified periodically. Takaful, by contrast, has been seen as providing guaranteed coverage. It is possible that a contract could be written whereby, if further funds are required, a "call" could be made on participants. However, no such contract has been developed or tested with either regulators or participants (or sharia council).

Transparency is a hallmark of these health-sharing arrangements. When individuals become members, they are asked to send an administration fee and their share for the first three months directly to the ministry. In later years, they only send a yearly administration fee to the ministry. The structure of benefit payouts is another aspect of transparency. Health claims are split into three categories, below US$300, US$300 to US$250,000, and above US$250,000. Claims below US$300 are considered deductible and are not covered. For claims between US$300 and US$250,000, a schedule of shares varies by family size and age.[1] Should claims be below the total shares of the group, everyone simply pays less. Thus, the issue of surplus ownership and payouts does not arise. With regard to actual payout, these plans cut out the middleman and ensure that members directly help each other and gain a personal responsibility toward each other. When a claim has been approved, a checklist is given to the claimant showing who is to assist in payment. Should some members not pay, this is reported and their claims are not accepted for payment. In such plans, a very specific set of circumstances for payment is given. For claims above US$250,000, members who want to participate pay an additional share into a savings account (which belongs to them). When a claim occurs, these funds are used for the claim. This structure is needed, as such claims are fewer but potentially much larger in size, so the law of large numbers does not work as easily. There are separate coverage and shares for other types of risk, such as injuries due to motor vehicle accidents.

Eligibility for Christian health-sharing programs is normally dependent on lifestyle requirements, such as regularly attending church and having such attendance verified by a pastor. There is normally a requirement to be healthy or, if not healthy, to work with a health coach to regain health. There is sometimes a requirement to be a non-smoker and to abstain from alcohol or not drink to excess. Maternity care for unwed women is often only allowed in rape cases, and members are expected to pay for and get preventive maintenance care. A testament of faith is generally required as well as a testament that the member will not smoke, do drugs, engage in extramarital sex, or drink alcohol to excess. In this way, to the greatest extent possible, homogeneous groups of people are covered.[2] In takaful, membership is open to all, subject to underwriting requirements similar to those of conventional insurance. An Islamic lifestyle is not a requirement for coverage.

Christian health-sharing arrangements are not without controversy. Due to the concept of mutual help and sharing without formal guarantees, they are not covered under insurance regulations. Therefore, there is no guarantee that benefits will be paid, and the numerous regulations put in place to protect consumers are not applicable (Boodman 2005). For nonemergency treatment, members need to call the ministry to determine the most appropriate course of action. The administrator is not necessarily a doctor and can recommend unconventional treatment in place of traditional medical treatment. Coverage that would normally be covered under insurance may not be covered, which the member might not understand. This includes coverage for things such as termination of pregnancy if the life of the mother is in danger and mental illness. There are also cases where administrators have taken shares meant to pay benefits and used them for their own purposes (Moll 2006). These types of issues would not apply to takaful, which is regulated similar to conventional insurance. These issues also point to the need for takaful regulations to keep pace with developments in the industry, especially if some operators opt for innovative models and solutions as opposed to following conventional insurance.

Christian Associations

Christian associations, as a subset of the more general association movement such as fraternals, friendly societies, and cooperatives, have their origins in the aftermath of the industrial revolution of the late 1700s and early 1800s. The industrial revolution created a gap between the owners of capital and the workers. In such a backdrop, people started forming groups for the following purposes:

- To negotiate for decent wages
- To market agricultural and other products
- To purchase unadulterated goods jointly at affordable prices
- To respond to the needs of small farmers, artisans, and business people for credit
- To provide affordable protection against the misfortunes of life.

Associations flourished because they put the needs of members ahead of profit considerations (Robb 2009). Takaful developed and flourished not due to the desire to avoid the negative aspects of capitalism, but from the need and desire of Muslims to participate in capitalism in an Islamic manner.

Associations have tended to get together based on race or religion and have provided insurance to their members in addition to giving out loans and scholarships and preserving the culture or religion of the association. Examples of such associations include the following:

- Catholic Knights
- Catholic Financial Life
- Polish Roman Catholic Union
- MAX (Mutual Aid eXchange), Anabaptist and Quaker
- Catholic Family Fraternal of Texas
- First Catholic Slovak Ladies Association
- Catholic Ladies of Columbia
- Protestant Alliance Friendly Society of New South Wales Limited
- Loyal Christian Benefit Association (LCBA).

The benefits of joining LCBA are typical:

- Death benefits if a newborn dies
- Orphan benefits for children whose parents die, including monthly benefit payments and a university scholarship
- Bereavement benefits such as telephone support and a series of booklets helping loved ones with their grief and telephone support
- Accidental death benefits
- Various scholarships, such as camping scholarships for juvenile members, scholarships to Christian elementary or secondary schools, and scholarships to postsecondary schools

- Discount programs such as identification theft protection and prescription drugs.

All Christians are eligible for membership. Branches of LCBA are set up to administer the association as well as to promote volunteer activities in the community.[3] To a certain extent, takaful operators have developed similar programs to assist their members and encourage sales, although this could be greatly extended to differentiate takaful from conventional insurance. This could include assistance with planning *hajj* (pilgrimage) and discounts in addition to the general wellness programs, benefits, and discount programs of Christian associations.

Christian associations have been in existence much longer than have health-sharing arrangements, since the 1800s in many cases. Some associations offer simple covers, whereas others offer the latest designs and types of products to rival traditional insurers. Compared to health-sharing arrangements, these associations are both regulated and offer a much more complete set of coverage.

Looking at the practices of the Catholic Knights, the surpluses (excess of assets over liabilities) are invested in socially responsible activities in accordance with the teachings of the Catholic Church. Instead of dividends, a tithe is paid to support the activities of the church or association. Should the solvency position become impaired, the board of directors has the option of allocating the deficit among all members, insured employees, policy owners, or any combination of the above. The member has the option of accepting a lower benefit, accepting a lien on the policy, or paying the deficit. The Catholic Knights appoints a priest, bishop, or cardinal as spiritual director to offer the president or board of directors advice based on Catholic teachings and practice. The spiritual director is a nonvoting member of the board of directors (Catholic Financial Life 2010).

In takaful, there is a wide range of practices with regard to surplus, ranging from keeping surplus within the fund to paying it to participants and the operator. A takaful operation that keeps surplus within the fund may have provisions for donating the surplus to charity, broadly similar to the Christian associations, but in practice this is rarely done. If a deficit arises in takaful, the operator provides an interest-free loan (*qard al hasan*) rather than asking participants to accept lower benefits or pay additional contributions. This reflects a combination of issues:

- The classification of takaful as a form of stock insurance rather than a nonprofit entity and the resulting need to protect the interests of participants
- The nature of coverage, which does not allow for reductions, such as with protection for mortgage loans
- Impracticality and marketing implications of asking for additional contributions.

These issues are practical in nature. In theory, considering a takaful fund to be a fund for participants to help each other in mutual solidarity, the solutions for resolving deficits in Catholic Knights would be valid for takaful as well. In takaful, a sharia council ensures that all aspects of operations are in accordance with Islamic law, similar to the spiritual director of Catholic Knights. The appointment of a sharia council member to be a nonvoting member of the board of directors is not common as of yet.

Christian Mutual Insurers

Christian mutual insurers are a subset of the wider group of mutual insurers and generally started from a need to find cost-effective means to insure church or related properties and risks. Some still focus on churches and related properties and risks, whereas others have branched out.

Examples include the following:

- Catholic Mutual Group
- Southern Mutual Church Insurance Company
- Brotherhood Mutual (Mennonite groups)
- Associated Mutual
- Church Mutual
- Goodville Mutual
- Ecclesiastical Insurance Group
- Catholic Super
- Christian Super.

Catholic Mutual insures church properties. It was founded by a group of Midwest Catholic bishops unable to obtain reasonable coverage for their churches. It provides services of particular interest to the Church, such as policies relating to hiring personnel, sexual misconduct policies, and counseling errors and omissions.[4] Brotherhood Mutual and Church Mutual also insure church properties.

Associated Mutual was started by a group of Jewish farmers who felt that they were being treated unfairly under the terms of available insurance contracts.[5] Goodville Mutual was started by a group of Mennonite men for automobile insurance on the principle of bearing one another's burden. Their mission is to provide comprehensive non-life products of the highest quality and to conduct their business on the biblical principles of love, justice, and integrity. Goodville Mutual's coverage includes needs that are specific to churches, such as stained glass coverage and protection for lawsuits relating to sexual acts.[6]

The Ecclesiastical Insurance Group was formed in 1887 by churchmen in order to protect churches against the risk of fire.[7] The group currently protects a wider range of risks. Ecclesiastical is owned by a charity, Allchurches Trust Limited. Allchurches receives its funding from Eccleciastical and has as its mission to promote the Christian religion, to contribute to the funds of any charitable institution or association, and to carry out any charitable purpose. Allchurches donated £6.8 million in 2009, with the majority used to support the dioceses and cathedrals of the Church of England.[8]

Similar to Christian mutuals, takaful started with a focus on specific products, in this case products needed by Muslims, such as obligatory motor, medical, and other non-life cover as well as coverage for mortgage loans. Some takaful operators continue to focus on such business, whereas others have diversified and offer coverage similar to a conventional insurance company. The major exception to this is with respect to maturity benefits. Conventional insurance companies provide guaranteed maturity benefits, whereas in takaful maturity benefits are not guaranteed. Guaranteed maturity benefits imply a guaranteed return on investment, which would fall under *riba* (giving or receiving interest) and therefore be prohibited in Islam. Thus far, takaful operators are generally not differentiated from conventional insurers; they do not have unique features or coverage, except for coverage relating to *hajj*.

Jewish Insurance

Halacha is the collective body of Jewish religious law, including biblical law and later Talmudic and Rabbinic law as well as customs and traditions. Interest (called *ribis*) appears to be forbidden in Jewish law (Lobel and Project Genesis n.d.; Halacha-Yomi, ch. 65). This extends from formal interest to "gifts" given before or after a loan or other contract. For situations involving something with a fixed market value, it is also prohibited to charge more than that value in exchange for delaying the time when payment is due. Although allowances are made for dealing with interest from non-Jews, there are restrictions, such as when a guarantor for the transaction is a Jew. The issue of surplus charity funds comes up in a business example (Hilchos Choshen Mishpat 1:16). Here the question asked is, if a campaign is conducted to raise money for a particular person to receive medical care and in the end surplus funds are available, what happens to the surplus funds? Four potential scenarios are given:

- If the cause for the surplus is that the sick person did not actually require all of the treatments that were originally anticipated or if money was collected for this cause and, ultimately, for whatever reason, the sick person did not undergo the treatments, the money must be returned to those who donated it. If it is no longer possible to identify who the original donors were, or if it would be a very large expense to identify and return the money to them, the unused money should be used to defray the medical expenses of another needy sick person. It should not be diverted to a different type of charity.

- If the patient received all or some of the treatments necessary, but more money came in than was actually needed, the surplus funds would belong to the sick person and his family. This would be true even if the patient passed away during the course of the treatment or afterward.

- In the above case, if the person (or organization) collecting is a well-known charity that collects funds for various causes, he would be permitted to divert these funds to another cause. If, however, he is just a friend who took the initiative this one time for this one cause, he would be obligated to give the surplus to the patient or his family.

- If the campaign is run on behalf of a recognized public charity fund or medical assistance program, the person collecting would be permitted to use the surplus funds for another charitable purpose, even if this is the only time that he has tried to raise money for charity. This is true even though the money was collected for a specific needy or sick person (Lobel and Project Genesis n.d.).

Thus, there are similarities between Jewish insurance and Islamic insurance, including the avoidance of interest and the sharing of surplus.

Using the Experience of Other Faith-Based Insurance to Address Current Challenges in Takaful

One challenge in takaful is defining exactly what takaful is. Iranian insurers (also labeled takaful) are not run as traditional takaful operators and do not have sharia councils. Some cooperatives in Saudi Arabia also do not have sharia councils. The Saudi Arabian Monetary Association (SAMA) has closed down the use of the takaful name and all differences between takaful and cooperative insurance regulations, as specified by SAMA in their regulations. This confusion, in conjunction with a lack of a worldwide body to collect statistics, hinders the ability of a potential entrant to understand what takaful is and to determine the size of the potential market. This issue is limited to takaful, as other faith-based insurance has not had profit as a motive (in general), thus making such analysis of secondary importance. Without a profit motive, the results of different operators' sharia councils could be published, which would likely lead to significantly more convergence of operations.

The wide variety of models currently in use has caused considerable confusion in the market as to what is acceptable under sharia law. Beyond this confusion in the market, regulation also becomes difficult, as there is no standard "takaful." Different operators develop their own version, which can vary substantially by company and by country. These differences, along with the interplay of religious and technical principles, make corporate governance very difficult. In many jurisdictions, AAOIFI (Accounting and Auditing Organization for Islamic Financial Institutions) guidelines are simply used as a reference, although in several jurisdictions they are binding. The following AAOIFI guidelines are useful with regard to corporate governance:

- Sharia Supervisory Board: Appointment, Composition, and Board
- Sharia Review
- Internal Sharia Review
- Audit and Governance Committee for Islamic Financial Institutions.

Corporate governance issues in takaful also arise from the use of *qard al hasan*, or interest-free loans, when there is a deficit in the risk fund.[9] The structure normally used is for the *qard* to be considered as an injection from the point of view of the risk fund, but a loan from the point of view of the operator's fund. This discrepancy potentially allows operators to show impressive results, while selling unprofitable business.

This also extends to the commissions paid for retakaful, which is similar to conventional reinsurance. No retakaful commissions should be paid up-front, as they are at present. Such benefits should only be attributable if a surplus is generated and shared with the operator and eventual participants. There is a belief that such commissions are permissible only if the operator is not able to cover the *wakala* fees of the policy concerned. The result is a deficit for the business, which would likely be made up by other profitable plans, which would not be equitable (Odierno 2009).

As noted, the significant diversity in takaful models has led to regulatory difficulties. Takaful is sometimes grouped with conventional insurance for the purposes of regulations, which ignores fundamental differences. Even when takaful is regulated separately, issues arise with regard to implied benefits and guarantees, even where none formally exists (Odierno 2007). This seems to be an issue for mutual insurers as well, with mutual insurance tending to be an afterthought in regulations, as well as for faith-based organizations offering discretionary benefits or voluntary sharing of medical expenses, which are not regulated at all.

In some takaful operations, the operator does not share in underwriting surplus due to concerns over uncertainty. The concern is how to keep the operator interested in maximizing underwriting surplus under such conditions: the operator is best served by charging cheap rates and reinsuring most of the risk so that large volumes of sales will result. Alternatively, the operator does not share in losses, so sharing in surplus seems one sided (Rabiah and Odierno 2008). Again, this is not faced by other types of organizations, as profit is not a motive. Even with the sharing of surplus among participants, myriad issues need to be considered when attempting to share surplus in a manner that is fair to all, such as the need to separate short-tailed policies (where claims are settled quickly) and long-tailed policies (where delays in payments due to court cases can render estimates of reserves and provisions little more than a guess), the need to determine the level of surplus to be kept inside the fund for contingencies, and the need to build similar levels of conservatism into rates for all plans in a takaful fund. Information technology issues also can force a simplified solution to be used, even though a more complicated solution would result in greater fairness (Odierno 2008). The IFSB (Islamic Financial Services Board) has defined solutions for these issues in its Takaful Governance and Takaful Solvency Guidelines. Further guidance will be offered when the Takaful Risk Management Guidelines are published next year. AAOIFI has tried to move from its "no surplus to operators" stance to a very peculiar "30 percent of surplus to be shared with staff members of the underwriting team."

Many issues arise with respect to *qard al hasan* to cover deficits. In this area, there is significant room for learning from others. Can surplus be maintained in the risk fund at all times, such as is done under other approaches? Can participants be asked to top up their contributions in periods of deficit or to accept lower benefits? Should a savings fund be developed and then charges dripped to the risk fund only when needed?

Determining who has final authority over whether the operations are truly Islamic in nature is also an issue. Is this the responsibility of the sharia council, the board of directors, or management? Should shareholders put processes in place to ensure compliance with Islamic principles? Does this need to be more stringent if management is non-Muslim? Here, the equivalent is the spiritual director of a Christian association.

Should participants have a say in operations and the hiring of the sharia council? Here as well, significant guidance can be gleaned from other organizations. Potentially, an advocate could be used to stand up for the rights of participants.

Notes

1. Samaritan Ministries International, http://www.samaritanministries.org/cost/.

2. Samaritan Ministries International, http://www.samaritanministries.org/faq/.

3. Loyal Christian Benefit Association, http://www.lcbalife.org/index.php/benefits.html.

4. Catholic Mutual Group, http://www.catholicmutual.org/.

5. Associated Mutual Insurance Cooperative, http://www.associatedmutual.com/index.php?q=history.

6. Goodville Mutual, http://www.goodville.com/aboutus/.

7. Ecclesiastical Group Insurance, http://www.ecclesiastical.com/aboutus/index.aspx.

8. Allchurches Trust, http://www.allchurches.co.uk/index.aspx.

9. Use of the term *qard al hassan* is disappearing in Malaysia and is being replaced simply by the term *qard*.

References

Boodman, Sandra G. 2005. "Seeking Divine Protection." *Washington Post*, October 25. http://www.washingtonpost.com/wp-dyn/content/article/2005/10/22/AR2005102200046.html.

Catholic Financial Life. 2010. "Articles of Incorporation of Catholic Knights." Catholic Financial Life, Milwaukee, WI, April 1. http://www.catholicfinanciallife .org/About/ArticlesandBylaws.htm.

Lobel, Rabbi Ari, and Project Genesis. n.d. "Halacha Yomi Archives." *Torah.org.* http://www.torah.org/learning/halacha/business.html.

Moll, Rob. 2006. "After the Scandals." *Christianity Today*, December 13. http:// ctlibrary.com/newsletter/newsletterarchives/2006-12-11.html.

Odierno, Hassan Scott P. 2007. "Achieving Common Standards in Takaful Regulations." *Middle East Insurance Review* (January): 71–72.

———. 2008. "The Sharing of Surplus in Takaful." *Middle East Insurance Review* (December): 51–52.

———. 2009. "Corporate Governance in Takaful." *Takaful Articles* 19 (November).

Rabiah, Adawiah Engku Ali, and Hassan Scott P. Odierno. 2008. "Managing Risks in Takaful through Pricing and Reserving Practices." In *Essential Guide to Takaful (Islamic Insurance)*, 83–99, edited by Engku Rabiah and Hassan Scott P. Odierno. Kuala Lumpur: CERT Publications.

Robb, Alan J. 2009. "Mutuality in Uncertain Times." Address to the Unimutual Twentieth Anniversary Conference, Canberra, Australia, September 10.

Sullivan, Amy. 2010. "Faith-Based Insurance: Christian Health Care Sharing." *Time,* June 7. http://www.time.com/time/magazine/article/0,9171,1992385,00 .html.

CHAPTER 5

Hybrid Insurance Structures: Reciprocals, Hybrid Mutual Insurers, and Takaful

Zainal Abidin Mohd Kassim, Hassan Scott Odierno, and Sabbir Patel

The previous chapters introduced major institutional structures for transferring and sharing risk and outlined the nature and background of mutual and faith-based insurers in the West. This chapter explores the concept of reciprocal inter-insurance exchanges (reciprocals), as employed in North America. These most often are unincorporated entities established to meet the special insurance needs of professional groups (for example, doctors), universities, and municipalities. Their legal status varies, with some treated as mainstream insurers for regulatory purposes and others as captive insurers.

A reciprocal exchange involves two distinct entities. With the reciprocal inter-insurance exchange, subscribers share their risk through a risk exchange. The reciprocal is overseen by a board of governors whose responsibilities include selecting the attorney-in-fact (AIF), monitoring the performance of the AIF, and approving rates. Reciprocals typically

The authors would like to thank Colin Heavyside (Capricorn Society Limited, Australia) for his contribution to this chapter.

maintain a range of surplus distribution accounts, all of which are available to pay claims. One of these types of accounts is the subscriber savings account, from which subscribers may receive a payment upon withdrawal from the exchange. Most policies these days are for fixed premiums, although it is possible for a reciprocal to issue a contract subject to further assessment.

The attorney-in-fact is a distinct legal entity that runs the day-to-day affairs (other than claims management) of the reciprocal. This may be owned either by the reciprocal or by a separate enterprise. The subscribers provide a power of attorney to the AIF, giving it legal authority to act on their behalf in managing and administering the reciprocal under the terms of a formal management contract, which may be in perpetuity or for a specified term. If the AIF is a company, its board of directors may include one or more members of the board of governors of the reciprocal.

An example of a reciprocal that sells to the general public with a commercial link is Farmers Insurance Group (FIG), which acts as attorney-in-fact to the Farmers Exchange (consisting of three reciprocal insurers: the Farmers Insurance Exchange, the Truck Insurance Exchange, and the Fire Insurance Exchange), which are owned exclusively by their policyholders. As a management company, FIG (currently owned by Zurich Financial Services) manages the policies under the Farmers Insurance Exchange. FIG provides non-claims-related management services to the Farmers Insurance Exchange in return for a fee determined as a percentage of the gross premium. These non-claims-related services extend to selection of risk, preparation and mailing of policy forms and invoices, collection of premiums, management of the investment portfolios, and other administrative and managerial functions. Farmers Insurance Exchange is responsible for the claims function, including the settlement and pay-ment of claims as well as the payment of agents' commissions and bonuses.

Farmers Insurance Exchange can issue bonds to FIG and other external parties, which contribute toward boosting its solvency margin. These bonds are termed either surplus note certificates (if not issued to affiliates) or contribution certificates (if issued to affiliates). These certificates have a fixed term and carry a coupon. They are different from ordinary bonds in that interest and capital payments are subject to the availability of surplus in the policyholders' pool and to the agreement of the regulators. To ensure solvency even further, Farmers Insurance Exchange issues contingent surplus note certificates to lenders who are obliged to subscribe on preagreed terms on the occurrence of a contingent event (for example, when a catastrophe exhausts the reinsurance lines of protection).

The success of this model is reflected in both its rating and its profitability. According to A.M. Best, Farmers Insurance Exchange has been rated as high as third in the personal lines property casualty market in the United States.

Discretionary or Hybrid Mutuals

A discretionary mutual is a cooperative in which the board of directors has the authority to decide the following:

- Whether or not to accept applications for membership
- The level of protection it will grant—each member is individually rated according to his or her risk profile and pays contributions accordingly
- The payment it will make on receipt of a claim.

The board is guided by the principles of fairness and justice, governed by its constitution, rules, and protection wordings, balancing the interests of individual members with those of the group as a whole. A feature here is that the board can accept a claim it considers to be fair in circumstances where a stock insurer would decline it (Robb 2009).

Discretionary mutuals have grown mainly from arrangements with certain professions, where groups of professionals agree jointly to meet the costs of certain risks that members face. They generally focus on specialized cover that segments of society find difficult or expensive to purchase. This is done on a discretionary basis and generally does not fall under insurance regulations. There are significant cost savings due to exemptions from state taxes and costs of supervision. However, discretionary mutuals need to be regulated with regard to the following:

- Levels of risk retained by the mutual, above which reinsurance should be obtained
- Deficits in the mutual fund, when members may be called on to pay additional contributions (Australian Government, Treasury 2004).

A distinction between discretionary and hybrid mutuals is that hybrid mutuals purchase insurance coverage above a certain retention level.[1] Generally speaking, external management companies manage the operations of discretionary mutuals. For instance, Capricorn Mutual in Australia is managed by Capricorn Mutual Management. The management fees are fixed and paid monthly and may also include performance-related remuneration as well as a bonus fee of 20 percent of the audited surplus of the operations.[2] However, not all managers take such performance fees.

The sharing of surplus is a sensitive issue in takaful. Although the sharing of investment profit is well accepted and allowed, the sharing of underwriting surplus is considered unacceptable from an Islamic point of view in many parts of the world (Malaysia being a major exception). The structure of a discretionary mutual represents one possible reality of takaful. This is what takaful ideally should look like, as takaful funds are set up to help participants to share in one another's risks, with retakaful used above a certain level. At the present time, takaful tends to focus on mandatory products such as coverage for mortgage loans and motor coverage, which require guarantees of coverage to be in place.

An example is the Capricorn Society, an Australian-based cooperative that has 12,000 automobile repair and service center businesses in membership, primarily in Australia but also in New Zealand and South Africa. Among other things, Capricorn Society enables its members to take advantage of a range of benefits, including access to joint purchasing, business credit, and financial services.

In 2003, the Capricorn Society directors looked into ways in which their members could benefit from a commercially feasible alternative to insurance, at that time an area of considerable dissatisfaction for many in the society. Capricorn Mutual, the vehicle established, now has several thousand members. It is not legally deemed to offer insurance and is therefore not regulated under the Australian insurance regulatory regime. Instead, it is treated as a financial services provider and holds an Australian financial services license.

Capricorn Mutual is at pains to ensure that its members and potential members understand this distinction. As its website puts it, "Capricorn Mutual is not an insurance company, but a discretionary mutual run solely for the benefit of its members. The Board of Capricorn Mutual exercises the following discretions: who to admit to membership; what protections to grant and the level of protection to apply; to accept or reject a claim for assistance made by a member; to pay in full or in part a claim for assistance made by a member. The Board's discretion in these matters is absolute."[3]

Members of the mutual pay a small subscription, currently $A 10, and if admitted to the society can then apply for protection against different risks. For each category of risk selected, a contribution—legally not considered an insurance premium—is payable. As Capricorn Mutual explains, "If the application for discretionary protection is successful, a member will be issued with a Schedule of Protection that confirms the protections in place and the amounts of discretionary protection available to the member."[4]

Claims are assessed by the board, which decides whether or not to pay out. Nevertheless, since the board is democratically elected by the mutual's members, in practice it is highly unlikely that legitimate claims will be denied.

Capricorn had chosen at inception to use the services of a specialist company, Regis Mutual Management, one of a handful of firms aiming to meet the needs of discretionary mutuals. According to Regis's chief executive Paul Koronka, a necessary prerequisite for a successful new mutual like Capricorn is that its members have shared interests and concerns. Typically, Koronka works with groups that consider their premiums to be unrelated to their claims experience and believe that they can achieve results as a group that are not available to them as individual members. Having developed sufficient in-house management expertise in administering all facets of the mutual, in July 2011 Capricorn deployed its own management services to the mutual, concluding its long and fruitful relationship with Regis.

The idea of using existing affinity groups as the basis for a new insurance (or quasi-insurance) mutual has deep roots. U.S. employers in the dock, ship repair, and offshore industries established their own Signal Mutual Indemnity Association back in 1986, for example, and Canadian, Australian, and U.K. universities have long-established mutuals dating to the 1980s.

An added refinement of the discretionary mutual model is the hybrid solution, in which the mutual externally takes insurance on behalf of its members for very large claims. One mutual deals with claims up to £50,000 on a discretionary basis, for example, but arranges a group insurance policy for risks above this threshold (ICMIF 2008).

Capricorn Mutual's parent, Capricorn Society, stresses its status as a cooperative, pointing out on its website that it identifies with the seven international principles of cooperatives (see the overview). It is also a member in its own right of the International Cooperative Alliance.[5]

Takaful

Similar to Christian health-sharing arrangements, takaful has a relatively short history (although the underlying concepts go back many centuries). Takaful was conceived in the late 1970s out of the need for Islamic banks to have insurance coverage consistent with Muslim principles. The first takaful operators, such as the Islamic Insurance Company, established in

1979, reflected this need. This company was developed out of the desire of Faisal Islamic Bank to obtain insurance in an Islamic manner and a fatwa (religious ruling) by its legal control committee in 1978.[6] As profit was not a prime consideration, the company was set up on pure cooperative principles. All surpluses remained in the fund, and actual expenses were charged to the risk fund. Profit for the operator was purely on investment income generated by capital. Similarly, the Islamic Arab Insurance Company of Saudi Arabia was established in 1979 as part of the Dallah Al Baraka Group to support its operations. This model functioned very similarly to that of other faith-based organizations, but whereas other faith-based organizations were developed to spread religious values or forge ties within a community, takaful sought to support banking operations.

In Malaysia, Syarikat Takaful Malaysia (STM) was established in 1984 to support the operations of the owner, Bank Islam. STM used a *mudharaba* model for its family takaful (life insurance) operations, in which the operator and the participants shared the profit from investments of capital (operator only) or policyholder funds (operator and participants). Management expenses were paid out of the profits shared with the operator. As general takaful and yearly group takaful developed, underwriting surplus was also shared. This was a practical consideration, as investment income for such plans was not sufficient to cover expenses, and thus surplus was treated as "profit" under the STM *mudharaba* model. In this sense, STM was developed under profit motives as well as to support banking operations. When STM started operations, there were only a handful of takaful operators worldwide. Since then, a wider variety of models has been developed, and the *mudharaba* model itself has evolved.

The basis for takaful was clarified by the Islamic Fiqh Academy, emanating from a meeting of the Organization of the Islamic Conference in Jeddah in December 1985 (Taylor n.d.), where it was resolved that

1. The commercial insurance contract, with a fixed periodical premium, which is commonly used by commercial insurance companies, is a contract which contains major element of risk, which voids the contract and, therefore, is prohibited (*haram*) according to the sharia.
2. The alternative contract, which conforms to the principles of Islamic dealings, is the contract of cooperative insurance, which is founded on the basis of charity and cooperation. Similarly is the case of reinsurance based on the principles of cooperative insurance.
3. The Academy invites the Muslim countries to work on establishing cooperative insurance institutions and cooperative entities for the

reinsurance, in order to liberate the Islamic economy from the exploitation and violation of the system, which Allah has chosen for this *umma*.

This ruling is important as much for what was stated as for what was not mentioned in the text. What was clearly stated were three principles that must apply for insurance to be considered Islamic:

- Islamic principles (sharia compliant)
- Charitable donations (*tabarru'*)
- Cooperative principles.

The following was not mentioned:

- The operating principles for a takaful operator
- Separation of risk, whereby insurance risk can be shared only with participants, not with the operator
- The basis of the relationship between the participants and the operator—that is, *wakala* (agency), *mudharaba* (profit sharing), or any other acceptable Islamic contractual foundation
- Whether any underwriting surplus can be shared between the participant and the operator or whether it should be distributed solely to the participants or be used for some other purpose, that is, as reserves or charitable donations (Taylor n.d.)
- The appointment of a sharia advisory board or similar arrangements
- The issuing of a fatwa
- Ongoing sharia review of the operations.

During the 1980s and early to mid-1990s, other operators, both in Malaysia and in countries such as Bangladesh, Indonesia, and Sri Lanka, followed suit with similar models. With many of these operations, the motive was to earn a profit rather than to support banking operations. Of course, ensuring that Muslims could obtain coverage and save in an Islamic manner was also a motive. In general, the vast majority of participants were Muslim. The *mudharaba* model had a disadvantage in that it was not universally accepted, especially in the Middle East with regard to the practical implementation of Islamic finance including takaful. An attitude of "us versus them" prevailed between Southeast Asia and the Middle East, with Southeast Asia being seen as progressive, at the expense of Islamic acceptability, and the Middle East being seen as overly conservative.

As it applies to takaful, a *mudharaba* contract is generally not acceptable where underwriting surplus is to be shared with the operator. Where no underwriting surplus is to be shared, a *mudaraba* contract is universally permissible.

While many of the products developed during this time were needed to support compulsory coverage, such as motor and mortgage loans, voluntary coverage also was being developed. STM developed bancatakaful operations that pioneered savings products. Etiqa, consisting originally of two separate companies, Maybank Takaful and Takaful Nasional, brought the development of bancatakaful to new heights with the products sold by Maybank Takaful. Whereas STM products looked distinctly different from conventional products, Maybank Takaful products were designed to look identical to the products sold by its sister company Maybank Insurance. This allowed potential participants to choose either conventional insurance or takaful, depending on their needs. Takaful Nasional pioneered the use of an agency force to sell takaful, dealing with issues such as paying commissions to agents directly from contributions received rather than from income attributed to the operator.

In the late 1990s, Bank Al Jazira in Saudi Arabia made popular the *wakala* model, in which the operator is paid fees to run the takaful fund. In this sense, the takaful fund is set up as a pure cooperative or mutual, but pays the operator a fee to run the business. The operator makes a profit by ensuring that its actual costs are lower than the fees charged. This is similar to a mutual insurer or reciprocal that is run by a stock company, with the stock company taking fixed or volume-based fees. This model quickly spread to Malaysia through its development by Takaful Ikhlas, thus uniting the Far East and the Middle East with a mutually acceptable model.

The late 2000s has seen the emergence of large multinationals interested in offering takaful. Here the motive is purely profit, as many of these companies market to non-Muslims as well as Muslims. Such multinationals are stock insurers rather than mutuals. For example, Prudential is a market leader in Malaysia and Indonesia, with Allianz also setting up operations in Indonesia. AIA has shown interest through the development of operations in Indonesia as well as Malaysia. ING, Great Eastern Life, and Friends Provident (in conjunction with AM Assurance) have just started operations in Malaysia. The large reinsurers have also entered the field of retakaful, with players such as Munich Re, Swiss Re, and Hannover Re all offering retakaful. Faith is seen as a means of marketing takaful rather than the sole reason for its attractiveness. Whereas most of these multinationals have flourished under the agency distribution system, some have ventured into bancatakaful. Prudential in Malaysia developed bancatakaful through Bank Simpanan National in addition to its agency force, whereas HSBC Amanah and CIMB Aviva focus completely on bancatakaful. Compulsory products such as coverage for mortgage loans are the mainstay, but, similar to Etiqa, pure savings products (whether through a traditional framework or a unit-linked design) have been developed along with single-contribution structured unit-linked plans, or closed-end funds (Odierno and Ismail 2009).

Thus far, there has been a distinction between development in the Middle East and development in Asia. In Asia, family takaful has developed in addition to general takaful, whereas in the Middle East, with the exception of a few players such as Bank Al Jazira, FWU Group, HSBC, and the National Commercial Bank in Saudi Arabia, the developments have been either purely general takaful or general takaful plus compulsory coverage for mortgage loans. In the Middle East, there has been resistance to family coverage in general.

The market for takaful is growing. Currently there are local takaful players in many Muslim-majority and some Muslim-minority countries. In the Muslim-majority countries with no takaful, interest continues to grow, mainly in line with the development of Islamic banking. In this sense, such markets perceive the need for compulsory coverage acceptable to Muslims, as Muslims awaken to the need for acceptable solutions to their insurance needs. Awareness of the need for coverage as well as the ability to develop takaful operations profitably are seen as factors in growth. As takaful continues to flourish in countries such as Indonesia, Malaysia, and Saudi Arabia, more Muslim countries are expected to develop takaful. This extends as well to Muslim-minority countries where Islamic finance is being developed. In such countries, the awareness of Islamic finance stimulates the corresponding awareness of takaful. Multinationals continue to see the potential for profit in takaful and tend to look to the established takaful centers of Malaysia and highly populated Muslim countries such as Indonesia as stepping stones to more global developments. In the future, takaful should continue to be developed, initially by local players developing in line with Islamic finance, and then expanded by multinationals. In less affluent countries, takaful may require the assistance of the government or other international bodies or the will of existing cooperatives.

Takaful Models

Profit motives are front and center for today's takaful operators. In some markets, competition has been cutthroat with respect to fees, charges, and projected levels of savings. For most takaful operators, the focus is not on savings products, which are the focus of mutual insurers, but on risk products, either non-life insurance or mortgage term products.

Takaful companies are not purely stock insurers. The takaful operator sets up a takaful fund, which is put together for groups of participants to assist each other in times of need. The direct link between contributors and those in need is not present. There is less focus on religion and religious observance, although a religious council (sharia council) carefully reviews the practices of these firms to ensure compliance.

Therefore, takaful can be considered a mutual insurance hybrid, operating in a new segment of the universe of insurance models. Takaful is similar in structure to a mutual insurance company, which is run by a stock insurer for a fixed fee, but also to a faith-based insurance company, which needs to comply with religious principles.

This structure is manifest in the main business models in takaful—namely *mudharaba*, *wakala*, and *wakala* with *mudharaba* on investment profit. In addition, there is the pure cooperative model in which all profit belongs to the participants. This type of model is not common in takaful, as it does not allow profit for the operator, but it would be an excellent choice for either a cooperative interested in making its operations compliant with Islamic concepts or for a government interested in helping segments of the population to help themselves in an Islamic manner.

The *mudharaba* model was used by the early takaful operators and continues to be used in various forms in countries such as Bangladesh, Brunei, Sri Lanka, and Sudan. In this model, shown in figure 5.1, the participant pays a contribution to the takaful operator, who splits this into two portions, a savings portion (participant's account) and a risk portion (participants' special account or risk fund). The funds in the participant's account belong to the individual participant, whereas amounts in the participants' special account become a community pool of money for assistance against the covered risks—that is, a common account. Thus, the pooled account operates in a manner similar to a mutual or cooperative. The takaful operator receives a portion of investment income as well as a portion of underwriting surplus, which is used to pay expenses as well as to provide profit. There are several variations of this model, depending on the country as well as the interpretation of the sharia council as to what is acceptable (Mohd Kassim 2007).

The most common model is the *wakala* model, either on its own or in conjunction with the *mudharaba* model. Naming conventions vary by

Figure 5.1   The *Mudharaba* Model

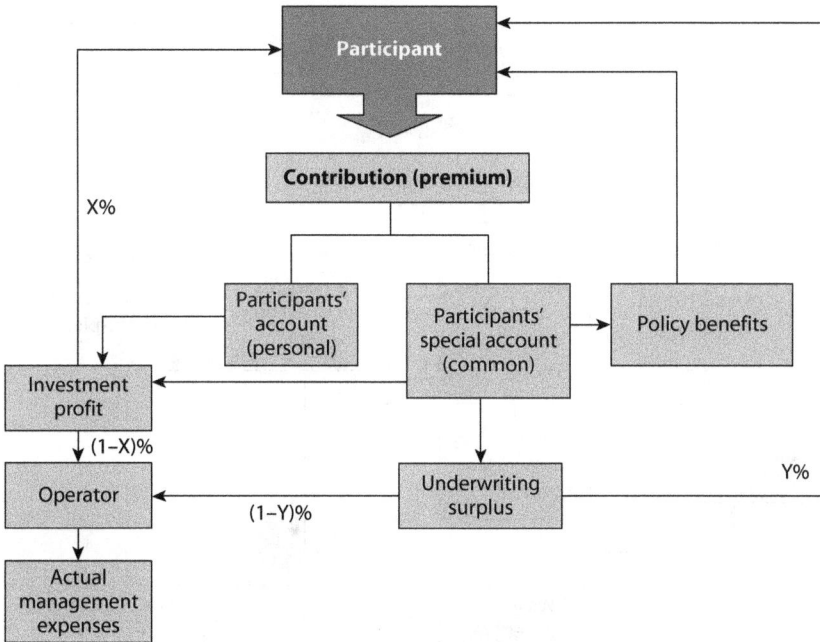

country and by operator, with some operators using a *wakala* model in conjunction with *mudharaba*, but calling it *wakala*. In the *wakala* model, the participant pays a contribution to the participant's account, and drips are taken on a monthly or yearly basis for the participants' special fund (risk fund) to cover benefits. For yearly renewable products, the contribution generally goes directly into the risk fund. All investment profit and underwriting surplus is given back to participants. The operator receives fees, called *wakala* fees, from which expenses are paid as well as profit. These fees can be defined in a variety of ways and ideally relate to work performed and expenses incurred to ensure fairness and minimize the mismatch between expenses and income. The participants' special account is again a common account operating on lines similar to cooperative or mutual principles (Odierno 2006). This is shown in figure 5.2.

The *wakala* with *mudharaba* on investment profit operates very similarly to the *wakala* model, but with the operator sharing in investment profits. Technically, two models operate within the overall operations, one for running the company and one for handling investment activities. Some sharia councils prefer to call this model *wakala* due to a dislike for

Figure 5.2   The *Wakala* Model

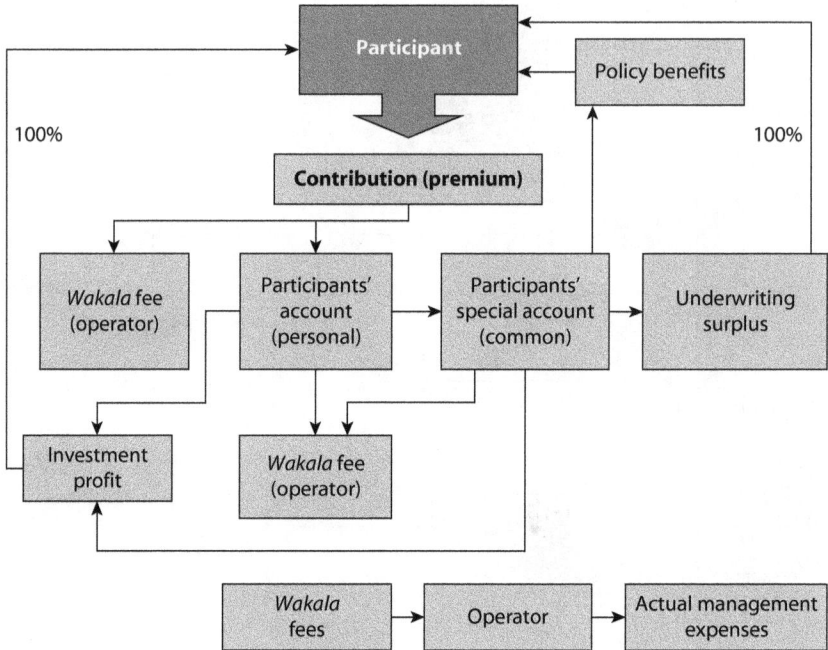

having more than one model in operation at the same time. Under both the *wakala* and the *wakala* with *mudharaba* on investment profits, some operators also share in underwriting surplus. In such a model, this sharing is considered incentive compensation for managing operations efficiently. Unfortunately, such incentives can lead to practices such as charging conservative rates to ensure a significant surplus. Whereas in the *wakala* model, there tends to be a *wakala* fee on the total fund value (normally just the savings fund) to cover investment expenses and allow for profit, in the *wakala* with *mudharaba* on investment profit model, the *mudharaba* replaces this fee (Mohd Kassim 2005). This is shown in figure 5.3.

In some countries and markets, especially where Muslims are a minority, takaful operations are set up as a department within a conventional insurance operation (called a takaful window). This is useful where there is an insufficient number of Muslims or insufficient interest to justify separate takaful operations. Such an approach can be problematic, however, with regard to the segregation of funds, cannibalization of funds, and infighting between conventional and takaful operations, antiselection between conventional and takaful products where they are similar,

Figure 5.3   The *Wakala* with *Mudharaba* on Investment Profit Model

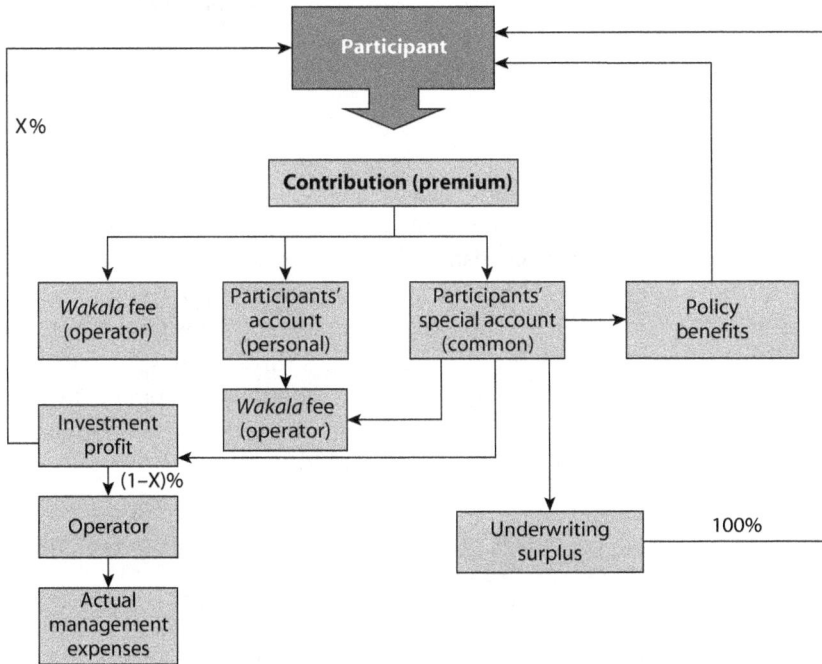

and potential dilution of branding, such as the difficulty of convincing Muslims of the acceptability of such operations from an Islamic point of view (Odierno and Iqbal 2006).

Although takaful is not quite the same as mutual or cooperative insurance, in countries where takaful is either new or nonexistent and cooperatives are popular, Muslim groups have tended to set up operations with the support and help of a cooperative or in some cases as an agency of the cooperative. This is seen in the setup of pilot takaful operations in Canada by Ansar Cooperative Housing working with the Cooperators Insurance Company and the Swedish Muslim Council working with Folksam. The ability to market takaful through windows and cooperatives provides opportunities to spread takaful to markets not traditionally thought of as takaful, but where significant Muslims exist and have a need for such products. A case in point is China: 60 million Muslims constitute an insignificant portion of the Chinese population, but a huge market in their own right (Odierno 2007). Similarly, in European countries such as Belgium, Finland, France, Germany, Spain, and Sweden, mutual or cooperative insurance constitutes more than 20 percent of total insurance, making these companies a simple yet viable means for offering takaful. Other countries in Europe also have a significant mutual or cooperative presence (AISAM 2007).

Conclusion

Understanding the similarities and differences in the structures of different types of insurance can help to inform the development of takaful. Takaful can move from being unknown and poorly understood to taking its proper place in the overall universe of insurance options. Takaful can be adapted to developing markets through existing cooperatives or be developed from government initiatives to target specific segments of society. This is the traditional strength of the cooperative approach and a potential strength of takaful as well.

Notes

1. Regis Mutual Management, http://www.rmml.com/index.html.
2. Capricorn Mutual, http://www.capricornmutual.com/view/home/.
3. Capricorn Mutual, http://www.capricornmutual.com/view/about/faq/.
4. Capricorn Mutual, http://www.capricornmutual.com/view/about/faq/.
5. Capricorn Society, http://www.capricorn.coop.
6. ICMIFtakaful, http://www.takaful.coop/index.php?option=com_content& view=article&id=70&Itemid=50.

References

AISAM (Association Internationale des Sociétés d'Assurance Mutuelle). 2007. *Mutual Insurance in Figures.* Belgium: AISAM.

Australian Government, Treasury. 2004. "Key Findings of the Review of Discretionary Mutual Funds and Direct Offshore Foreign Insurers." In *DMF Review.* Canberra: Treasury, Australian Government, May. http://dmfreview. treasury.gov.au/content/_report/key_report.asp.

ICMIF (International Cooperative and Mutual Insurance Federation). 2008. "Promoting New Mutuals." *Voice* 61 (April).

Kassim, Zainal Abidin Mohd. 2005. "Takaful: The Islamic Way of Insurance." *Contingencies* (January–February): 33–38.

————. 2007. "Takaful: A Question of Surplus." In *Islamic Insurance Trends, Opportunities, and the Future of Takaful*, ed. Sohail E. Jaffer, 48–52. London: Euromoney.

Odierno, Hassan Scott P. 2006. "Setup Issues in Starting Takaful." *Middle East Insurance Review* (November): 62–63.

————. 2007. "Potential for Takaful in China." *Middle East Insurance Review* (February): 53–55.

Odierno, Hassan Scott P., and Muhaimin Iqbal. 2006. "Takaful Windows: An Initial Stepping Stone to Bigger Islamic Insurance Market." *Middle East Insurance Review* (December): 65–66.

Odierno, Hassan Scott P., and Muhammad Ismail. 2009. "Takaful Marketing and Distribution: The Asian Perspective." *Middle East Insurance Review* (December): 50–51.

Robb, Alan. 2009. "Discretionary Mutuals." *New Zealand Cooperatives Association*, October 14. http://nz.coop/discretionary-mutuals/.

Taylor, Dawood. n.d. "To Be or Not to Be (Takaful), That Is the Question." *ICMIFtakaful*. Takaful Ta'awani, Jeddah, Saudi Arabia. http://www.takaful.coop/index.php?option=com_content&view=article&id=70&Itemid=50.

CHAPTER 6

Trade-offs in Takaful

Hassan Scott Odierno and
Zainal Abidin Mohd Kassim

Mutual operations started from a need for fairness and mutual assistance due to the rise of capitalism. Groups of people with a similar background—be it profession, religion, or culture—formed cooperatives to assist each other in many aspects of life, including insurance. Many times, these groups perceived themselves as being treated unfairly by insurance companies, so they decided to band together and help themselves. The initial push into mutual structures took place in the mid-1800s. Over the past several decades, there have been some widely publicized conversions from mutual into stock insurance companies, due in theory to the need to raise capital. Since then, some have questioned whether this need could have been satisfied in alternative ways.

Takaful was started in 1979, when Faisal Islamic Bank formed the Islamic Insurance Company of Sudan in response to demand for insurance in accordance with Islamic principles (Kloewer 2011). This was also the key driver for development of the first takaful operator in Asia, Syarikat Takaful Malaysia Berhad, in 1984.[1] Later takaful operations started for various reasons, foremost being the need to satisfy the demand of Muslims for insurance and savings in accordance with Islamic laws.

In the late 2000s in Malaysia, large multinationals were attracted to takaful, with the result being a wider acceptance of takaful beyond

Muslims. In some takaful operations, upward of 60 percent of participants have been non-Muslims. The driving force for such business is the perceived fairness of takaful and the allure of profit sharing and transparency (Bhatty 2007).

Mutual insurers are 100 percent owned by the participants, so there is no question of profit motive or other such concerns. In takaful, an operator earns profit from the takaful operation. To the extent that takaful models and products entail significant profits, takaful could be seen as just another product line of stock insurance. However, there are differences in the type of needs being satisfied. Whereas mutuals tend to satisfy the basic needs of a local community, many takaful operators allow participants to access global investment markets in a manner acceptable to Islam. Thus, whereas mutual operations could be seen as satisfying basic needs and as an alternative to stock insurance, takaful fine-tunes stock insurance mores to make them acceptable to Islamic laws.

Variation in Approaches

Mutual operations have developed for the past 150 years. The approach has traditionally been for a group of people to join together to help each other in a variety of ways, including insurance. The approach in reality has been varied: some operations have stayed close to the founding groups, while others have evolved into huge enterprises competing head on with stock insurers.

Takaful historically developed in response to conditions at a local level, but with the advent of the Internet and globalization, it has become less varied and more consistent. Takaful can be split into several broad categories:

- Companies only selling takaful and with a sharia council
- Companies selling both takaful and conventional insurance and with a sharia council
- Companies only selling takaful but with no sharia council.

Operations in the first group can easily be considered takaful, such as the operators in Bahrain, Malaysia, Sudan, and many other countries. Within this group, practices vary widely. These variations have arisen partly through regulatory practices (which are discussed below) and partly through tradition within each country. For instance, the sharing of surplus of the takaful fund with the operator can be a sensitive issue.

In Malaysia and other Asian countries, this is allowed, and some takaful operators in the Middle East share in surplus through a *wakala* performance fee. Companies that do not share surplus with the operator resemble a mutual, whereas companies that give a significant amount of surplus to the operator resemble a normal stock insurer. This leads to a rainbow of practices, with mutuals at one end and stock insurers at the other. From a technical point of view, however, this oversimplifies the issue, as the operator receives fees as part of the model of operations. To the extent that the fees are higher than the actual costs of managing the operations, the operator indirectly obtains the surplus from the operations of the takaful fund.

Differing practices within the design of the fees themselves can lead to a wide variation in practices and, which is more important, a wide variation in practices expected for the future. For instance, in Sudan fees consist of the sharing of investment income of the fund, with actual expenses being covered from the fund. Thus, the profit of the operator is based solely on the level of investment income sharing. This naturally leads to cases where significant portions of investment income are shared with the operator. In such cases, savings products such as for children's education or retirement will not be competitive with other savings channels such as banks, but they will be competitive with regard to coverage. This would lead to lower profit for the operator, as such products have less investment income. An optimal strategy might involve products that predominantly offer risk coverage, but with some elements of savings, such as single-contribution mortgage-reducing term plans and other plans that form a core need of Muslims.

For models where the fees consist of a percentage of investment income as well as a percentage of contributions, a wider range of products is feasible. With a smaller proportion of investment income given to the operator, the takaful operation can compete with banks and other providers for the investment savings of Muslims and non-Muslims alike. Because the fees are a percentage of contributions, the trend is still toward higher-contribution products, as this maximizes profit to the operator. Thus lower-contribution products, such as products for lower-income groups, are not favored. For companies with unit-linked products, investment profit sharing would be replaced by fees as a percentage of net asset value. Similar issues are also present with such plans, as lower fees allow these products to compete with banking products such as unit trusts.

A full range of products can be provided where fees are obtained from a variety of sources, such as a percentage of investment income or net asset value, a percentage of contributions, fees per policy, or even fees as a percentage of transactions such as claims, surrenders, or drips from a savings fund into a risk fund. In such models, reasonable profits can be obtained from a variety of products, thus providing incentive to market takaful to all classes of participants.

For operators sharing in surplus, differences can arise in the level of conservatism built into product pricing. For instance, if the operator receives 50 percent of the surplus of the takaful fund, there is a strong incentive to price products very conservatively to ensure that significant surplus arises in practice. This is an element of some models in Malaysia and is in contrast to operators that do not share in surplus, where pricing is very competitive, which is good for the participant but leads to concerns over solvency and profitability of the fund. Such a concern pertains to Bahrain, where takaful operators have been known to undercut each other as well as conventional insurers (Odierno 2008). This is more evident for general than for family takaful.

Thus, the products of two takaful operators might have very different looks and feels. Some operators prefer to make their products look exactly like conventional insurance, while others do their utmost to make their products and outlook uniquely different, even to the extent of community service. A takaful operator with a conventional insurance sister company might offer products that look and feel like conventional insurance, as the same agent might sell both takaful and conventional insurance. Such operators might also import products and systems from the conventional insurance company, leading to further similarities in look and feel. Operators active in bancatakaful might design products with a conventional insurance look and feel due to the lack of time needed to explain the nuances of takaful models and operations properly to potential bank customers.

In addition to being sold alone, takaful can also be sold as simply another product line. Such operations are called takaful windows. In Indonesia, most takaful operators are windows, ranging from multinationals to local companies. There is significant variation not only between these windows and operators selling only takaful, but also within such windows. Such windows raise concerns about the ability to segregate conventional and takaful operations properly—for example, assets and the flow of funds to and from the participant (Odierno and Iqbal 2006). There is a range of window operations beyond Indonesia, such as insurers selling takaful in Singapore and Thailand. In such operations, it is felt that there is not enough business to warrant separate takaful operations, but sufficient volume to develop separate products. In Singapore, the products sold tend to be unit linked, as this fits with regulatory requirements, whereas in Indonesia a range of products are sold. The effects of regulations are discussed more fully below. The concept of takaful windows is similar to that of the friendly societies in Australia, where there is a separate fund for each type of product. Takaful would be just one type of product. The viability of takaful windows points to the ease with which a friendly society could sell takaful if desired.

Another category of takaful is one in which the company does not have a sharia council. In takaful, the sharia council is responsible for ensuring that all aspects of operations are in accordance with Islamic law. This raises concerns over whether operations without a sharia council are truly in accord with Islamic law. In Saudi Arabia, cooperative principles require that 10 percent of surplus from operations be shared with participants, with the other 90 percent belonging to the operator. This is a significant variation from takaful in other countries. In the Islamic Republic of Iran, operators can function without a sharia council. Here, reliance is placed on the regulators council, and rules follow Shi'a Islamic laws rather than the Sunni Islamic laws followed by most other takaful operations.

Innovation and the Role of Regulations

Chapter 3 discusses the regulatory treatment of cooperatively and mutually structured insurers. As mentioned, concerns have been expressed recently that, internationally, regulatory bodies are much more focused on conventional insurers and are less well informed about other structures for insurance companies. In particular, chapter 3 discusses the reservations about Solvency II expressed in France by ROAM (Réunion des Organismes d'Assurance Mutuelle).

Notwithstanding these concerns, the recent growth in the share of global insurance markets held by mutuals and cooperatives suggests a strong culture of innovation among these insurers. Case studies from Australia, France, and Sweden are given in chapter 3, but other examples could be cited as well. In Kenya, for example, the Cooperative Insurance Company (CIC) has grown to be the third largest player in the Kenyan insurance market and has demonstrated a sharp understanding of the value of new technology in its introduction of M-Bima, a mobile phone payment system for microinsurance products. CIC has also played a key role in the launch of Kenya's takaful operator, Takaful Insurance of Africa.

Another example is the Philippines-based mutual CARD Mutual Benefit Association, the insurance arm of a group of mutually reinforcing institutions that includes CARD Bank and CARD Foundation, a nongovernmental organization. CARD has been a pioneer in developing the microinsurance market in the Philippines and is helping to launch microinsurance products in Cambodia.

In other words, cooperatives and mutuals are operating creatively within the current legal and regulatory frameworks. The role of the International Cooperative and Mutual Insurance Federation (ICMIF), the global federation for cooperative and mutual insurers, is significant in this respect, both for disseminating best practice from within member organizations and for lobbying at the international level as the voice of the sector.

Innovation in design has allowed some mutual operations to fall outside the purview of insurance regulations. As mentioned in chapter 4, this is true of the Christian health-sharing networks in the United States, such as the Samaritan Ministries. Here, benefits are not guaranteed at all, thus allowing the operations to avoid insurance regulations. Insurance regulations provide market discipline and protection for policyholders, but also add expense and complexity. For a mutual, since policyholders and shareholders are one and the same, the risks are significantly lower than for a stock insurer, where one party promises benefits to another. This nuance has not been taken into account in many insurance regulations worldwide, although the European Union has special regulations for mutual operations.

Unfortunately, it is the rule rather than the exception that a lack of understanding of the inherent differences between mutual and stock operations has resulted in regulations that stifle innovation and make it extremely difficult for new mutual insurers to start.

Innovation and regulations go hand in hand in takaful. In countries such as Singapore and the United Kingdom, where the Islamic population is in the minority, there are no takaful-specific regulations. Rather, takaful must satisfy conventional insurance regulations like any other insurer. With this in mind, a takaful operator in these jurisdictions must determine the best strategy for the circumstances. For instance, risk products such as yearly renewable life (family) products as well as general insurance products generate little investment income. This is useful for such countries, where Islamic assets are not generally available and where those that are available likely have solvency risk charges. Savings products in these jurisdictions likely will need to be unit linked in nature, as unit-linked products generally do not incur solvency risk charges. In some jurisdictions, a minimum holding of government bonds is mandated. In such cases, either the emergency (*darurat*) principle applies and the operator holds these assets or the operator decides not to hold such assets and incurs penalties accordingly. In Bangladesh, one operator has consistently incurred fines, as it cannot hold such assets. In Kenya, the operator worked with the regulator to change the regulations.

In some countries, for one reason or another, selling products labeled as takaful might not be possible. Here, innovation can occur in the form of product being sold. For instance, in India it might be difficult to get approval to sell products labeled as takaful, but there is nothing to stop a company from developing a product that is takaful in its operations but is labeled as community insurance. Such a product could be marketed to both Muslims and non-Muslims, with Muslims being aware that the product is in line with their beliefs.

A country developing takaful regulations needs to decide the extent to which innovation will be allowed and encouraged. For instance, in Bahrain the model to be used is *wakala* for underwriting and *mudharaba* for sharing investment returns. This is explicitly cited in regulations and ensures that all operators use the same model and compete based on technical aspects such as price as well as service and reputation rather than on the model of Islamic insurance. This avoids unpleasant disagreements over which company is right or wrong, but could stifle innovation. Takaful is a new field, with new models and ideas being developed each year. To declare one model as the only correct one is premature at this stage.

Malaysia is recognized as a leader in regulating takaful, with specific regulations in place since 1984. Regulations are split between acts, such as the Takaful Act 1984, and guidelines. Guidelines deal with range of topics and aspects of takaful, including the following:

- Capital adequacy
- Financial reporting
- Anti-money laundering
- Prudential limits and standards.

Capital adequacy relates to margin of solvency requirements, dynamic solvency testing (DST), and risk-based capital (RBC) requirements; although there are no formal requirements for DST and RBC in takaful, these are expected in the near future. RBC requirements are one place where regulations can allow for innovation in takaful, while maintaining parity with conventional insurance. For instance, in takaful, in theory the operator is managing rather than accepting benefits risk. With this in mind, charges must be taken out of the risk fund or other participants' funds rather than out of the operator's fund. While some operators might want to run the operation similar to a conventional operation, with risk charges located in the operator's fund, other operators should have the option to maintain consistency with takaful concepts. Some risks, such as expense risks and operational risks, are the responsibility of the operator in both takaful and conventional insurance.

Ideally, RBC guidelines allow for structures where takaful concepts are followed carefully. For instance, one structure might be such that each participant pays not only his contribution but also a loading to cover his portion of RBC charges. When the participant leaves, he is entitled to receive his RBC loading, subject to the approval of the actuary. Here the participants still own their own risks and cover each other, with the operator managing these risks and handling its own risks with regard to expenses and operations.

Financial reporting guidelines for takaful and conventional insurance are distinct. This allows for the reporting of separate risk, savings, and operator's funds. Regulations that do not allow for this type of reporting force operators to hold two sets of books, one with these separate funds, or more precisely subfunds, and another in accordance with the regulatory format. This increases the regulatory burden of takaful operators.

Anti-money-laundering guidelines affect both takaful and conventional insurance equally and are applicable to both.

Prudential limits and standards are a wide-reaching category, with guidelines for both takaful and conventional insurance. Some guidelines apply to both, such as the role of the appointed actuary, guidelines for the audit committee, fit and proper guidelines for key responsible persons, guidelines on the introduction of new products (with small differences here between takaful and conventional insurers), and guidelines on data management and management information systems. Some guidelines specifically relate to conventional insurance, such as those related to derivatives (although takaful has an equivalent in the guidelines for investment management) and reporting on financial conditions. Other guidelines have been developed specifically for takaful, such as guidelines for the governance of the sharia committee and guidelines for the establishment of retakaful operations.

The majority of prudential limits and standards have separate, but similar, guidelines for takaful and conventional insurance, which allows for the particular circumstances of takaful to be taken into account. There are similar guidelines for stress testing, related-party transactions, Internet business, appointment of external auditors, and valuation basis for family and general business. Corporate governance is significantly different: conventional insurance has corporate governance and prudential management guidelines, and takaful has the takaful operating framework, which details the types and forms of models allowable in takaful. This provides a minimum level of consistency and recognizes that the choice of model used affects corporate governance but also can limit innovation.

Takaful is a business. As a business, the operator strives for a certain return on its capital. This return on capital is related to both the profit margin and the amount of capital that is held. This is where a proper understanding of regulations is vital. If regulations force takaful to hold more capital than it should considering the risks it carries, then it will need to find ways to increase its return. This could be done by taking on increased risks (which could result in even more capital being required) or by increasing fees or charges to participants. Value is created in takaful through the minimization of such fees, thus regulations need to be precise in requiring the appropriate level of capital from takaful operators (Odierno 2010).

One aspect unique to takaful is that of *qard al hasan*, or interest-free loan. The original intention of *qard* was to provide for situations where cash was needed in order to pay claims. However, *qard* has become a method of funding statutory deficits. From a technical point of view, a loan—whether *qard* or any other loan—should not be used for such purposes, as statutory deficits need to be covered through shareholder injections or be subjected to the onerous rules and *riba* (interest) concerns in dealing with surplus (solvency) notes, including seeking supervisory approval before repayment. Jurisdictions with separate takaful regulations generally have provisions for *qard*, whereas other jurisdictions require the takaful operator to cover deficits through more traditional mechanisms (Odierno 2009a).

A potential innovation in health takaful is for the development of a takaful pool for long-term health plans considered risky, such as long-term care. In such plans, the policyholder pays premiums for many years in order to receive health care in the last few years of his or her life. Here there are significant risks with respect to future costs of health care as well as investment returns many years into the future. Risk-based capital regulations hinder takaful companies from selling such a product. However, such a product will be needed in the developing world—for example, in Asia—as demographics change, families have fewer children to care for aging parents, and children live farther away. In this case, a takaful structure that does not guarantee benefits, sets contribution rates conservatively, and gives all surplus back to participants would minimize risks while providing satisfactory coverage (Odierno 2011). Regulations will need to allow such product structures in order to realize the potential for innovation in takaful.

Mutual Insurer: Lessons for Takaful

The discussion so far in this chapter has focused on regulatory trade-offs. However, to the extent that takaful adopts mutual insurance principles, it is instructive to explore the strengths of mutual operations, faith based or otherwise, to identify which can be accommodated by takaful.

A main strength of mutual insurers is their longer-term focus. Mutual insurers are (theoretically) immune from takeover, so there is no need to monitor the stock price or focus on short-term profits. Charges are generally lower in mutual insurers as opposed to stock insurers, especially where savings products are concerned. This has led to increased value for policyholders. The agents of mutual insurers tend to be tied rather than independent, which has led established agents to think more long term and to build stable businesses.

Takaful also has a longer-term focus and a tied agency force. However, this is due mainly to the markets in which takaful operates rather than to the underlying characteristics of takaful. Takaful operators tend to be listed on the stock market, but with few concerns about takeovers in the developing world, where takaful is common. In most markets where takaful is popular, tied agency forces are common for conventional insurance as well as takaful.

Mutuals are considered to have superior financial strength, as mutuals are generally very well capitalized. This has arisen because surplus tends to be held in insurance funds rather than paid out as dividends to shareholders. The strong focus of mutuals on participation policies also lends itself to financial strength, as such policies are considered to be among the lowest-risk policies for an insurer. This superior financial strength is further enhanced by the generally less complicated liabilities and less volatile earnings due to captive agents.

Thus far, there has been very little in the way of solvency regulations for takaful, and it is difficult to discuss the financial strength of takaful operators. The Islamic Financial Services Board (IFSB) has introduced takaful solvency guidelines for the industry, and takaful operators functioning under conventional insurance regulations have been subject to the same solvency regulations as conventional insurers. This is theoretically conservative for takaful, as takaful products generally do not contain formal guarantees or carry the risks of conventional insurance. Having said that, takaful entails numerous informal guarantees: participants have reasonable expectations that the operator will honor its projected benefits and will pay out as expected. This is especially true for compulsory products, such as coverage for mortgage loans, as the bank providing the loan will want benefits paid in full upon the death of the participant. Failing this, the bank will likely reconsider any relationships with the takaful operator. In takaful, liabilities tend to be fairly uncomplicated and earnings to be less volatile than for conventional insurance (Pask 2009).

Mutual insurers have the following pluses:

- Self-help
- Equality
- Solidarity
- Openness
- Social responsibility.

With respect to self-help, the driving force in most modern takaful operations is about the operation making a profit rather than about participants helping themselves. The underlying principle in takaful, however, is about participants helping each other. Takaful greatly values equality, although putting it into practice is a challenge due to the complexity of insurance in general and takaful in particular. Ensuring that each participant pays a fair share and that surplus is distributed fairly is always a challenge. It is true that takaful binds participants together for a common purpose. This is the goal, but it is unclear if this is happening in practice. It is not clear to what extent takaful operators satisfy their social responsibilities. Currently takaful mirrors conventional insurance contracts and markets. This is one point of difference with cooperatives. Thus, takaful has several points in common with mutuals in theory, but fewer in practice. Two reasons are generally given for why takaful mirrors conventional insurance: the use of similar distribution channels and the need to broaden the appeal of takaful products.

The key principles of mutuals are the following:

- Open membership
- Democratic member control
- Concern for the community.

Takaful allows for open membership, but not for democratic member control, although there is no reason why this could not be done. A participants' advocate would be needed to ensure that the needs of participants are met. Such an advocate could use means such as Internet voting to ensure that the wishes of the members are taken into account. Takaful does have a concern for the community, but perhaps much less than it could have and certainly much less than mutual operations have.

The key success factors for mutuals are considered to be the following:

- The cooperative is established by the members and for the members to meet a common need. It is imperative for the cooperative to be in constant communication with its customers and be ready to respond to their needs—whether or not these are the most profitable opportunities available. This is a distinct difference from takaful, which is established for a particular need, but takaful could differentiate itself by communicating better with members and responding to their needs.

- In a competitive world, the cooperative insurer cannot rely on ethics alone; it has to demonstrate value for money. This is absolutely true in takaful. People will not line up to buy takaful, as takaful is still insurance, which must often be sold. In a perfect world, Muslims will exclusively purchase takaful plans rather than conventional insurance, but if takaful is of inferior value, then Muslims will still purchase conventional insurance (at least for the most part).

- Members should feel closer to the cooperative each time they are in contact with the organization—high levels of customer service and claims management are fundamental. The extent to which this is true in takaful is still unclear.

- The customer is, in effect, the owner of the company; close involvement and communication are needed in all key decision making. This is not currently the case in takaful.

- The cooperative culture must be nurtured internally and extended externally; staff must understand the organization's principles and believe in this business approach. In the past, this was clearly the case for takaful. However, the multinationals active in takaful today readily employ non-Muslims, with differing levels of understanding of the uniqueness and beauty of takaful.

- Some larger cooperative insurers have undertaken a prevention and risk management approach, which has led to better underwriting. This again shows the concern that the company has for its members' welfare. Risk management capabilities in takaful, especially those of the multinationals, rival those of conventional insurance.

- Cooperatives also tend to be involved in the local communities, helping to address livelihood issues and supporting community projects, sometimes offering unique coverage that fulfills the distinct needs of the local population and providing services that are beyond traditional insurance. This does not seem to be actively done in takaful, although some takaful operators do coordinate benefits and activities such as *hajj* (pilgrimage). More can be done in takaful to integrate services and to integrate into the local community.

- Many cooperatives are active in responding to the needs of unserved segments of the population who may not have access to insurance due to financial, geographic, religious, or ethnic reasons (Patel 2007). This segment of the population has not generally been served by takaful, especially multinationals, which have focused on the more affluent market.

Cooperatives offer the following lessons for takaful:

- Ensure good corporate governance and transparency. The decision-making process of the organization should be clear and equitable between the needs of the operator and the needs of the participants.
- As takaful and cooperatives grow, members base their decisions not on the values and ethics of the organization, but rather on price alone. Takaful operators need to ensure that consumers understand that takaful works under principles different from those of conventional or stock insurers.
- Takaful principles should be embraced by employees and managers and integrated with a business strategy that is supported by consistent takaful values-based management practices. Managers must understand the responsibilities of being a takaful provider, and frontline staff should deliver the message that takaful is different from other insurance.

- Greater awareness of and involvement in the operations by the participant will lead to greater customer loyalty, thereby providing a competitive edge over conventional insurance. This can be facilitated by developing a participant advisory committee or allowing participant representatives to be elected to the board.
- Spending more resources in supporting community projects and ensuring wider access to protection for the poor is at the heart of takaful. This builds affinity with the local population and a better understanding of what Islamic insurance is.
- Closer cooperation is needed between operators, with open sharing of information (Patel 2007).

The number of demutualizations has declined since the late 1990s and is expected to remain low, as the advantage of mutuals has started to shine through, especially since the recent financial crisis. As an example, the lack of access to capital markets has generally been considered a key disadvantage of mutuals. However, during the recent financial crisis, the inability to access capital markets became a strength, not a weakness.

A concern for mutuals is with respect to governance issues, such as compensation, successor planning, and risk oversight. These aspects receive less attention in mutuals, as there is no open market scrutiny. This is exacerbated by the reality that policyholders have little say in management of the mutual. Corporate governance, risk oversight (or more precisely a clear understanding of the underlying risks and who bears them), and lack of policyholder say in the management of the company are issues for takaful as well.

Mutuals need the support of government in several areas. One is in ensuring a fair playing field. In this respect, regulations regarding mutuals need to keep up with stock companies. In many cases, consideration of the interests of mutuals seems to be simply an afterthought. This is an issue for takaful as well, as in many cases takaful is regulated together with stock insurers in a "one size fits all" approach. In many cases, even where there are separate regulations for takaful, regulations tend simply to follow the regulations for stock insurers, with little accounting for the differences between takaful and stock insurers or for the differences between different takaful operations.

Mutuals can bring value to society:

- Bring choice and competition to the market.
- Offer low premium products and thus cater to all segments of society.

- Respond to changing needs, as mutuals are close to their members and understand their needs.
- Encourage self-help and personal responsibility for planning.
- Bring economic stability by taking a long-term view.
- Provide greater value to policyholders.

Governments should provide incentives to mutuals, such as tax incentives to encourage savings and provide protection in the less affluent segments of society. Government should also use mutuals to stimulate innovation (Mutuo 2010).

Takaful potentially can provide similar values to society. The takaful model and plans can be designed to look exactly like conventional insurance products or to look different. To the extent that takaful is allowed to be different, this provides innovation and choice to the market, expanding the choice of investment and protection products. Similar to mutuals, takaful requires an understanding to ensure that innovation is allowed and encouraged. Takaful thus far has tended to follow the market of conventional insurance, with relatively less focus on the less affluent segments of society through plans such as microtakaful. With creativity, microtakaful could be made successful, such as by using the organization of mosques and *imams* to sell microtakaful to members of local communities (Odierno 2009b). Thus far, the extent to which takaful has responded to the needs of its members, encouraged self-help or planning, and taken a long-term view is unclear. Currently there is strong pressure to collect market share and fees, which is more similar to the operations of stock insurers than to those of mutuals. Takaful, being generally smaller and newer than conventional insurers, has struggled to provide greater value than conventional insurers. However, the recent success of multinational operators—in particular, at selling takaful to non-Muslims—shows the value in takaful concepts, such as sharing in surplus and transparency.

Conclusion

The mutual and takaful approaches share similarities. Both are likely to be at the forefront of a push toward fairness in financial transactions involving the general public. Takaful will continue to be driven by the desire of Muslims to join world markets in a controlled and acceptable manner. In this sense, takaful could be considered a middle ground between stock insurers and mutual operations. Both mutual and takaful operations have significant variations in their approach and practices.

There is no one definition of exactly what a takaful operator is, any more than there is a standard definition of exactly how a mutual operates. Regulations have played a key role in the development of both takaful and mutual operations and will likely continue to do so in the future: both depend on a proper understanding by regulators of the risks and nuances of their operations to flourish and develop.

Note

1. Syarikat Takaful Malaysia Berhad, http://www.takaful-malaysia.com.my/corporate/aboutus/Pages/companybg.aspx.

References

Bhatty, Ajmal. 2007. "The Growth and Global Market for Takaful." In *Islamic Insurance: Trends, Opportunities, and the Future of Takaful*, 3–21. London: Euromoney.

Kloewer, Gerd. 2011. "Comments to: Kenya's First Takaful Company Licensed." *Financial Islam–Islamic Finance*, February 17. http://www.financialislam.com/2/post/2011/1/kenyas-first-takaful-company-licensed.html.

Mutuo. 2010. *The Mutuals Manifesto 2010*. London: Mutuo.

Odierno, Hassan Scott P. 2008. "The Sharing of Surplus in Takaful." *Middle East Insurance Review* (December): 51–52.

———. 2009a. "Corporate Governance in Takaful." *Takaful Articles* 19 (November).

———. 2009b. "Takaful Health Insurance in Asia." In *A Quick Guide: Health Insurance in Asia*. Singapore: Asia Insurance Review.

———. 2010. "Regulating Takaful." *Islamic Finance News*, April 21, 19–20.

———. 2011. "Health Takaful in a Changing Environment." *Middle East Insurance Review* (October): 72–74.

Odierno, Hassan Scott P., and Muhaimin Iqbal. 2006. "Takaful Windows: An Initial Stepping Stone to Bigger Islamic Insurance Market." *Middle East Insurance Review* (December): 65–66.

Pask, Adrian. 2009. "In the Midst of the Downturn, Many U.S. Mutuals Aren't as Down as Their Publicly Held Peers." Standard and Poor's, October 16.

Patel, Sabbir. 2007. "The World of Cooperatives and the Takaful Twist." *Middle East Insurance Review* (September).

CHAPTER 7

Principal-Agent Issues in Takaful

Zainal Abidin Mohd Kassim

Islamic finance and takaful take as their guide the sharia law of *muamalat* (sharia's version of commercial law) and therefore are separate from the sharia law of *ibada* (laws governing belief and the worship of God). Thus, participants in Islamic finance and takaful need not subscribe to the religion of Islam as a precondition of entry, and the principles underlying Islamic finance and takaful are not proprietary to Muslims. Indeed, takaful shares many of the same principles that have made mutual insurers a success around the world. In addition to these shared principles, the sharia law of *muamalat* prohibits the taking of interest income and imposes many other restrictions and conditions, as detailed earlier in this book, to ensure complete transparency in any bilateral transaction.

Unlike the early mutuals, takaful was born into a world driven by regulations. These regulations contain onerous capital requirements, as they are designed to ensure that the insurer meets its obligations to the insured. Thus, the evolution of takaful has been affected by the regulations within which it operates. In order for takaful to succeed, its implementation must be on a holistic basis, and, in particular, regulations must cater to its unique features.

Takaful as currently practiced is neither a proprietary nor a mutual activity. Partly as a result of regulations and partly due to the inherent difficulties in starting a mutual insurer from scratch, the existing takaful operations are structured as hybrids, part mutual and part proprietary. This unique structure gives rise to many issues with regard to corporate governance and solvency.

Takaful is a mutual with regard to indemnifying losses but a proprietary company with regard to managing the operation. Put simply, takaful policyholders as a group are deemed to have "contracted out" the management of the business. This is different from a typical mutual insurer, where the management team is directly in the employ of the mutual and the mutual pays all wages and distribution costs. Premiums less expenses less claims incurred give rise to surpluses that are distributed either directly or indirectly to the policyholders cum owners. Furthermore, the business of selling insurance is owned by the policyholders in a mutual insurer, and thus the "equity" in the operation resides with the policyholders. Under takaful, however, policyholders have no "equity" in the operation.

In a mutual insurer, the owner and the insured are one and the same, whereas in a proprietary insurer the two are distinct: the shareholders are distinct from the policyholders, and the owners are clearly the shareholders. If we consider a typical property, casualty, and general insurance operation, the premiums collected constitute direct income to the company. Any subsequent claims constitute an outgo. The profit or surplus arising after allowing for expenses and any contracted distributions accrue directly to the shareholders of the company.

To analyze further, there are three major sources of profit (applicable to both proprietary insurers and mutual insurers):

1. Any excess of expense loadings in the premium over actual management or commission expenses incurred
2. Any investment profit or losses on the assets under management, with assets of the company made up of shareholder capital, technical reserves backing future claim payments, and retained earnings
3. The underwriting surplus, being the excess of expected claims (estimated from past experience) over actual claims.

For the typical takaful operation, profit from the excess of expense loadings in the premium accrues to shareholders, profit or losses from the assets under management are shared between shareholders and policyholders, and underwriting surplus is for the account of policyholders (although some takaful setups do take a share of underwriting surplus for shareholders).

In a proprietary life insurance company and in what is called the "participating life fund," the shareholders contract to share underwriting surplus or investment profit with the policyholders (usually accompanied by a higher premium than otherwise). Within the participating fund, there is usually a defined "bonus policy" as to how surpluses are distributed among the policyholders. Unlike takaful, however, the profit to be shared originates from all three of the above, as all expenses are charged directly to the participating life fund.

A takaful company's operational structure is driven by the sharia-approved contracts it employs. These contracts are grouped by contract *types.*

Islam was born in the trade routes of the Arabian Peninsula centered in the holy city of Mecca. Trade in the peninsula was conducted through certain standardized contracts that were identified by the name attached to them. These include, among others, the *wakala* contract, the *mudharaba* contract, and the *murabaha* contract. The principles were set by sharia *muamalat* and survived to become the basis for Islamic finance and takaful. This is not to say that the list of available sharia-compliant contracts is a closed group; rather, there has been no sustained effort by sharia scholars (in conjunction with financial practitioners) to create new types of contracts that adhere to the principles of *muamalat.* These principles can be summarized as follows:

- No *riba* (interest, usury)
- No *gharar* (uncertainty)
- No *maysir* (gambling)
- Engagement in permissible *(halal)* dealings and avoidance of prohibitive *(haram)* dealings.

The prohibition against *gharar* can best be explained by considering a few examples:

- Sale of the unborn calf in the womb of a pregnant cow. *Gharar* is present in the sale, as the buyer and seller do not know whether the calf will be born alive and, if alive, be healthy or deformed. Such a sale is not sharia compliant.
- Sale of tomorrow's daily catch of a fisherman. This is an advance sale of an unknown quantity of fish. Neither the buyer nor the fisherman know how much fish will be landed tomorrow or even if the weather tomorrow will permit the fisherman to go to sea. The presence of *gharar* invalidates such a sale from the sharia perspective.

The prohibition against *gharar* attempts to ensure that the contract is fair to both buyer and seller by removing the possibility of exploitation due to asymmetry of information between the two parties to the transaction. In an insurance and takaful contract, many elements of uncertainty are involved. For example, the amount payable should the insured event transpire can be uncertain, and whether the event will happen during the period of insurance is also unknown. *Gharar* in takaful is forgiven with the use of a *tabarru'* (donation) to pay the risk premium. *Gharar* is forgiven in this way, but never negated or alleviated. It still exists in the takaful contract.

The predominant contract used in takaful is the *wakala* contract. This literally means an agency contract. A principal contracts an agent to perform a task in exchange for a preagreed fee. There is total transparency in this contract, and it meets all of the requirements for sharia compliance. In a takaful operation based on this contract, there are at least two distinct funds (three where a savings element is attached to a life takaful product); the shareholders' (operators) fund and the policyholders' (participants, as they "participate" in a pool) fund. The premiums (contributions, as they "contribute" toward the pool) are deposited into the participants' fund, which in turn pays *wakala* fees to the operator for managing the takaful business on its behalf. In practice, the *wakala* fees are deducted from the contributions before they are deposited into the participants' fund. The services provided by the operator include management, investment, information technology, and distribution. The participants' fund can also be multiple in nature (that is, made up of more than one separate individual fund), depending on its purpose. For example, in a takaful savings plan, there could be a choice of investment options, each represented by a distinct fund.

However, the challenge in takaful is to manage the portion of the premium paid that is designated to pay claims. Certainly it should involve a sharing of risk among the pool's participants. However, it is impossible to rid the inherent uncertainty even in this mutual risk-sharing arrangement. The eventual claims on the (risk) pool cannot be determined with certainty at the outset. The (risk) premiums are an estimate based on past observations and observed trends. Any commercial contract among the participants in the pool is certain to run afoul of the prohibition against uncertainty under sharia law. The solution (which is not necessarily unanimously agreed among sharia scholars) is to treat the risk premium as a donation (*tabarru'*). Being unilateral in nature (the receiver of the donation does not have any obligation to the person donating it), donations circumvent the sharia laws against *gharar,* which apply to bilateral contracts. These donations can be thought of as indirect contributions through the pool to alleviate the losses of the unfortunate participants who are subsequently struck by the insured event.

By treating the premiums as donations, takaful policyholders do not have equity in the takaful operation. Contrast this with the premiums paid by the policyholder to a mutual insurer, where the policyholder effectively owns part of the business through his or her contract with the mutual. This unique definition of risk premium has practical implications for the sharing of surplus.

What happens if the premiums prove insufficient, especially as the risk pool has no capital at inception? It is not practical to ask participants to top up their premiums after all claims have been accounted for. The practice in takaful is to require the operator to provide an interest-free loan to the risk pool to cover any shortfall. This loan will be a first charge on future distributions of surplus arising in the pool. How these loans (termed *qard*) should be treated in the accounts remains a source of debate in the industry, especially among regulators. The Islamic Financial Services Board (IFSB) has attempted to address this important issue through its IFSB-11, Standard on Solvency Requirements for Takaful Undertaking.

An important ingredient of success in any venture is to align the interests of all stakeholders toward a common goal. In a proprietary insurer, the stakeholders are the shareholders, management, and policyholders (when they participate in profits). Shareholders exercise control over management through the board of directors. Management's interests are aligned with those of shareholders through the compensation structure. Finally, shareholders' interests are aligned with those of policyholders through the sharing of surplus (if applicable). Occasionally, however, such alignments are insufficient and even destructive, if not structured correctly. Many failures of insurers are due to management trying to maximize immediate gains (usually by making risky investments or maximizing sales at the expense of proper underwriting or improper pricing), as their remuneration structures are linked to the company's immediate growth and profits, potentially at the expense of its long-term financial stability.

In takaful, a very difficult conflict must be addressed. In any agent-principal arrangement, the agent is driven by a need to maximize fee income. Where the *wakala* fee is determined as a percentage of premium income, it is to the benefit of the agent to increase turnover. The danger is when this increase in turnover is achieved through poor underwriting and improper pricing of premiums (relatively lower premiums attract more policyholders), where the portion of the premiums allocated to meet claims is insufficient. Higher turnover not only results in higher *wakala* fees (expressed as a percentage of premiums), but also results in deficits in the risk pool. For conventional insurance, deliberately under-pricing while temporarily increasing turnover eventually will result in underwriting losses and deplete shareholders' capital. For takaful, any deficits in the risk pool are for the account of policyholders, not the shareholders. Clearly a straight agent-principal relationship in this instance does not adequately align the interests of the agent (operator) to those of the principal (participant). A valid question is, can the principal terminate the services of the agent should the agent not manage the business prudently? We have yet to see takaful structures that would allow such sanctions against the operator.

Any loss in the risk fund is carried by the participant, *not* the operator. Given this, if there is a profit (usually termed a surplus, a significant component of which is from underwriting), should the operator share in the profit? Clearly, if this is the case, asymmetry in the risks and rewards of stakeholders can result in a conflict of interest. In many classes of insurance, profit is a function of claims incurred, where claims incurred are claims paid plus change in technical reserves. Technical reserves are estimates and are set by the operator. Should the technical reserves later be deemed to be inadequate, the profit in one year can turn out to be a loss later. Currently, no mechanism is in place to claw back past profit distributions from the operator. Another component of surplus is investment profits. Without proper controls in place, the investment policy of the operator toward the participants' fund can be overly risky, as the operator shares in any upside, but not in any downside. Proponents of surplus sharing see this as another form of fee income to the operator. As a counterargument, sharing in underwriting surplus could incentivize takaful operators to underwrite prudently, as they would also benefit from any upside.

The sharia community itself is divided on whether the takaful operator should be allowed to share in underwriting surplus. Some sharia scholars see this sharing as contrary to the concept of mutuality and as diluting the "purity" of the underlying sharia-approved contract (under the *wakala* or agency contract, the agent is entitled to a predetermined and quantifiable fee before the service is rendered). Other sharia scholars consider surplus sharing as an acceptable extension of the *wakala* contract. These scholars justify surplus sharing as an "incentive fee" for good performance.

Another touted preference for mutual insurers over proprietary insurers is their expected focus on customer service rather than on profits alone. In an agent-principal relationship such as takaful, the operator as the agent may seek to maximize profit by minimizing expenses, which inadvertently can affect service to the policyholders.

How fees are structured also favors the operator, as participants have no say on the fees payable other than to shop around before deciding on any particular takaful operation. However, comparing insurance products is difficult. How surplus is determined and distributed is also determined by the operator. These examples of agent-principal conundrum are not easily resolved, thus making proper and adequate corporate governance an important issue in takaful.

The hybrid operating model does present certain advantages that can offset some of the challenges in corporate governance. The stock ownership structure of the takaful operator offers a means of managing owner-manager conflicts. The board of directors can do this by setting clear performance targets and carefully monitoring their achievement.

An ongoing principal-agent issue in takaful is the treatment of surplus. In this regard, the sharia board is primarily responsible for ensuring that the operation is run on a sharia-compliant basis. However, sharia scholars are rarely versed in the technicalities of insurance. Their decisions are based on the input provided by the technicians, and faulty input results in inappropriate rulings. In some instances, the rulings on important issues are taken as final, without due consideration of the appropriateness of the input that went into the deliberations. Disagreements between sharia scholars are common, and sharia scholars are known to revise their own decisions over time.

An example of where sharia scholars can differ in their opinions serves to illustrate the point. One burning issue of contention is the sharing of surplus in the risk pool. Two subjects are related to this topic: (a) the right of participants to share in surplus and (b) the right of shareholders to share in surplus.

On the first subject, the disagreement lies in the application of the concept of *tabarru'* to the contributions of participants in the risk pool. The issue relates to the finality of donations: specifically, once an amount has been donated, the donor loses all rights to the donation. This is the principal reason why participants in takaful do not have equity in the risk pool, unlike policyholders of mutual insurers. When a surplus transpires, why should participants expect to receive a refund of part of their contributions when they have given up their equity in that contribution?

Should the takaful fund be obliged to pay any benefits when a claim occurs if the contributions are deemed to be donations? Sharia scholars have no issues with regard to the payment of claims, as the payment covers a financial loss and the participant does not profit from it; they do have issues with the repayment of *tabarru'* for sharing surplus. Technically, there are no major issues with the distribution of surplus back to policyholders. From an actuarial perspective, the distribution of surplus is a useful "price correction" mechanism. The issue is principally a sharia one. Distribution of surplus back to policyholders is also a major marketing attraction for takaful, as the participants have no ownership in the business itself, unlike mutuals. This would not be an issue if premiums were set at the end of the term of the policy rather than at the beginning!

The subject of shareholder participation in surplus gives rise to very strong disagreements among sharia scholars. Sharia scholars who support shareholder participation in surplus point out that the share in surplus acts as an incentive for the operator to manage the risk pool correctly. Surplus is equated with profits, which in turn are equated with the setting of adequate premiums and the application of appropriate underwriting. This is seen as a means of aligning the shareholders' interest with that of participants. Technically, there are serious concerns with this argument. Earlier it was noted that takaful operators may underprice premiums to generate turnover, which likely will result in underwriting losses for which participants are solely responsible. Furthermore, surplus is not profit; it is only an estimate of eventual profit. If the technical reserves prove insufficient (and there are many legitimate reasons why they may eventually prove insufficient), an initial profit may turn out to be a loss later, when all claims are settled. As shareholders do not share in losses, any subsequent losses due to an underestimate of reserves cannot be recouped.

A compromise is for shareholders *not* to share in the first dollar of profit, but instead to share only above a threshold. If the threshold is set high enough, this would provide a margin for any subsequent upward adjustment in technical reserves. A second mechanism to consider is placing a maximum limit on surplus to which the shareholders are entitled. Placing a maximum limit on the amount of surplus to which shareholders are entitled would ensure that the takaful operator does not take excessive risk. Notwithstanding the technical arguments and constraints mentioned here, some sharia scholars are against shareholder participation in surplus from a purely "legal" perspective.

Before leaving the role of sharia, it is appropriate to mention the prohibition on combining two types of contracts into one. For example, it is not possible to combine a *mudharaba* contract (typically used in Islamic investment and financing under which one party contracts to receive a share of profits from a venture in exchange for his entrepreneurial efforts and for bearing all of his own expenses, while the other party provides capital for the venture and receives a share of the profits) with a *wakala* contract. This is logical, as otherwise there is no reason to have different types of contracts. There are, however, no objections to having different contracts for different undertakings. In many takaful operations, there is a *wakala* contract between the operator and the participant for the management of the distribution and underwriting of the business and a separate *mudharaba* contract, again between the operator and the participant, in which the operator undertakes to manage the investments of the takaful funds.

Clearly, the relevant regulators will have a role in mediating principal-agent conflicts. Since the 2007–08 financial crisis, the regulator has had multiple roles. On the one hand, there is pressure to ensure that customers are treated fairly, while on the other hand, there is a need to ensure that the institution regulated (here it would be the insurer) remains solvent at all times. This is not an easy task for one institution to manage, as the two roles can be contradictory. The United States has a Consumer Protection Agency that is separate from the regulator and is responsible for ensuring that consumers are treated fairly; the original regulator remains primarily entrusted with ensuring the solvency of banks and insurers. The United Kingdom is also pursuing this route with the breakup of its Financial Services Authority into two separate regulators.

Suffice it to say, the issue of how to ensure the continuing ability of takaful companies to meet their obligations is foremost on the minds of regulators in those jurisdictions where takaful companies operate. The position is complicated by the fact that policyholders are, in fact, indemnifying each other, with no financial obligations toward the pool other than the premiums paid, and the fact that the takaful fund usually has little or no capital with which to meet claims volatility.

This problem stems from the inappropriate premise that benefits from takaful companies are guaranteed in the same way as those of proprietary insurers and that policyholders can assume that their claims will be met. Such guarantees can only be given either by putting capital at risk (not possible where the insurers are also the insured and the position is one of a new start-up) or by passing the risk through a back-to-back arrangement with a third party (for example, through reinsurance). Where the obligations include an accumulation of premiums toward the payment of an eventual benefit, there is an implicit guaranteed return on those savings. For such investment guarantees, this requires a ready supply of sharia-compliant investments with income and capital guarantees. Such investments do not exist in an interest-free financial system. Furthermore, using derivatives to transfer risk is not possible, as only "asset-based" transactions are truly sharia compliant.

What should be the premise underlying a takaful contract? Is it appropriate for takaful companies to provide guarantees when no capital is available other than the accumulation of participants' premium income? Would products with no guarantee of full payment in the event of an insured event be acceptable to the public?

The ability of the takaful risk pool to solicit an interest-free loan from the shareholders to cover occasional deficits is a wonderful innovation, as it enables a takaful fund to generate capital indirectly *from future surpluses of the fund.* Instead of participants having to pay up capital at the outset, shareholders will come up with any necessary capital should a deficit occur, and this would be financed (repaid) from future surpluses of the fund. Two implicit assumptions are necessary for this to be possible. The first is that the business will continue profitably into the future. The second is that the ability of participants to subsidize across cohorts can be minimized. However, there is a limit to the availability of this notional capital, and that limit depends on the volatility of the risk assured. It is not prudent to depend on future surpluses when the risk assured has high volatility. For a true risk-sharing experience and where the retained surplus in the risk pool is limited, takaful should be restricted to low-volatility claim events. Life (termed family) takaful, where mortality is predictable, is suitable in a risk-sharing platform such as takaful. At the other end of the spectrum are specialized risks such as aviation and oil and gas, where claims volatility makes risk sharing impracticable.

Retakaful

One way to have a greater spread of risk is through retakaful, the sharia-compliant equivalent of reinsurance. The purpose of reinsurance is two-fold: (a) to spread risks across a bigger pool of risks, allowing the insurer to take on more capacity, and (b) to allow the insurer to better manage its capital. Retakaful is similar to reinsurance, but with some important differences. Perhaps the most important is that the ceding entity in a retakaful arrangement is the takaful risk pool and *not* the takaful operator. This fact is often overlooked.

The difference between retakaful and reinsurance is obvious considering that the insurance risks are shared among participants rather than transferred to shareholders of the takaful entity. This is also true in retakaful, but the risk sharing is elevated to a higher level across independent pools. This understanding needs to be applied consistently in the conduct of the retakaful arrangement. In particular,

- All retakaful commissions should be payable to the takaful risk fund from which the retakaful contribution originated. To pay this commission to the takaful operator could compromise the integrity of the originating agent-principal relationship between the takaful operator and participants. Another option is to pay no retakaful commissions at all and only allow participation in surplus sharing.

- A retakaful pool (there can be many pools of risks, as in a reinsurance arrangement) should not be confined to risks from one cedant only. Such a pool is not retakaful, as it simply extends the originating takaful risk fund and does not entail any diversification benefit other than access to the capital of the retakaful provider should the need of a *qard* arise.

Retakaful, if well implemented, supports the development of risk sharing rather than risk transfer. To succeed, takaful has to lessen its dependence on shareholder capital (whether it be takaful or retakaful shareholder capital) and turn more toward spreading and diversifying risk to manage claims volatility. Retakaful's role is to allow that spread and diversification to happen, not just across classes of risks but across geographies.

One other mechanism for dealing with principal-agent issues is corporate governance. Corporate governance in takaful refers to the manner in which the board of directors, sharia board, and senior management oversee the takaful business. The business of takaful is a hybrid that requires some modification in the structure of corporate governance found in conventional insurers. The organizational structure is summarized in figure 7.1.

The sharia advisory board (SAB) represents an additional layer of corporate governance in takaful. It is entrusted to ensure that the operation

Figure 7.1   Organizational Structure of Takaful

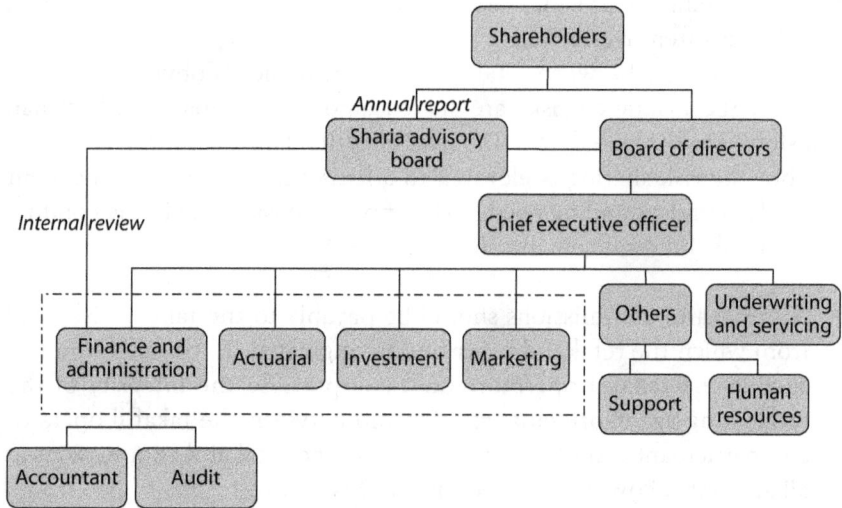

does not contravene sharia principles. The Islamic Financial Services Board has published IFSB-10, Sharia Governance System for Islamic Financial Institutions, to provide guidance in this area.

The board of directors is responsible for ensuring that the business aspect of the operation is optimized, and the sharia board is responsible for ensuring that the operation is run on a sharia-compliant basis. Who, then, is responsible for protecting the rights of policyholders? IFSB-8 is of particular interest when considering this question. This standard recommends the establishment of a separate independent body—a governance or policyholders committee—responsible for giving due consideration to the policyholders' rights and interests in the takaful operation. While the theory is sound, the practicality of resolving a conflict between the board of directors and their policyholders committee can be challenging. This structure recognizes that there are areas in the operation of a takaful company where the interests of shareholders and policyholders may diverge.

Risk permeates all aspects of life. The fundamental question is whether risk transfer is the best means of managing risk. Perhaps it is, but only if the price is fair and there is no risk of default. Both conditions are difficult to meet. Sharia's solution is to share, not transfer, risk. Under the application of risk sharing in takaful, the "price" is adjusted through surplus sharing and the guarantee is shared among all of those at risk.

This chapter highlights some of the principal-agent issues that arise in implementing takaful. The presence of these issues does not mean that there is no feasible sharia-compliant alternative to conventional insurance. There is an alternative, if at the outset a holistic approach is taken to implementation, the current limitations of takaful are recognized, and the appropriate guidance is in place. The latter must come from the regulators, as only they can command the respect of the whole industry.

The role of regulators is paramount in takaful, especially where the industry is fragmented, with different sharia contracts being used. Such diversity may result in innovations, but in the short to medium term an effective means of managing policyholders' expectations and the industry's well-being is needed. This requires creating a standard takaful contract, or at most two contracts, and devising regulations for ensuring the industry's continuing solvency and aligning the interests of all stakeholders. This may include restricting takaful initially to personal lines of business, thus leaving commercial lines to the next phase of development. Managing the interests of various stakeholders is difficult, given the scarcity of persons knowledgeable about both the principles and the limitations of takaful. This is compounded by the public's very limited knowledge about their rights in takaful. A simple solution in the short run is to impose tariffs on takaful premium rates so that takaful companies do not have to compete purely on rates. Distributing surplus back to policyholders could address the issue of equity within a tariff environment. To address sharia concerns about the validity of surplus refunds within a *tabarru'* arrangement, the distribution of surplus could take the form of a reduction in the policyholders' renewal premium.

A role that life insurance has taken up very successfully is that of an accumulator of savings, be they for retirement income or for important lifestyle changes like parenthood and children's college education. This should be the primary aim of takaful, and takaful is well suited for it. Volatility in insuring life is manageable, and, being long term in nature, expected future surpluses can be reasonably counted as capital for managing year-to-year underwriting and investment volatility. Family takaful can galvanize the savings of the *umma* (community of believers) toward sharia-compliant investing, which is basically a subset of socially responsible investments. Savings through family takaful are also a stable source of capital that is useful for long-term infrastructure investments, which are very much in demand in the developing Muslim countries.

CHAPTER 8

Investments in Takaful

Hassan Scott Odierno

This chapter discusses investments in takaful, starting with the types of investments needed, the types of products being sold, and the models being used. The main assets used in takaful are then explained, along with the criteria for selecting assets as Islamic. Finally, risk-based capital is highlighted and linked to the choice of investment strategy as well as the strategies for structuring liabilities.

Investment Needs of Takaful

The investment needs of takaful vary greatly by the type of product. Takaful products can be classified as savings products or risk-coverage products. Coverage products may also include savings, but the focus is on the coverage being provided. Savings products in conventional insurance can be either guaranteed or not guaranteed, with a range of alternatives in between that use guaranteed maturity values plus nonguaranteed bonuses. In takaful, there generally are no guaranteed maturity benefits. However, promotional materials can build up the expectations of participants, forming an implicit guarantee, and corresponding investments, such as the holding of stable rather than volatile assets, are needed to honor it.

An exception to the lack of guarantees in takaful are the closed-end unit-linked funds popular in Malaysia in the mid-2000s. With these funds, a single contribution is paid to the takaful operator, who takes a small percentage (around 5 percent) for the *wakala* (agency) fee and *tabarru'* (donation) and invests the rest. In this type of product, the contributions are collected for several months and then invested at once. The fund could be either capital guaranteed or capital protected. Implicit in both is the existence of a guarantee of capital at maturity of the plan.

Other than the closed-end unit-linked funds mentioned above, savings plans in takaful are generally through either a unit-linked structure or a traditional savings structure. Both tend to focus on long-term goals, such as savings for retirement or children's education. Unit-linked plans tend to be straightforward from an investment point of view. There is normally an equity fund, a safe fund (Islamic equivalent to a bond such as a *sukuk*, a cash fund, or a *murabaha* fund), and a mixture of the two (a balanced fund). In some cases, there can be significantly more types of funds, such as for various categories of equities. Whereas mature conventional markets have a variety of safe funds, takaful generally does not, due to a lack of assets. Given the ease in determining which equities are Islamic, unit-linked takaful tends to be the product of choice in predominantly non-Muslim countries with little or no other Islamic assets. With unit-linked plans, investment risk is passed to the participant, as volatility and minimum or no returns are expected.

Whereas unit-linked takaful plans have unit prices that change every day, traditional savings structures are more stable. Here, investment return is allocated on a yearly basis, with the operator choosing the mix of assets. This means that participants with short-term plans receive the same investment arrangements as participants with long-term plans. There is no differentiation. Depending on how the plan was marketed, there could be expectations for a minimum level of return. Savings takaful plans are mainly regular contribution plans, with the exception of the closed-end fund or single-contribution plans.

Unlike savings products, risk coverage products normally have clear expectations as to expected returns. This is true for both family and general takaful products, but especially for long-term family products. In many countries, risk coverage products dealing with a particular basic need are the most common, in particular mortgage-reducing term takaful (MRTT) to cover Islamic loans. This includes credit policies attached to other loans such as automobile and personal loans, but the average duration of MRTT plans is significantly longer.

The challenge with long-term coverage products pertains to pricing, where a particular discount rate is used to determine the present value of future benefits. As a simplified example, suppose there is a two-year policy with expected death benefits of US$100 in year one and US$100 in year two. The single pure risk contribution is not simply the addition of the two benefits, that is, US$200. Assuming a discount rate of 5 percent, the contribution rate is US$100/(1.05^0.5) + US$100/(1.05^1.5) = 190.53. An implicit guaranteed return of 5 percent per year is embedded in the product, which the investment strategy needs to account for. If there is investment profit sharing, then this needs to be accounted for as well, which could significantly increase the required return. MRTT plans can have an average duration of 15 to 20 years or more, while other credit plans have a duration of about five years or so. These plans tend to be single contribution, as in Malaysia.

Another popular long-term family plan is the stand-alone medical plan. This is a regular contribution plan that pays for medical expenses. There are a number of variations to this plan, such as payment for specific hospital and surgical expenses or payment of a fixed daily amount for hospitalization. Although the term for this plan can be as long as that of MRTT plans, it is a regular contribution, so there is less need for investments. The contribution rates generally are not guaranteed, so there is a degree of flexibility. This plan can also be sold in rider form attached to a unit-linked or traditional savings plan. With regular contribution products, the contribution is level, but the benefits might have an increasing cost. This is true of products covering death, as the probability of death increases over time. For these products, the participant pays too much in the early years and not enough in the later years. The investment income is not used to pay a return to the participant.

The other family coverage plans tend to be short term in nature. The main type of product is yearly renewable group term takaful and group hospital surgical takaful. These plans have lower investment needs, both because they are yearly in nature and because the claims liabilities are short tailed (claims are processed relatively quickly).

One family plan that is not commonly sold but that presents a challenge from an investment point of view is the annuity plan. Annuities were sold for a short period in the early 2000s in Malaysia. The plan was structured in two portions, an accumulation period and a payout period. Both periods were generally long term, with the payout period being particularly long term. Due to the promotional materials, the plan, although not guaranteed, was taken to be implicitly guaranteed and treated as such by the regulators. This created difficulties due to the long-term nature and guarantee of high returns.

General takaful products tend to be short term in nature, with the exception of long-tailed business, which has a longer-term view, although not as long as most long-term family funds. For long-tailed general business, claims take a long time to settle and might not surface for some years after the claim is incurred. The long settlement time usually arises when lawyers and lawsuits are involved, such as third-party motor, workman's compensation, and third-party liability.

In addition to the product design and expected claims settlement experience, the takaful model chosen also plays a part in the investment strategy, but only to a point. For instance, with the MRTT plans, the two main structures are the long-term risk fund and the drip fund. With the long-term risk fund, a single contribution is paid into the risk fund, which explicitly guarantees the investment return used as a discount rate in calculating the contribution rates. In the drip model, regular drips are taken from the savings fund and moved to the risk fund. In this case, the savings fund does not have a guaranteed return per se, but as a practical matter it is difficult to ask participants to make additional contributions. It also is difficult from a marketing point of view to deny coverage should the savings fund run out before the policy is contracted to expire.

Although the products sold and resulting liabilities are similar worldwide, the available investments vary widely. Malaysia has the widest selection of Islamic assets, but still does not have the ability to fully match liabilities with corresponding assets. In other countries, this challenge can be significantly more acute. In such cases, the pricing of products might need to account for this. For instance, where no *sukuks* (bonds) or other fixed-income assets are available, a unit-linked structure may be the only product possible. This would increase the riskiness of such products (to participants), but with the absence of *sukuks*, this is unavoidable. It might also be necessary to limit the duration of liabilities or policy terms sold if *sukuks* with suitable terms are not available.

Types of Investments in Takaful

The type and amount of Islamic investments available vary greatly by country. The one asset class available in most countries is equities. Equity as an asset class is acceptable, but there is a process for determining which companies are suitable for investment. For example, Dow Jones Indexes provides several screens for both industries and financial ratios in Islamic markets. Excluded industries are alcohol, pork-related products, entertainment (hotels, casinos and gambling, cinemas, pornography, music), tobacco, and weapons and defense. Financial ratio screens ensure that the total debt, the sum of the company's cash and interest-bearing securities, and accounts receivables, each divided by the trailing 24-month average total market value, is less than 33 percent. The wide availability of Islamic equities is seen in the breadth of indexes offered by Dow Jones: more than 20 regional and global indexes and 69 country indexes (Dow Jones Indexes 2011). Some companies in these indexes have a small amount of activities in nonpermissible activities. A purification process is used in these cases, whereby some of the profits are donated to charity in order to cleanse the investment.

In conventional insurance, bonds are used primarily to back liabilities. Equities are used primarily to invest free assets as well as assets backing bonuses to provide additional long-term yield. With fixed-income assets such as bonds, either corporate or government bonds normally are used. Ideally, the duration of these bonds matches the duration of liabilities, with corporate bonds being used to take on credit risk. In takaful, there is *sukuk*, the Islamic equivalent of a conventional bond. Whereas conventional bonds promise to repay a loan, with *sukuk* there is partial ownership in a debt (*sukuk murabaha*), asset (*sukuk ijara*), project (*sukuk istisna'*), or business (*sukuk al musharaka*).

Sukuk structures are used for government as well as private bonds, with private bonds called Islamic private debt securities and government bonds called government investment issues. Islamic private debt securities include *sukuks*, commercial papers (short term, up to one year), and medium-term notes (up to seven years). Malaysia has the deepest and most diverse range of *sukuk* structures. Table 8.1 presents the amount outstanding in Malaysia as of October 26, 2011, for a range of instruments.

Table 8.1   Amount of *Sukuks* Outstanding in Malaysia, by Type of Instrument, 2011

Financial instrument	Amount outstanding (RM billions)
Islamic medium-term notes	125.9
Government investment issues	104.0
Corporate bonds (Islamic)	69.1
Asset-backed securities (Islamic bonds)	5.1
Islamic commercial papers	2.9
Malaysian Islamic Treasury bills	2.0
Others	0.6

Source: Bank Negara Malaysia 2011a.
Note: US$1.00 = RM 3.10, as of October 2011.

Although *sukuk* instruments are issued worldwide, availability is still very limited, in terms of both quantity and duration. Most *sukuks* have been issued in Malaysia. Unfortunately, there is controversy regarding the structure of Malaysian *sukuk*. In November 2007, Sheik Muhammad Taqi Usmani, president of the Sharia Council of the Accounting and Auditing Organization for Islamic Financial Institutions (AAOIFI) estimated that 85 percent of all *sukuks* in issuance were not sharia compliant due to the existence of guaranteed returns or repurchase obligations from the issuer. To be sharia compliant, *sukuks* must have three key elements:

- *Sukuks* must represent ownership shares in assets or commercial or industrial enterprises that bring profits or revenues.
- Payments to *sukuk* holders should be the share of profits (after costs) of the assets or enterprise.
- The value payable to the *sukuk* holder on maturity should be the current market value of the assets or enterprise and not the principal originally invested (Usmani 2007b).

The structure in Malaysia causing this controversy is the *bai' bithaman ajil* (BBA) and sale with immediate repurchase (*bai' inah*), which, due to the fixed coupons and rates, makes the structure appear to be identical to that of conventional bonds. BBA is a contract where an asset is financed on a deferred and an installment basis with a preagreed payment period, with the sale price including a profit margin (which does not need to be specified). *Bai' inah* is a contract where the buyer purchases the asset on a cash basis and immediately sells it back on a deferred payment basis at a price that is higher than the cash price (Securities Commission Malaysia 2011a). As a result of this controversy, as long as these structures prevail, Malaysia will continue to have assets that provide fixed returns to back liabilities, though not generally in the full range of durations needed. Without these structures, the traditional concept of backing liabilities with assets of fixed returns at similar durations must be reconsidered. With floating-rate assets backing long-term liabilities computed on a predetermined expected rate of return, it is imperative that such liabilities be priced conservatively. This would provide the security that the assets will be sufficient to back the liabilities, with excess investment returns being shared between the operator and the participant. The greater the uncertainty in the asset returns, the more conservative the liabilities should be priced. Unfortunately, this has not been the practice in reality, with takaful products being priced even more aggressively than conventional products in many countries.

Although there are constant developments in the application of Islamic structures to *sukuks*, the following summarizes the main contracts:

- *Musharaka*. A joint enterprise in which all the partners share the profit or loss of the joint venture. It is the alternative to interest-based financing, with return based on the actual profit earned by the joint venture. The financier in an interest-bearing loan cannot suffer loss, while the financier in *musharaka* can suffer loss if the joint venture fails to provide profit (Usmani 2007a, 27).
- *Mudaraba*. A special kind of partnership where one partner gives money to another for investing in a commercial enterprise. The first partner provides the investment, while the second partner does the management and work. Any losses are the sole responsibility of the first partner (Usmani 2007a, 82).
- *Diminishing musharaka*. Another form of *musharaka* where the share of the financier is divided into units, and it is understood that the client will purchase the units of the share of the financier over time. This structure works well for mortgages (Usmani 2007a, 82).
- *Murabaha*. Most Islamic banks and financial institutions use *murabaha* as an Islamic mode of financing, and most of their financing operations are based on this. In reality, *murabaha* refers to a contract where the seller agrees to provide the purchaser with a specific commodity with a certain profit added to the cost. The payment might be at spot or deferred. There is transparency in the amount of profit being received (Usmani 2007a, 95).
- *Ijara*. Something that is given in exchange for rent, that is, leasing (Usmani 2007a, 157).
- *Salam*. Advanced purchase, a sale whereby the seller undertakes to supply some specific goods to the buyer at a future date in exchange for an advanced price fully paid at spot (Usmani 2007a, 186).
- *Istisna'*. A purchase order, where a commodity is transacted before it comes into existence. It orders a manufacturer to make a specific commodity for the purchaser (Usmani 2007a, 195).

Table 8.2 presents the share of contracts used in Malaysia as of December 2011.

An additional challenge with *sukuks* is the definition of assets backing the structure. Structures can be classified as asset based versus asset

Table 8.2   Contracts Used in Malaysia, 2011

Type of contract	% of total
Murabaha and BBA	48
Ijara	30
Musharaka and *mudharaba*	3
Others	19

Source: Bank Negara Malaysia 2011b.
Note: BBA = *bai' bithaman ajil.*

backed. Normally structures are asset based, defined here as where the *sukuk* holders rely on the company seeking to raise finance. In theory, however, in asset-based structures the lenders own the assets until the loan is repaid and reliance is placed on the assets of the *sukuks* for security (Norton Rose 2011). Asset-backed structures appear safer due to the link between the *sukuk* and the underlying assets, but in reality the legal structure can be extremely complicated, putting into question whether any extra safety is really being afforded. This was seen in the problems with Dubai World Nakheel *sukuks* in November 2009. At that time, Dubai World requested restructuring of its US$26 billion in debts, which became known as the Dubai debt crisis. The main concern was repayment of the US$4 billion *sukuks* of Dubai World's developer, Nakheel, best known for its construction of the Dubai Palm Islands. In this structure,

• The originator of the structure was Nakheel Holdings, a subsidiary of Nakheel World. Nakheel World is owned by Dubai World, a 100 percent state-owned company.

• Nakheel Holdings sold the leasehold rights to the underlying tangible assets for a period of 50 years (the *sukuk* assets) to Nakheel SPV. The underlying tangible assets were the land, buildings, and other property known as DWF South and Crescent Lands at Dubai Waterfront. The aggregate amount for the entire lease period of 50 years was paid by Nakheel SPV to Nakheel Holdings.

• The amount paid by Nakheel SPV was raised by the issuance of *sukuks*. Nakheel SPV issued *sukuk* certificates for a period of three years.

• Nakheel SPV acted as agent and trustee for and on behalf of the *sukuk* holders, in accordance with an agency declaration and a declaration of trust. Nakheel SPV declared a trust in favor of the *sukuk* holders over its title to the *sukuk* assets.

- Nakheel SPV leased the *sukuk* assets to Nakheel Holdings for a period of three years. The lease comprised six consecutive periods of six months each. The rental payments matched the periodic distribution payments on the *sukuks*, so Nakheel SPV essentially paid the lease payments to the *sukuk* holders. At the redemption date of the *sukuks*, the lessee had to purchase the *sukuk* assets from the lessor at a certain exercise price. This exercise price was equal to the redemption amount of the *sukuks* and was used to pay back the principal amount to the *sukuk* holders. In this way, the *sukuks* were redeemed.

- Nakheel Holdings granted a guarantee to Nakheel SPV for payment, delivery, and other obligations. Under this guarantee, various covenants were given, such as a negative pledge, change of control provisions, limitations on financial indebtedness, asset sales, loans, dividends, the granting of security, and the granting of undertakings to maintain insurance and provide financial information. In addition, Dubai World issued a guarantee to Nakheel SPV for the payment obligations. Under that guarantee, Dubai World also entered into certain covenants such as a negative pledge and maintenance of ownership undertaking (stating that it would maintain ownership and control over its subsidiaries).

- For greater *sukuk* holder security, a collateral security structure was set up to secure the payment obligations. Nakheel Holdings granted two mortgages to hold the underlying tangible assets for and on behalf of Nakheel SPV as agent for the *sukuk* holders. The security agent was Dubai Islamic Bank PJSC, which entered into a security agency agreement with Nakheel SPV pursuant to which it held the two mortgages granted by Nakheel Holdings for the benefit of the *sukuk* holders.

- At first glance, the *sukuk* holders were sufficiently protected and their position was secure. First, Nakheel Holdings had guaranteed the payment obligation of Nakheel SPV. This guarantee was the first form of credit enhancement built into the structure. Second, Dubai World guaranteed the payment obligations of Nakheel SPV. So if the obligors failed to pay, Nakheel SPV had recourse to Dubai World's credit enhancement. Lastly, in accordance with a purchase undertaking, Nakheel Holdings agreed to purchase all of Nakheel SPV's interests in the *sukuk* assets at maturity date or at the occurrence of a dissolution event. In reality, none of the parties was in a position to fulfill its payment obligations. There was implied assistance from the government, as Dubai World is state owned, but this did not end up being the case (Salah 2010).

This structure was very dependent on the legal structure of Dubai. Although the law mentioned in the agreements was English law, due to the physical location of the assets, Dubai law likely had ultimate jurisdiction. This was a concern for the *sukuks*, but the government of Abu Dhabi granted a loan to Dubai to repay the *sukuks*, so they were, in fact, repaid (which is just as well, as the bulk of the assets in the SPV were yet-to-be-reclaimed land from the sea).

Complicated structures also lead to potential issues regarding double taxation. For instance, where there is a physical transfer of assets, there could be multiple stamp duties and land taxes. This is due to the inherent nature of Islamic structures in requiring assets to back the *sukuk*. This is further complicated by the continued innovation in structures, such as convertibility options (Dubai Port Authority *musharaka sukuks*), exchangeability (Aabar Petroleum *mudharaba* structure), put and call options (Investment Dar *musharaka sukuks*), co-ownership structures (Sharjah Islamic Bank), and medium-term note programs (Sa'ad Group). Fortunately, many jurisdictions are passing tax-neutrality laws, such as the U.K. Finance Acts from 2005–07 (Testa 2007). The dual issues of regulation in complicated legal structures as well as taxation need to be dealt with at a governmental level in order to facilitate the growth of *sukuk* in a jurisdiction.

The complicated nature of *sukuk* structures poses a challenge for the risk management departments of takaful operators. These departments need to balance the theoretical differences in Islamic structures from their conventional equivalents, with practical issues making such structures rather similar. Legal aspects discussed above will also need to be considered when determining appropriate assets for investment. This is exacerbated by the lack of a secondary market for *sukuks*, as very few *sukuks* are traded. As the example of the Nakheel *sukuks* shows, *sukuks* were not immune to the problems of the global financial crisis, which arose due to high risk, complex financial products, undisclosed conflicts of interest, and the general feeling that through such products intermediary banks were simply printing money risk free (U.S. Senate 2011). If risk is minimized in one aspect, then it is inherently being taken in another aspect. The takaful operator needs to understand the risks involved with each *sukuk* structure.

Risk-based capital regimes determine the level of capital required to be held to ensure the solvency of the takaful operations. The various risks of the operation are determined, along with who should be accountable for them. They include risks related to the products being sold, investments, expenses, and operations. Of relevance to *sukuk* structures are the risk charges for investments. It is quite likely that many regimes might not account for the differences between *sukuk* and conventional structures. This means that risk management departments will need to assess the risks of each type of investment independently and to ensure that sufficient capital is maintained for these risks. Charges may also be required for mismatches between assets and liabilities, where such charges tend to be determined by stressing both assets and liabilities through increasing and decreasing investment returns. Thus, strong knowledge of the practical workings of each *sukuk* structure is needed.

Takaful operators can invest in the equity and *sukuk* markets through Islamic unit trust funds. These funds provide coverage ranging from equities to *sukuks*, as well as a combination of the two. A multitude of coverage is also available for specific subsets of risks such as equities in certain regions. In Malaysia, as of September 30, 2011, there were 165 approved Islamic unit trust funds with a total net asset value of RM 25 billion (Securities Commission Malaysia 2011b). The issue with such unit trusts is that the underlying cost structures can be high relative to direct investment.

Another major investment by takaful operators is in Islamic deposits with banks, the Islamic version of fixed deposits. These accounts have durations up to five years. In Malaysia, total deposits were RM 20 billion in December 2010, shown by type of instrument in table 8.3.

Mudharaba general investment accounts are profit-sharing accounts where account holders expect a specific rate of return. In *mudharaba-*specific investment accounts, the account is earmarked for particular

Table 8.3   Islamic Fixed Deposits in Malaysia, by Type of Deposit, December 2010

Type of Islamic deposit	% of total
Mudharaba general investment account	33
Mudharaba specific investment account	14
Demand deposits (*wadia*)	15
Commodity *murabaha*	9
Savings	9
Others	20

Source: Bank Negara Malaysia 2011b.

investments and the account holder bears the investment risks. The vast majority of takaful operators' deposits are in *mudharaba* general investment accounts. Demand deposits operate under the *wadia* or safe-keeping principle and do not provide investment income except in the form of *hiba* (a gift). Under a commodity *murabaha*, the bank purchases and takes title to a relevant asset (normally precious metals) from a third-party broker and then sells the assets to the borrower at cost plus a specified profit. The borrower then enters a contract to sell the assets to the broker at cost. The commodity *murabaha* has been criticized because the commodity rarely changes hands and may not even exist (Harrison 2010).

Another potential option is to invest in properties, either directly or through real estate investment trusts (REITs). In determining acceptable properties for investment, the tenants of the property need to be screened in a process similar to what is done for equities. The proportion of rental income from unacceptable sources must be given in charity to cleanse the investment. The rules for Islamic investment property vary slightly by jurisdiction, but for REITs in Malaysia, the Securities Commission imposes the following restrictions (Ting and Noor 2007):

- Rental income is derived from permissible business activities according to *sharia*. If a portion of the rental is from nonpermissible activities, these rentals shall not exceed 20 percent of total turnover of the Islamic REIT.
- An Islamic REIT is not permitted to own properties where all the tenants operate nonpermissible activities.
- For new tenants, the Islamic REIT shall not accept new tenants whose activities are fully nonpermissible.
- For tenants who operate mixed activities, only 20 percent of the total floor area can be occupied for nonpermissible activities.
- For activities that do not involve the use of space, the sharia committee or sharia adviser will base its decision on *ijtihad* (the process of reasoning by which Islamic jurists obtain legal rulings from sources of sharia).

Activities that are not permitted vary by jurisdiction, but include conventional financial services, gambling, manufacture or sale of non-*halal* products, nonpermissible entertainment activities, hotels, and resorts. Takaful operators generally do not invest in Islamic investment properties.

Although these represent the main investment choices of takaful operators as of the writing of this book, this is a new and developing field, with innovative structures continually being developed. The choices available will likely continue to expand and develop over time.

Risk-Based Capital, Investment Strategy, and Product Design

The main investment strategy challenge in takaful right now is matching the needs of participants with the availability of assets. Products such as MRTT, with implicit guaranteed returns built into the pricing for 20 years or more, require guarantees on investment returns to match this risk. This is simply not possible in most countries. If such investments are not available, then the takaful operator will be hit with a hefty risk charge. Even in Malaysia, where some assets have fixed returns, these products are controversial, and they are not accepted in many parts of the world. If Malaysia were to move to more globally acceptable products, the mismatch would be significantly worse. This is also seen in savings products, where a takaful equivalent to the guaranteed maturity benefits in conventional insurance is needed. In many parts of the Muslim world, this has meant that family takaful has been avoided. This is prudent from a risk management point of view, but ignores the basic needs of Muslims. The need for coverage products is seen in the following *hadith* (saying of the prophet):

> A dead person was brought to the Prophet so that he might lead the funeral prayer for him. He asked, "Is he in debt?" When the people replied in the negative, he led the funeral prayer. Another dead person was brought and he asked, "Is he in debt?" They said, "Yes." He [refused to lead the prayer and] said, "Lead the prayer of your friend." Abu Qatada said, "O Allah's Apostle! I undertake to pay his debt." Allah's Apostle then led his funeral prayer. (Bukhari, vol. 3, book 37, no. 492; translation by Khan 1984.)

With more and more Muslims having significant levels of debt through house and vehicle purchases, takaful coverage products clearly are needed.

The need for Islamic savings products is also seen in the following verse from the Qur'an (2: 278–79): "O ye who believe! Fear Allah, and give up what remains of your demand for usury, if ye are indeed believers. If ye do it not, Take notice of war from Allah and His Messenger: But if ye turn back, ye shall have your capital sums: Deal not unjustly, and ye shall not be dealt with unjustly."

Conclusion

Simply limiting takaful products to appropriate sharia-compliant assets will not fulfill all the insurance needs. Thus, a strategy is needed to fulfill these basic needs of Muslims, while following proper risk management processes. Through risk-based capital guidelines, regulators seek to link capital requirements to the risks taken. The effectiveness of this guidance is limited by the ability to account properly for the risks involved. In particular,

- Liabilities for long-term coverage plans assume a particular investment return and "guarantee" this return, either explicitly or implicitly. The risks of this guarantee need to be accounted for.
- Islamic assets might look and act similar to conventional insurance counterparts, but the recent financial crisis shows the need to understand the complicated investment structures involved and to quantify these risks.
- The interaction between assets and liabilities under adverse conditions needs to be understood and quantified.
- In takaful, the operator manages, but does not take on, risks. Who is responsible for each risk and where capital for each risk should be held must be clarified from a theoretical and a practical point of view.

With Islamic investments continuing to evolve, takaful operators will need to go beyond risk-based capital guidelines and truly understand the risks being taken on. This entails showing discipline in the pricing of liabilities, using conservative investment returns where necessary, and allocating any excess back to the participant over time.

References

Bank Negara Malaysia. 2011a. "Financial Instruments Outstanding as at 26 October 2011." Islamic Interbank Money Market. Bank Negara Malaysia, Kuala Lumpur. http://iimm.bnm.gov.my/index.php?ch=5&pg=8.

———. 2011b. *Financial Stability and Payment Systems Report 2010.* Kuala Lumpur: Bank Negara Malaysia.

Dow Jones Indexes. 2011. *Dow Jones Islamic Market Indexes.* Princeton, NJ: Dow Jones Indexes.

Harrison, Hermione. 2010. "Commodity Murabahah: Concerns, Challenges, and Market Appetite." *Islamic Finance Asia* (February): 31–33.

Khan, Muhammad Muhsin, trans. 1984. *The Translation of the Meanings of Sahih Al-Bukhari,* Vol. III. New Delhi: Islamic University, Al Medina al Munawwara, Kitab Bhavan.

Norton Rose. 2011. *Islamic Finance Library.* London: Norton Rose.

Salah, Omar. 2010. "Dubai Debt Crisis." *Berkeley Journal of International Law* 4 (Spring): 19–32. http://www.boalt.org/bjil/.

Securities Commission Malaysia. 2011a. "Approved Syariah Concepts and Principles for the Purpose of Structuring, Documenting, and Trading of Islamic Securities." Securities Commission Malaysia, Kuala Lumpur, October. http://www.sc.com.my.

———. 2011b. "Unit Trust Funds in Malaysia: Summary of Statistics." Securities Commission Malaysia, Kuala Lumpur, October 27. http://www.sc.com.my/main.asp?pageid=302.

Testa, David. 2007. "Cross-Border Sukuk Issues." Speech for the London Sukuk Summit, London, June 21.

Ting, Kien Hwa, and Abdul Rahman Md. Noor. 2007. "Islamic REITs: A Syariah-Compliant Investment Option." Speech for the Twelfth Asian Real Estate Society Annual Conference, Macao SAR, China, July 9–12.

U.S. Senate. 2011. "Permanent Subcommittee on Investigations, Committee on Homeland Security and Governmental Affairs: Wall Street and the Financial Crisis; Anatomy of a Financial Collapse." 112 Cong., 2nd sess. S. Rept. Government Printing Office, Washington, DC.

Usmani, Muhammad Taqi. 2007a. *An Introduction to Islamic Finance*. Karachi: Maktaba Ma'ariful Qur'an.

———. 2007b. "Sukuk and Their Contemporary Applications." November. http://www.muftitaqiusmani.com.

CHAPTER 9

Challenges for Takaful Going Forward

Hassan Scott Odierno, Zainal Abidin Mohd Kassim, and Serap O. Gönülal

If we consider a stock company (a company capitalized by stockholders' capital), the loyalties are clear: management works for the shareholders, while the board of directors ensures that management performs to the shareholders' expectations. In regulated industries such as banks and insurance companies, another layer of responsibilities is placed on the board to ensure that the company adheres to the stringent financial and operating standards imposed by the regulator.

There is also a relationship between the stock insurer and the policyholders. In most cases, there is only one balance sheet and one profit and loss account, so the policyholder transfers risk to the insurer's balance sheet by paying a premium. The insurance contract clearly sets out the legal basis of the exchange, and the insurer is obliged to pay out the loss if the insured event transpires. The price of this risk transfer is the premium payable. The policyholder can shop around for the lowest premium and the best policy terms. The profits of the company are tightly linked to the underwriting performance of the insurance business and the returns earned from investing the assets of the company. The insurer keeps the regulator at bay by ensuring that adequate capital is maintained at all times to guarantee that claims will be paid. As far as the insurer is concerned, the less capital that is required the better, but the regulator will usually insist on more. In setting the amount of capital to hold, the insurer will take cognizance of the fact that it is often difficult to increase capital quickly and will therefore keep an appropriate margin in excess of the minimum required to satisfy the regulator.

How is this different in takaful? The answer is complicated. The complexity arises from the hybrid nature of takaful, it being a cross between a stock company and a mutual. The basis of determining how the income of the operator (stockholders) is determined has a profound impact on how a takaful company is run (assuming that regulations do not place impediments on its execution). For example, as has already been pointed out, if the company gets a percentage of all contributions (premiums) collected and is not responsible for the sufficiency of the rating structure of its products, then the inclination to maximize income can result in underpricing the product itself to the detriment of the ability to pay claims, adversely affecting the solvency of the takaful funds.

Similarly, if the company shares in the profits on the investment performance of the takaful funds, there is a risk that management will overinvest in volatile assets. Although stockholders take a percentage of investment profits, in takaful they do not share in investment losses due to the type of contract generally used for managing investments (the *mudharaba* contract).

This asymmetry in the sharing of profits but not losses is the direct consequence of sharia's insistence that there should be no transfer of the insurance or investment risks to stockholders, only a sharing of these risks among participants.

If we were to accept the premise that the stockholder is not responsible for underwriting the insurance and risks, then how should takaful companies compete? The operator does underwrite risk on behalf of the participants, but it does not share in any underwriting loss. How should potential participants (policyholders) choose between different takaful operators? Certainly, the choice should not be based entirely on the price of contributions (premiums), because, unlike the case with stock insurers, paying the premium does not transfer the risk to the insurer; moreover, similar to mutual insurers, the actual price of cover is the premium net of any surplus refund, not the initial premium. Furthermore, inadequate contributions can jeopardize the solvency of the takaful fund, thus leading to the possibility that an eventual claim will not be honored.

Implications of the Takaful Model Adopted

Several takaful models (or more specifically sharia-approved contracts) are in practice globally. These include the *mudharaba* model as applied in Sudan, the *wakala* on insurance and the *mudharaba or wakala* on investment services as applied in Bahrain and Saudi Arabia, and a combination of sharia-approved contracts as applied in Malaysia. Before examining the implications of the various takaful models for the risks in takaful, we review the types of risks inherent in a takaful operation and where they reside.

The same risks are inherent in any takaful operation, irrespective of the model used, but who is responsible for the risks varies. Models can vary within a jurisdiction, but differences are more significant between different regions. For instance, the model and what is considered acceptable is significantly different in the Middle East than in Southeast Asia, where liberal policies have sought to encourage the growth of takaful. Some Middle Eastern scholars might not even consider the operations in Southeast Asia as takaful. Similarly, some operations in Saudi Arabia are cooperative operations, but 90 percent of profit goes to the shareholders, which some might not consider as takaful. The same goes for countries such as the Islamic Republic of Iran, where Shi'a rules can make takaful look significantly different than in other countries. In all of these scenarios, the risks examined here are present. In operations where takaful describes not the entire company but simply one product of the company (offered through a takaful window in a conventional insurer), additional risks are related to ensuring the sanctity of the takaful product within the larger operations of the insurer. Differences in the operations and methods of implementing takaful make it difficult to determine even how many takaful operations are in existence worldwide, which hinders efforts to standardize the regulation of takaful activities globally, another risk in and of itself.

Of major concern is how and by what means the public should choose the takaful operator or products that provide the best value. For the public, another criterion with which to make a choice is which operator is more "sharia compliant"! The risk of misselling in takaful is considerable.

Expense Risk

Like any business, some operating expenses are fixed in nature (so-called overhead), some are variable (for example, sales commission), and some do not fit neatly in either of these categories. In pricing its services and products, the entrepreneur needs to load its costs of services or goods to recover these expenses. Apart from variable expenses, overhead cannot be recovered on a per sale basis, but only on a specified volume of sales. If the sales volume is not met, there will be expense overruns, while if sales volume is in excess of target (termed "critical" size), this "excess" expense margin will contribute to profit.

Other than on the *mudharaba* model as practiced in Sudan, this expense risk is borne by the shareholders, as all management expenses are for the shareholders' account. The shareholders' income is through a fee (a so-called *wakala* fee), a share of investment profits, a share of the surplus in the underwriting experience, or a combination of these.

Underwriting Risk

There are two basic determinants of the risk premium: the estimated likelihood of a claim occurring and the estimated average size of the loss when it occurs. In the real world, there will be fluctuations and volatility in the actual number and size of claims realized. The law of large numbers works on the basis of a large number of claims. This can happen only if the expected frequency of claims is high in one year or, if it is low, if claims are accumulated over a sufficiently long time horizon.

As mentioned earlier, the underwriting risk in takaful rests with the participants, not the stockholders of the company. Should a deficit occur, the stockholders would extend a *qard* (interest-free loan) to the takaful fund, which would be paid from future surpluses in the takaful fund. A complication arises because the stockholders share in underwriting surplus, but not in underwriting losses.

Consider a situation where the pricing of the policy is on a best-estimate basis (50 percent likelihood that the risk premium is just sufficient to pay claims in any one year). In such a situation, any surplus arising in any one year should not be automatically distributed; when the period of observation is stretched over a long enough period, say five years, and the pricing is correct, then no surplus arises over the period, as total surpluses over the years are exactly balanced by losses in other years. Thus, when the risk premium is determined on a best-estimate basis, the issue of sharing surplus, but not losses, with shareholders goes against the basis of how the risk premium was calculated. The example below illustrates this issue. The Islamic Financial Services Board (IFSB) recommends that no surplus should be paid out before the actuary has set aside an amount of surplus into a reserve account.

A takaful fund has a one-year-term renewable product and prices its risks on a best-estimate basis. Its five-year underwriting experience is shown in figure 9.1. First, let us assume that there is no surplus distribution to either the participant or the takaful operator. Deficits are covered first by retained surplus from past underwriting years and, if that is insufficient, by a *qard* from the takaful operator, which would be repaid from future underwriting surplus.

In the example in figure 9.1, over an observation period of five years, the cumulative profit or loss is zero (20 – 10 + 30 – 50 + 10), with deficits being made good either by retained surplus or by a temporary loan from the takaful operator.

Let us now assume that any underwriting surplus is shared equally between the takaful operator and the participants. The resulting distribution is shown in figure 9.2. Any deficits in this example would be met from a *qard* from the takaful operator, as there would be no retained surplus.

The alternative scenario in figure 9.2 would result in an outstanding *qard* of 40 after five years. Where has this 40 been used? In this example,

Figure 9.1   Five-Year Underwriting Experience of a Takaful Fund

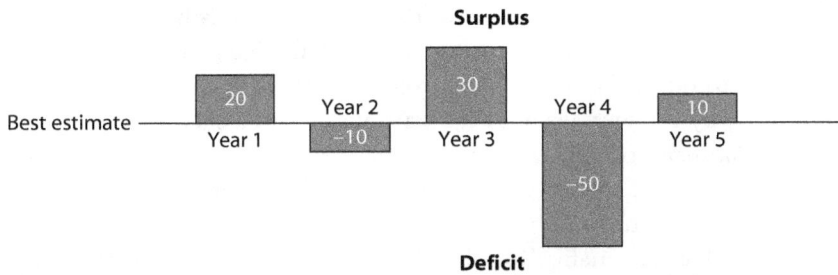

Figure 9.2   Underwriting Surplus Shared Equally

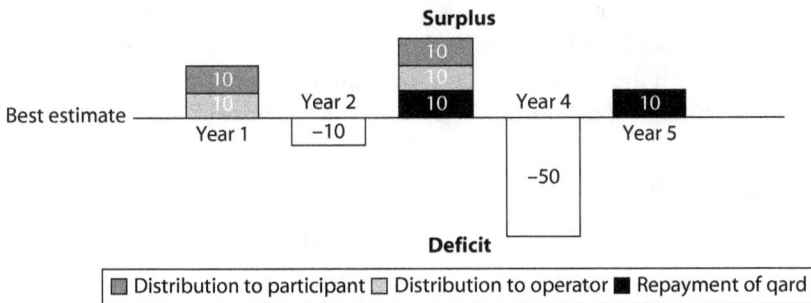

we have mistakenly (in hindsight) distributed (false) surplus of 20 to participants and 20 to the takaful operator.

For claims that take many years to settle (for example, liability claims), and in order to eliminate the risk of overdeclaring any underwriting surplus, it is preferable to wait until the claim amounts are reasonably certain before determining the underwriting results. Indeed, this is practiced in Lloyd's, as this is seen as a fairer way to settle underwriting accounts among different stakeholders. Perhaps even for short-tail risks, this basis of surplus distribution should be adopted to reduce the possibility of false surplus being distributed, as illustrated earlier.

Investment and Investment Profits

Several takaful models look at the investment of the assets of a takaful pool as another service that justifies a separate fee. The basis for determining the fee can be a percentage of funds under investment (the *wakala* fee approach) or a percentage of investment profits (the *mudharaba* approach). The *wakala* performance fee can be applied to either underwriting or investment returns. The former is straightforward, and the fee is easily calculable, but it does not align the interests of stockholders tightly with the interests of participants. This is because, regardless of whether the funds perform well or not, the fee is still payable. The incentive to outperform by taking excessive risk is there, but it is partly countered by a lower absolute fee payable should assets underperform. The *mudharaba* contract, however, ties the stockholders' interests more tightly to the participants' interests, because, if there are no profits, there is no income for the shareholders. The only issue here is whether unrealized capital gains qualify for distribution to *stockholders* because the actual profit is only made when assets are eventually sold.

Long-term family coverage plans such as mortgage-reducing term takafuls deserve special mention. Here the participant pays a contribution and receives coverage in return. When pricing these products, the actuary assumes a particular investment return. Investment risks for these plans are effectively with the stockholders, as there are practical difficulties with asking for additional contributions later or reducing or eliminating benefits.

Operational Risks

Operational risks are clearly the responsibility of the stockholders, as management runs the business on their behalf and participants usually have no say in the decision-making process. Unless the takaful model is a

Table 9.1   Risks, by Type of Takaful Contract

Type of contract	Expense risk	Underwriting risk	Investment risk	Operational risk
Pure cooperative	Participants	Participants	Participants	Participants
Mudharaba only	Stockholders or participants[a]	Participants	Participants	Stockholders
Pure wakala	Stockholders	Participants	Participants	Stockholders
Wakala with surplus sharing	Stockholders	Participants	Participants	Stockholders
Wakala for underwriting, mudharaba for investment	Stockholders	Participants	Participants	Stockholders

a. Participants in the Sudan version; stockholders in the Malaysian version.

pure cooperative model, where there are no stockholders, this risk sits clearly with the takaful operator. Operational risks would include mispricing risks and misselling risks and, uniquely for takaful, sharia compliance risks. Table 9.1 summarizes where the risks reside under various takaful contracts.

Risk-Based Capital

The risks in table 9.1 are combined in risk-based capital (RBC) regulations to determine how much capital a takaful operation should hold. Risk charges are developed for each risk, generally grouped into liability (benefit) risks, asset risks, asset-liability mismatch risks, and operational risks. RBC regulations normally involve not only the calculation of such charges but also the specification of how much excess should be held, with one level being the regulatory minimum and a higher internal capital adequacy ratio (ICAR). For risks belonging to the participant, by right the capital for such risks should be with the participant. In practice—regardless of the contention that the operator manages, but does not take on, risks—if stockholders provide the capital, the operator has taken on the benefit risks. Ideally, RBC regulations should allow for capital up to the target ICAR to be funded by participants for risks belonging to them. At the outset, where there are no retained surpluses, the stockholders would be responsible for providing any necessary *qard*, and some capital would have to be allocated for potential *qard*.

Simply providing for all such solvency requirements from the operators' fund results in risk transfer, which is not acceptable from the sharia perspective. Assuming that the pricing of the takaful products allows surpluses to arise, the takaful fund can build up sufficient retained surplus over time to relieve the necessity of requiring a *qard* from the stockholders. However, if the solvency requirements are provided for through the takaful fund, it could be many years before participants share any surplus. This places an unfair burden on early participants compared to later participants, who can receive surplus right away because the accumulated surpluses are already sufficient to fund the required solvency capital. Balancing the theoretical desire for participants to fund their own risks with the practical issues of fairness and simplicity is a challenge. It would be possible to require each participant to pay an additional amount (that is, to price risk premiums in excess of best estimate) to fund his own solvency requirement. When the participant leaves the takaful fund due to death, surrender, or maturity, he would receive the "excess" premiums back, subject to approval of the actuary.

Product Structure Issues

One risk inherent in takaful is the risk that the model or product structure chosen now will be considered unacceptable by sharia at a later time (so-called sharia risk). For instance, in the earlier takaful structures, a common feature was a long-term risk fund, where a single contribution is paid into a fund and benefits are paid from it. In the development of this contribution, certain mortality experience and investment return are assumed. Although the assumed mortality may eventually prevail (as life expectancy is expected to increase), the same may not be true of estimated investment performance. Over time, this structure could be considered unacceptable to sharia, as this product could be seen as guaranteeing future investment returns.

Similarly for retakaful (the sharia-compliant version of reinsurance), an issue is whether conventional reinsurance can be accepted under a retakaful program. Although not prevalent at the current time, as a ready supply of retakaful arrangements exists, some companies still use reinsurance to protect their takaful fund. Whereas conventional reinsurance is considered to provide coverage against losses for shareholders, retakaful is intended to protect participants against the risk that their takaful fund will go into deficit. Among retakaful operators, how risks are pooled can also differ. For example, some retakaful programs maintain separate funds for each cedant. It is possible that, over time, a retakaful program can only be considered if the pooled risks are ceded from various takaful pools, not from just one cedant. This is the case now in Malaysia. This should also be the case worldwide, but it is not, causing major problems with retakaful, specifically in the area of general-casualty takaful insurance in the Middle East.

Issues related to product structure can also be present for certain types of products currently included in takaful. Payor benefit riders to the base policy provide coverage for the payment of contributions when certain adverse events occur, such as when the parent or spouse dies or the payor incurs a critical illness. Under these conditions, where should these contributions be paid from? Obviously, payment is from the takaful fund in some manner, but where provision is made for total future contributions, what happens if the beneficiary (for example, the child or the wife) also passes away before the policy matures? Then, an immediate death benefit is paid along with any investment, if applicable, to the structure. There will be a gain or a loss on this provision. Who does this gain or loss belong to? By right, this is an annuity structure, but at the present time this methodology is not used for these plans. It is possible that this kind of structure will be redesigned in the future, leaving questions about the structures currently in place. The same can be said for children's education plans, where the concern is over how to ensure that the benefits of the plan will remain with the child and not be distributed via *fara'id* (Islamic inheritance) laws. The underlying concern is whether later sharia developments will change how we look at takaful and the various takaful structures, throwing earlier structures into doubt.

Corporate Governance and Regulation

Due to the potential misalignment of interests among stakeholders, the role played by corporate governance and regulation is particularly important in takaful. An important question to ask is, who takes care of the participants' interests in a takaful operation, when, unlike a stock company, underwriting and investment risks are squarely on the shoulders of participants? Having a proper structure of corporate governance in place is preferable to being overly dependent on regulations, as the latter are unlikely to cater to everything that can possibly go wrong in a takaful setup. However, given the lack of a standard on how takaful should be structured and the lack of experienced human capital (in takaful), the regulator needs to have adequate rules in place for takaful.

In nearly all takaful companies globally, participants are not represented on the board of directors. Even if participants were represented on the board, conflicts could arise between the different board members representing stockholders and participants, as their interests may not be aligned.

Sudan requires participants to be represented on the board, but this can be easily manipulated by ensuring that some board members are themselves policyholders. Thus, instead of the board of directors, should the sharia advisory board (SAB) be responsible for protecting the interests of participants? What regulatory role should the SAB take on? This is related to the larger issue of who is ultimately responsible for ensuring that the takaful operations are considered sharia compliant. Does being sharia compliant mean that takaful participants should be given priority over stockholders? It is easy to place this responsibility on the SAB, but in reality the SAB is responsible only for the queries that are presented to it. If the management does not refer specific questions to the SAB, then the SAB will not rule on the issue. The Accounting and Auditing Organization for Islamic Financial Institutions (AAOIFI) has given management the responsibility for ensuring that operations comply with sharia. This bypasses potential problems when management or board members are not Muslims.

The SAB's role is to ensure compliance with sharia law and not to determine the parameters within which the business is run, as long as these parameters do not go against sharia principles. Indeed, Islam encourages businesses and the earning of profits through legitimate trade. The IFSB goes so far as to recommend an independent entity that would be responsible for ensuring that the interests of participants are not compromised in any takaful setup (IFSB 2009). The practicality of this structure of corporate governance is debatable, as the recommendation does not mention who is responsible for arbitrating between this independent group and the company's board of directors when differences of opinion remain unresolved. Nevertheless, this recommendation has merit, as participants have very little say about the running of a takaful operation. With an advocate set up to represent participants in SAB meetings, the SAB would at least receive a balanced view of the issues and hear the voice of participants.

The solution would still be with the regulator. It is for the regulator to set rules and standards for takaful that protect the legitimate rights of participants while allowing stockholders to make an acceptable return on their capital. A concern here is that different regulators could have very different opinions as to what is reasonable and acceptable. As yet, no global organization ensures consistency in takaful. Organizations such as AAOIFI and IFSB exist, but their rulings are not accepted worldwide or even in a majority of countries with takaful.

A related question in takaful is, who is responsible for ensuring that participants are treated fairly? The simple answer is that everyone is responsible, from management to the SAB and the appointed actuary.

Ensuring fairness is a complicated matter. For instance, it is generally accepted that different types of products can be kept in the same takaful fund. However, what if some products are expected to be very profitable, whereas others are expected to lose money (possibly due to the use of tariffs)? Should the profitable products be allowed to subsidize the unprofitable products? The SAB may not be aware of this issue unless the actuary brings it to the board. Regulators do play a key role, but they cannot develop regulations for all potential issues. Similarly, management cannot be expected to police itself, as pressures to be competitive and profitable may lead management to present issues to the SAB in a manner that makes a favorable response likely. The actuary is in a unique position to determine issues of fairness and needs to work closely with the SAB to ensure that participants are treated fairly.

Ultimately and notwithstanding the difficulties, a workable takaful structure combined with strong corporate governance and supporting regulations is the way forward.

The use of *qard* or interest-free loans is a potential corporate governance or regulatory issue facing the takaful world. Qard was originally used when a takaful fund did not have enough cash to pay claims. In this case, the operator would give the fund a *qard*, which would be paid back once the takaful fund had the necessary cash flow. In recent times, *qard* has been used to deal with statutory deficits at year end. A statutory deficit can arise when the required technical reserves are in excess of the available takaful fund and not just when there is inadequate cash flow. In this situation, *qard* is considered a loan from the point of view of the operators' fund, but an injection (as it covers the deficit) into the risk fund from the point of view of the regulators. This does not align with the sharia view that debt must be repaid irrespective of how long it takes. This is also an issue with accounting standards, which state that any outstanding loan must be "impaired" (written off) if it is not repaid within a certain period of time.

Lack of Suitable Investment

The concept of pooling in takaful also extends to how contributions are invested. It is not for the operator to guarantee the performance of these investments; if for no other reason, to be sharia compliant, such guaranteed investment performance has to be "free" (that is, no contingent-based fee can be extracted from the party enjoying the guarantee); otherwise, it is tantamount to a risk transfer.

In order for investment returns to be less volatile, allocation should be weighted toward *sukuks*, the sharia equivalent of bonds in conventional finance. Instead of interest, *sukuks* pay a rent earned on the underlying assets on which they are based (for *ijara* or leasing-based *sukuks*). Unfortunately, other than in Malaysia, the availability of *sukuks* in the currency of the jurisdiction is restricted by lack of supply. Generally, the tenor of *sukuks* is also limited (usually a five-year term at issue). The supply and availability (in differing tenures) of *sukuks* in the currency of the takaful product are crucial for takaful to succeed as a dependable form of saving.

Marketing and Distribution Channel

The best insurance product in the world will not sell unless there is an effective distribution channel for it. This statement is generally true of takaful unless the cover is compulsory by law (for example, third-party motor liability takaful). Although takaful provides a means for Muslims to obtain coverage in a manner acceptable to their religious beliefs, takaful must still be sold. People will not line up to purchase it. This is consistent with insurance in most of the developing world (that is, a push rather than a pull strategy is needed). Experience has been that selling takaful through bank channels can only succeed if the banks put in sufficient resources to ensure its success. This is usually difficult, as the banks are simultaneously promoting their own competing products, which are probably easier to sell than takaful. It does not help that, as a "new" offering, takaful requires the intermediary to educate the public on exactly what takaful is and how it differs from insurance. Therefore, the more successful takaful companies are those with an extensive network of agents rather than those depending on a bancassurance channel. Such an agency network is expensive to build and maintain, thus requiring significant investment on the part of the takaful operator. However, operators can leverage off the existing distribution infrastructure of their more established sister insurance operation (in Malaysia, many conventional insurers now have a takaful sister company), with various degrees of success. Should takaful be designed and marketed to be similar to conventional insurance, or should it be designed to be unique and different? Ideally, takaful should look unique and different if it is to create its own market and niche. If takaful were to appear very similar to conventional insurance, there is always the risk that takaful will simply cannibalize its sister company's conventional insurance sales. With bancassurance sales, contact with the participants (policyholders) is limited given the short period of time involved in the sales process, and it is common for takaful products to look very similar to conventional equivalents.

Customer Loyalty

One concern in takaful has arisen from the way takaful is promoted. Many takaful operators highlight the surplus-sharing aspect of takaful as being superior to the insurance version of the same product. This raises the question of whether participants would remain loyal to any operator that has a *qard* outstanding in its takaful pool. Deficits are to be expected when claims are volatile, but when the *qard* remains unpaid, any future surplus in the takaful pool will be used first to repay the *qard*, thus depriving participants in that year of any surplus dividends. It is therefore important for the takaful operator to minimize the probability of a deficit in any one year. There are several ways of doing this. Risk sharing could be structured among different groups of risks. By grouping types of risks that are not directly correlated with one another, the underwriting experience of the pool as a whole can be made less volatile. Alternatively, retakaful could be used to handle the peaks of claims experience.

Conclusion

Managing a takaful operation involves rethinking the norms of insurance. Takaful is not simply another name for insurance. In order for takaful to succeed, there is a need to understand how risks in takaful are distributed and how they should be managed so as to align the interests of the various stakeholders as closely as possible. The challenge in takaful is how best to work within the constraints imposed by sharing rather than transferring risk. This is key, as only when risk sharing can be optimized to minimize volatility in claims experience can there be less dependence on speculative shareholders' capital. We also need to realize that modern takaful is about savings and prefunding of benefits. Thus, there is also a need to expand the variety and depth of sharia-compliant asset classes to mitigate the investment risks inherent in long-term takaful savings and protection products.

Reference

IFSB (Islamic Financial Services Board). 2009. *Guiding Principles on Governance for Takaful Undertakings*. IFSB: Kuala Lumpur.

CHAPTER 10

Oversight in Takaful

Hassan Scott Odierno and Zainal Abidin Mohd Kassim

The unique characteristics of takaful make its success somewhat dependent on a friendly regulatory environment. The hybrid nature of its setup
(a combined management company and mutual risk pool) makes it difficult to thrive in an environment that promotes only stock companies or
only mutual insurers. The current regulatory approach in countries where
takaful coexists with conventional insurance has been to encourage takaful, but not to favor one form above the other.

The Proposition: Why Takaful?

The role of the state in managing its population's well-being has never
been easy. This has to do with the limited resources at the disposal of
government, the deteriorating dependency ratios (with the ratio of working to retired population declining year by year), and the tendency of the
population to consume too much and to go into debt. The dependency
ratio is expected to continue falling due to a combination of lower birth
rates as populations urbanize and general increase in longevity. The tendency to consume too much has been exacerbated by the recent availability of cheap credit. The need to encourage saving by the population is
therefore a crucial part of the sustainable development of a country.

Insurance, specifically life insurance, has traditionally been a conduit for such saving, as it doubles as a safety net if a contingency were to happen that affects the family unit's ability to continue to enjoy their current standard of living. With the spread of urbanization and the resulting breakup of the family unit, the importance of this safety net has grown. Insurance for the protection of capital also plays an important role in modern society, as individuals tend to borrow money to purchase assets. The loss of assets due to a calamity before the associated loan has been fully paid can decimate the balance sheet of the family.

While insurance has become an essential component of individual risk management in financially aware societies (indeed, for some, insurance is as important as food and shelter), it is easy to forgo such an intangible offering. This may indeed be the reason why many Muslim families forgo insurance on the excuse that their religion prohibits conventional insurance. Islam prides itself for being a practical religion, but Muslims themselves tend to accept the prohibitions without seeking alternatives. Perhaps the point is missed that God would not prohibit some practices without providing a better alternative to them.

For insurance, the solution for Muslims is takaful. As originally envisaged, takaful was similar to mutual or cooperative insurance setups. Unfortunately, such setups are becoming increasingly rare and those that are still in operation exist because of the strength afforded by the capital that has accumulated as a result of retained surpluses over a long period of time. It would be a challenge for any new mutual insurers to be set up in the age of Solvency II.

Before we analyze best practices in takaful, we consider the objectives of various stakeholders—the state, the operator, and, most important, the participants:

1. Increase the penetration of takaful among those currently not insured.
2. Support the development of Islamic finance by making sharia-compliant insurance available to protect the assets underlying *sukuks* (Islamic bonds).
3. Make available a long-term source of financing for investment (to use for infrastructure projects and the like that have a long gestation period) through the savings component of takaful products.
4. Provide a sharia-compliant insurance alternative for compulsory personal coverage such as motor third-party insurance.

5. Encourage long-term savings for retirement through takaful savings plans so that the role of the state in providing for old-age retirement can be reduced to a manageable and sustainable level over the long term.

As a start, therefore, a real need for takaful must exist so that the distribution costs can be kept low and the risk of misselling can be minimized. In many instances, misselling arises from intermediaries who try to sell complicated products that the policyholder does not really need or fully understand or from products that incorporate unacceptable policy conditions. Best practices for the implementation of takaful start at the product design stage, including setting policy conditions, managing the distribution channel, and establishing an effective claims management process.

Takaful-Friendly Environment

Very different products are sold as takaful in the Middle East and Southeast Asia. General takaful products are predominant in the Middle East, while family takaful products lead in Southeast Asia. This has to do with several factors:

1. A higher savings ratio in Southeast Asia. Individuals in Southeast Asia tend to save more than their counterparts in the Middle East.
2. Lack of a comprehensive government social safety net in Southeast Asia. Middle Eastern countries tend to have a comprehensive state pension scheme for employed citizens.
3. Tax incentivized savings through life and family takaful in Southeast Asia. In many countries in the Middle East, no personal tax is payable, so there is no tax incentive to save.

Takaful also requires the presence of a developed secondary Islamic capital market. This includes not just sharia-compliant listed entities, but also a liquid *sukuk* (Islamic bond) market. Without *sukuks*, it will be difficult to manage investment risks in takaful. Indeed, the financial performance of takaful companies in the Middle East has been closely correlated with the performance of equities on the local stock market due to the predominance of equity investments in takaful company portfolios. This is unhealthy, as the ensuing volatility in equity performance can have a detrimental effect on the solvency of the takaful pool.

The most important ingredients for takaful to succeed are regulations in the host country. Success in takaful cannot be measured over a short period of time. Some takaful policies can extend for 20 years or more, so the responsibility for sustainability has to rest with the regulators.

We now trace the regulations and conduct of takaful from product design to distribution to claims settlement and comment on the issues that led to a particular regulation.

Why the Need to Regulate?

Takaful, like insurance, is one of the few services where you "pay first" and receive the "service" later. Thus, you will never be certain that you have bought the policy that you thought you bought until you actually submit a claim on it. Of course, the insurer must still be in business when you eventually make the claim! As such, it is important to keep the "insolvency risk" (the risk that claims will not be paid because the insurer is insolvent) to a minimum. This means ensuring that the takaful operator has put in place an appropriate pricing mechanism and good claims-reserving practice together with the availability of sufficient capital to ride out the volatility of claims over time.

In takaful, the concept of mutuality requires that the operator minimize reliance for solvency on the shareholders' capital. Capital alone will not necessarily mitigate insolvency risk. The near collapse of giant AIG during the 2007–08 financial crises is testament that abundant capital alone cannot guarantee the solvency of an insurer. The financial market cannot be left to regulate itself, sophisticated financial models in use by the market can and do fail, and the consequences of failure in a financially interconnected world have proven to be nearly catastrophic.

Regulate at the Source

In takaful, risks are pooled, and claim payouts are shared among the participants (that is, the policyholders). There is no reason for takaful companies to compete on price, as the contribution (premium) is not the final "price" for the cover. Similar to a policy with a mutual insurer, the ultimate price of cover is dependent on the premium less the eventual dividend (or surplus) payout. A mechanism is needed to ensure that takaful products are sufficiently priced.

What drives the takaful operator (the company that manages the business)? Depending on the takaful model adopted, the financial interests of the operator may lie simply in increasing turnover (similar to an insurance intermediary), as profitability is driven by the fee it receives per unit of sales. Regulation is required to ensure that sales are not made to the detriment of participants in the takaful pool.

Product design should be preceded by the following questions:

- Is this product what the participants need?
- What segment of the market should this product be targeted to?
- Are sufficient sharia-compliant assets available of the type necessary to provide a competitive return to participants' savings?
- What risks are inherent in this product to the participants and the operator? Are both parties aware of these risks? For the operator, what steps are taken to manage these risks?

In most instances, the participant or user of takaful is not financially savvy. One of the roles of the intermediary is to provide financial advice covering both the protection and savings aspects of the product. However, providing financial advice is fraught with difficulties. One size does not fit all. Intermediaries may not be sufficiently competent or, worse, may be biased. There is no reason why misselling will not be as significant a risk in takaful as it is in conventional insurance, as participants may not fully understand the products on offer and may participate simply on the basis of trust.

The next level of oversight is the contract itself. Takaful contracts should be simple enough to minimize such risks. Simple contracts may have an impact on pricing, but the management's consideration should be different from that of a pure stock insurer: in takaful, participants carry the contingent risk, so there can be some leeway in claims management.

Takaful is inherently more transparent than insurance. For example, in takaful the operator has to tell participants how much of their contribution is paid to it as a fee. Regulations should require such a declaration, together with a requirement for the operator to have a clear and written policy of how surpluses or deficits arising from the operation are shared with the various stakeholders.

Levels of Governance

Governance is an important aspect of risk management. Risks should be clearly elucidated, and risk management should be allocated to the appropriate stakeholder. Furthermore, to the extent possible, there should be minimal conflicts of interest among stakeholders to ensure the long-term sustainability of the operation.

In takaful, there are various levels of governance:

- *Board of directors.* Board members are responsible to the shareholders (which unlike a mutual are *not* also policyholders) and to the regulator (as the board, for all intents and purposes, manages the managers of the company).

- *Sharia advisory board.* Board members are responsible for ensuring that products and investments are sharia compliant. Clear standards are lacking among sharia scholars (in Islamic jurisprudence, what is specifically and clearly prohibited is surprisingly small in number, so how different sharia scholars interpret the prohibitions can vary significantly from region to region or within any one region itself). For this reason, a "supreme" sharia council is needed in each jurisdiction to ensure uniformity in the interpretation of Islamic edicts and avoid confusion in the marketplace.

- *Actuary.* Actuaries are charged with understanding how everything in takaful technically ties together. This knowledge needs to be guided by regulations, remembering that the competition complicates decisions about pricing and reserving within the takaful company. Actuaries often are used in family takaful, but also they are being used increasingly in general takaful for pricing and reserving.

Does Takaful Require Solvency Standards?

The short answer is yes. But there should be less reliance on capital and more effort made to achieve the same goals through a simplification of the industry. Simplification can be achieved by maximizing the pooling of risks, which brings the benefits of diversification and ultimately a more stable claims experience and therefore lowers the capital required to maintain solvency. Risk capital can be minimized by aligning as much as possible the interests of all stakeholders in the operation. This alignment will reduce the possibility of any one stakeholder unfairly "gaming" the system. The holding of capital can also be minimized by requiring predetermined standard models, as this will standardize different types of risks and allow for more efficient regulatory monitoring.

Innovation can also thrive with sensible rules in place. In Islam itself, there are limits as to what can be "innovated," yet Islam is one of the fastest-growing religions in the world. Would such standards stifle competition? The insured is also the insurer in takaful, and this question should be answered by looking primarily at the needs of the participants and not just those of the takaful operator. Indeed, as in mutuals, takaful companies should give top priority to service.

What about Surplus Distribution?

Many takaful setups refer to the potential distribution of surplus to participants as a major selling point. However, experience has shown that such an emphasis has led to disappointment among participants, as surplus distribution is unusual during the early phase of development. Managing participants' expectations is therefore very important in takaful. This requires that the takaful industry invest in programs to educate the general public on what takaful is and what to expect from it. It also means that takaful operators should be realistic in their promises to participants about when surpluses can be expected to arise and how such surpluses will be distributed.

Practices around the World

Regulations for insurance and takaful in many countries are the cumulative result of the regulator reacting to one crisis after another in the industry. The overhaul of banking and insurance regulations expected in the aftermath of the 2007–08 global financial crisis is an example. However, it is not appropriate simply to copy the regulations of one country without understanding the implications of the regulation in a different business environment. With takaful, there is also a need to consider the local sharia's interpretation of the various *fiqh muamalat* (sharia law applicable to business contracts), especially when regulations are transplanted.

This does not mean that regulations are less prudent as a result of sharia constraints, but it does point to the need to ensure that the product as a whole remains sharia compliant.

Considering the regulations in jurisdictions where takaful is practiced can assist in understanding the differing approaches to managing specific risks. Table 10.1 summarizes the practices in selected countries.

Much can be written about how takaful is managed in each of these jurisdictions. Malaysia has the most developed regulatory system for takaful, developed in tandem with the regulations for conventional insurance. The underlying principle of regulation is first to manage the allocation of

Table 10.1 Takaful Practices in Selected Countries

Type of contract	Malaysia	Bahrain	United Arab Emirates	Indonesia	Sudan	Saudi Arabia
Standardized takaful model or contract	There is no restriction on the takaful models to be applied, but any "nonstandard" contract requires approval of the regulators.	Yes, the *wakala* model. All takaful firms licensed in Bahrain must organize and operate their business according to the *wakala* model. In exchange for the provision of management services to takaful fund(s), the shareholders of the takaful firm are allowed to charge a specific consideration (a *wakala* fee). For insurance assets invested on behalf of takaful funds, the takaful operator can use the *mudaraba* model and receive a set percentage of the profits generated from the investment portfolio.	The regulations acknowledge and accept the use of *mudharaba* and *wakala* models, but are silent on the use of other models.	The operating framework allows the application of *wakala*, *mudharaba*, or *mudaraba musharaka*. Other models can also be considered.	The framework for the model is mixed: *wakala* for insurance activities and *mudharaba* for investment.	No reference is made to sharia contracts; rather, the industry is regulated as a cooperative, but with shareholder capital.
Regulatory requirement to treat customers fairly	Yes	Yes. The insurance code of practice is made up of overarching principles applied throughout the customer relationship.	Yes. Senior management should ensure that adequate standards of customer protection are adopted by the operation in each jurisdiction.	Yes. Regulation on insurance requires fair pricing that is nondiscriminatory and financially sound.	As a cooperative, this is implicit in the company's charter.	Yes. Specific rules govern professional conduct.

Requirement to certify pricing of takaful products by an actuary	Yes	No	Yes	No	Yes
Requirement for a sharia certification on its operation	Yes	Yes	Yes	Yes	No
Existence of a national supreme sharia decision-making body	Yes	No	Yes	Indirectly yes	No
Limitations on commissions to intermediaries	Yes	No	No	No	Yes
Solvency requirements	Yes	Yes	Yes	Yes	Yes
Regulation on the investment of takaful assets	Yes	Yes	Yes	Yes	Yes

risks and then to require the availability of sufficient resources to manage such risks. Resources here are not intended to be restricted only to capital. Risk-based capital extrapolates risks to required capital so that, should the ratio of available capital to required capital drop to a predetermined level, this is flagged early enough for regulatory intervention to occur. Regulations also seek to protect participants by making the takaful operator responsible for ensuring that participants are treated fairly, failing which the regulator can place sanctions on the operator. Such an extensive set of regulations has been criticized as being so prohibitive as to stifle innovation. This criticism is directed especially to restrictions placed on the fees the operator is able to extract from the participant, where treating customers fairly can be wrongly interpreted to mean charging the lowest fees.

Conclusion

A lot can be achieved if sufficient incentives are present both on the supply (operator) and on the demand (participant) side. The takaful operator expects to achieve a reasonable return on the capital employed, while the participant expects to save and receive protection in a cost-effective way. Certainly a holistic approach to establishing takaful can ensure its success over the long term. In this context, the role of regulations in ensuring a healthy industry cannot be overstated.

Much work remains to be done to get the right balance so that takaful can prosper and achieve its full potential among the world's 1.6 billion Muslims, if not the non-Muslim population of the world.

CHAPTER 11

Microtakaful

Alberto Brugnoni

The most sought-after commodity is neither staple food nor water, but the sort of empowerment that lifts people, whatever their religion or race, out of poverty and gives them some security and a real hope of becoming financially self-sustaining.

In this regard, the Muslim *umma* (community of faith), which represents 25 percent of today's world population, is paradigmatic, as it has three peculiarities: (a) most of its members live in low-income or lower-middle income countries,[1] where the incidence of poverty is in general very high;[2] (b) a tiny fraction of Muslims live in some of the richest countries in the world, with abundant liquidity and an accumulated wealth worth trillions of dollars; and (c) it has at its disposal equalization tools such as the compulsory *zakat* and voluntary *sadaqah* (charity) that are meant to redistribute wealth but do not really fulfill their raison d'être.[3] As a result, the divide between the rich and the poor remains high within the Muslim nations, and the widening gap is becoming a threat to peace and, as recent events have shown, is linked directly to the spread of unrest and civil war.

For the Muslim world, the word empowerment translates, among other things, into a savvy mix of sharia-compliant microfinance and microinsurance tools,[4] two components of a single proposition aiming to overcome the issues of poverty and societal divide. Both tools are a sharia version of the widely known "People, Planet, Profit paradigms"[5] that preach social, environmental, and economic sustainability. However, both microfinance and microinsurance are in their infancy, as the word micro is not yet consonant with the words Islamic finance and takaful.[6]

On the one hand, Islamic microfinance is indeed lagging far behind its conventional counterpart and is statistically almost nonexistent.[7] Of the conservatively estimated 77 million microcredit clients worldwide, only 380,000 adhere to Islamic microfinance—300,000 are reached by 126 institutions operating in 14 countries and 80,000 are reached by the well-known network of Indonesian cooperatives. The supply is concentrated in a few countries, with Afghanistan, Bangladesh, and Indonesia accounting for 80 percent of global outreach. In all other countries, Islamic microfinance is still in its infancy. No scalable institutions are reaching clients on a regional and national level. The average outreach of the 126 institutions is 2,400 clients, no institution has more than 50,000 clients, and the average Islamic microloan is similar to a conventional microloan.[8]

On the other hand, takaful, with a galloping growth of 20 percent a year and a unique hybrid business model—where shareholders and participants do not necessarily share the same interests—is in no hurry to add microtakaful to its current developmental agenda. Besides, the underwriting of even conventional insurance policies in the Muslim countries is traditionally very low, with less than 2 percent of gross domestic product (GDP) spent, on average, for insurance compared with a global average of about 7 percent;[9] the penetration of microinsurance among the poor is even lower. In 2006, only 80 million of the world's 2.5 billion poor were covered by some form of microinsurance, and in 23 of the world's poorest 100 countries, no microinsurance activity has been detected.[10]

The Essence of Microtakaful

Microtakaful essentially has the same technical apparatus as takaful, but it also has three peculiar features that relate to its social mission.[11] First, the changing nature of inherent risks it assumes when dealing with people at the base of the economic pyramid puts it much closer to the principles of cooperation than takaful itself. Second, its effectiveness is, to some extent, linked to the use of *zakat* funds, which can act as the ultimate *qard al hasan* for the payment of premiums. Third, its proposition is inextricably linked to the proper use of Islamic microfinance instruments.

Although better-off persons face essentially the same risks as the poor (that is, risks related to health, death, education, housing, and agriculture, among others), they have access to formal and sophisticated insurance schemes and often have a financial buffer for overcoming problems. In contrast, when faced with a shock, the poor rely on coping mechanisms based on self-insurance and informal solidarity groups.[12] In other words, the better-off manage risks *before* the event occurs by saving or purchasing insurance, whereas the poor manage risks *after* the event occurs, by selling assets, making out-of-pocket payments, or borrowing from family or moneylenders.[13]

Therefore, in order to come up with cost-effective business models that cope with the profile of the potential users of microtakaful policies, one needs to think outside the box, leave the conventional commercial ways of doing business, and understand that the poor have different needs and priorities. Designing insurance products for all types of needs will affect any insurance program adversely, as setting, gender, and degree of vulnerability must be considered. The risk profile also changes, as takaful deals with manageable risks for those who can afford them, while microtakaful targets the types of risk that are excluded using normal yardsticks. Finally, the distribution of microtakaful policies has its own peculiarities.

Needs

Demand-driven products are a prerequisite to be successful in the microtakaful industry, as financial resources of the target groups are very limited. Hence, it is important to gain a deep understanding of the needs of the policyholders. As a general consideration, the implementation of microtakaful has two broad goals: the first is to secure the revolving funds of the Islamic microfinance institutions (IMFIs), and the second is to secure the payment to the IMFI in case of disability or death. With regard to the latter, at present, the most widespread covers in conventional microinsurance are credit life and funeral insurance; others include life insurance, health insurance, and additional benefits for the deceased's family. These covers are naturally more widely available where the government makes coverage mandatory.[14] In addition, microtakaful can also offer other investment products to make life more secure for the poor, such as savings for education and pensions.

Risks

In microtakaful, the risks are a function of (a) the permanent state of poverty, (b) a low and often erratic income, and (c) excess vulnerability; they are triggered by the loss of property due to theft or fire, loss from natural and man-made disasters, losses in agricultural production, accidental death, disability, and various health issues. Under microtakaful, to contain and quantify these risks, the benefits have to be small, but the scale must be large: as a consequence, the profit margins per unit of sale also have to be small, but the scale of the business has to allow for attractive profits for the microtakaful provider. Some products will be profitable, and others will not be, but the point is that, even if there is a loss, the company's commitment to the social values embedded in microtakaful should be able to sustain it. Besides, because of the scale, the estimated claims ratios and mortality rates in microtakaful are likely to be closer to the experience, and this will make it easier to estimate provisioning and profitability and reduce the margin of error. Most important, the continuation in payment of premiums should be directly or indirectly linked to income-producing ventures. This is because premium persistency depends on the economic worth to the customer of continuing to seek cover where the insured is part of a household or affinity group linked to an income-producing venture. This could be related to agriculture, industrial production, a cottage industry, or some other form.[15]

The least risky approach to providing microtakaful is for IMFIs to outsource the whole business to a regulated takaful operator. In this relationship, which is commonly known as the partner-agent model, the IMFI acts as a microtakaful agent, selling policies to its clients on behalf of the takaful operator in exchange for a commission; the IMFI is also responsible for servicing the product, which involves verifying claims and submitting claims requests.[16] The takaful operator, in turn, manufactures the insurance product, which involves determining the product's features, such as the insured event, the waiting period, exclusions, the term, and the benefit. It also provides the actuarial, financial, and claims-processing expertise and absorbs all of the insurance risks.

The policyholder benefits by having better access to a wider range of products with increased coverage and greater sustainability; the partnering takaful company has access to a new market without having extensive marketing, distribution, or administrative costs. More important, the partner-agent model facilitates the pooling of risks between the formal and informal sectors.

Distribution and Risk Carriers

According to a majority of sharia scholars, sales targets are not desirable, and agents should not sell policies that are not in the customers' interest but instead serve their own sales targets. Furthermore, all delivery channels should operate according to sharia, to prevent the insurers' funds from being mingled with funds from *haram* (prohibited) activities.[17] In principle, microtakaful products should be distributed by partners who know the target market well and have an established relationship with potential customers.

As with conventional microinsurance, microtakaful is delivered with the help of agents and financial institutions (table 11.1 summarizes the major differences between takaful and microtakaful). However, to reach the poor, additional innovative distribution channels are used, including the following:

- *Full-service model.* Regulated takaful operators downsize their insurance services and charge a premium affordable by the poor. IMFIs can assume the role of insurers by offering basic credit life insurance to protect their loan portfolios.
- *Partnership model.* As discussed above, takaful operators, with products, pair with IMFIs and others to provide microinsurance in low-income markets.

Table 11.1   Difference between Takaful and Microtakaful

Consideration	Takaful	Microtakaful
Can it cover high risks?	Normally excluded	Yes
Is it an extension of social insurance?	No	Yes
What about preexisting conditions?	Excluded	Difficult to exclude
Customer segmentation	Formal economy, mostly employed or self-employed	Informal economy, outside the social insurance coverage
Affordability considerations	Upper- to middle-income classes	Bottom of the income and social pyramid; subsidies needed from *zakat* funds, government, donor agencies
Underwriting considerations	Easier to mitigate adverse selection and exposure to fraud	Need to mitigate risk from adverse selection and fraud through links with economic benefits of microcredit, microfinance, or schemes for community and affinity groups
Distribution	Agency, brokers, commercial banks, direct, electronic	Microfinance institutions, rural banks, mosques; no brokers

Source: Haryadi 2006.

- *Community-based model.* Local communities form groups that capitalize and manage a risk pool for their members.
- *Provider model.* Hospitals and clinics (or even dairy cooperatives) create prepaid or risk pooling coverage for people using their facilities.
- *Social protection models.* National governments underwrite cover for certain risks through social insurance programs, such as with health care, crops, and livestock, as well as covariant risks.[18]

Cost-effective Business Models

To ensure the success of its microtakaful endeavors, a takaful operator ought to look at and implement the following steps (extracted from Haryadi 2006): (a) real, integral partnerships with people's organizations; (b) products decided and agreed on by partner organizations; (c) trust and transparency between the partner and the takaful operator; (d) simple products; (e) group insurance; (f) minimal marketing costs and avoidance of commissions; (g) risk-only coverage; (h) automatic coverage linked to other activities; (i) aggregated premium payments; (j) streamlined administration; (k) simple claims procedure and verification; (l) rapid delivery for benefit payments; and (m) a profit-sharing mechanism.

The key challenge in microtakaful lies in containing the costs of developing and operating the system. Although microinsurance has used government subsidies to provide effective and comprehensive financial protection to the poor masses, the unique advantage for microtakaful is the additional money that may be available from institutionalized *zakat* funds to provide financial protection in the true spirit of cooperation between the haves and have-nots.

Market Education

In most developing countries, an insurance culture does not exist. People are not familiar with insurance or often with other financial services. The target groups do not know how insurance works or how they can personally benefit from it. In addition, insurance benefits are intangible, which requires trust from the policyholders. Therefore, staff and potential customers need to be educated on how insurance and takaful work, and the provision of capacity-building, training, and technical expertise becomes a critical ingredient for the success of the selling proposition.[19]

Sharia Supervisory Board

In terms of governance structure, microtakaful companies need to have a sharia board in addition to the usual board of directors. The role of the sharia board is to ensure that the takaful operation complies with the principles of Islamic law. Among other things, this involves ensuring both the acceptability of invested assets in terms of sharia and the equal treatment of shareholders and policyholders. The Governance of Takaful Operations Working Group of the Islamic Financial Services Board (IFSB) is addressing some of these issues.

The Use of Zakat

Zakat—the fourth pillar of Islam—is an obligation, imposed by God on men and women who possess enough means, to distribute to the poor and the needy a certain percentage of their annual savings or capital in goods or money. Zakat is assessed once a year on both capital and savings from income and is neither a tax levied by the government nor a voluntary contribution or charity; rather, it is a devotional act. Its literal meaning is "increase through purity," as it is deemed that wealth, having being purified through this disbursement, will increase. Zakat is compulsory on cash, cattle, and crops, and the computation differs for each of these categories. For cash, the minimum rate (there is no upper limit) is 2.5 percent, calculated on the net balance after all lawful expenses have been met at the end of the year.[20]

The disbursement of zakat funds to the eight categories[21] mentioned by Qur'an 9:60 as charity—to support living expenses and pay for emergencies—is increasingly debated. Although commendable, zakat is a short-term solution that does not change the long-run status quo. More proactive uses of zakat funds for the empowerment of the poor are often proposed as a way to move individuals permanently out of poverty and to prevent the forthcoming generation from living in the same conditions. For instance, one proposal is to move these funds into microenterprise programs where the poor can apply for qard al hasan as their microenterprise capital.[22] It is envisioned that, with the technical assistance of the IMFIs, the poor can develop their business and become self-sufficient, up to the stage where they repay the qard al hasan.

With regard to microtakaful, zakat monies could indeed be used to pay the premiums of the policies. This is the path chosen by the Selangor Zakat Centre, which has set up the Collective and Intensive Takaful Fund, funded by a monthly deposit deducted from the payments made to the poor. The fund, which represents a best practice, is jointly operated by Takaful Malaysia and Takaful Ikhlas, and the benefits it provides include payments in case of natural death, accidental death, permanent total disability due to natural causes, permanent total disability due to accidents, hospitalization, permanent partial disability due to accidents, difficult illnesses (40 listed diseases), obsequies expenses, and savings. The Selangor Zakat Centre is now widening the scope of its activities by setting up Education Takaful, an independent fund for the education and teaching of the subscriber's children.

A Possible Course of Action for a Start-up Operation

As a general rule, only major insurable risks should be covered by a small benefit package to keep premiums affordable; policy language should be simple, with either no or only a few exclusions; and group insurance policies should be used as a means to reduce administrative costs. Premium amounts and payments ought to be adapted to the cash flow of the customers; if possible, premiums should be linked to an existing financial service. Group pricing should be applied, policy application and claims documentation should be reduced to a minimum, and claims should be settled quickly. Needless to say, underwriting, investments, and reinsurance should all follow sharia prescriptions (no risks stemming from prohibited activities, investment categories needing to adhere to Islamic law, reinsurance only with retakaful companies, and so forth).

The following five short-term, credit-linked products represent possible building blocks. Beginning with credit life, each builds on the systems and experiences of the previous product. For example, if an IMFI has an effective system for managing a credit life product, it is easy to add credit disability and not too complicated to offer an additional benefit policy. It is anticipated that these products would be introduced one-by-one over a period of years as the IMFI develops expertise, although an IMFI does not need to provide all of them.

- Credit life with coverage for the outstanding balance (cost plus profit in the case of *murabaha*) of the financing if the client dies.
- Credit disability with coverage for the outstanding balance of the financing in the event of permanent disability.
- Additional benefit: a term life policy for clients that corresponds to the term of financing. If the recipient of the funds dies during the term of financing, his beneficiaries would receive a fixed payout to cover funeral and other immediate expenses. This is in addition to the credit life and credit disability policies.

- Additional lives: sold with additional benefit, this term life policy covers a certain number of additional household members. The insurance term corresponds to the term of financing.
- Continuation: a one-month renewable term policy as a continuation of the additional benefit policy. An IMFI's client could purchase it at the end of his term of financing if he wants to have insurance coverage without extending his financing.

As the complexity of these products increases, the value for policyholders increases too. With credit life and credit disability, the protection largely accrues to the IMFI, since insurance reduces its credit risk. Credit life is a simple product, so the degree of complexity is lower than term life or health insurance, and the degree of success in its offering is higher.

At a later stage, additional and more complex products can be added, such as (a) saving life with transition funds, pensions, endowments, and education life; (b) personal accidents and unemployment; (c) property insurance covering fire, theft, rainfall, floods, livestock, and agriculture prices; (d) annuities and endowment; (e) health covering optical, surgical, outpatient, hospitalization, dental, and critical diseases; (f) disabilities insurance and dismemberment insurance; (g) integrated insurance packages; (h) crop loss insurance; (i) flood and storm damage insurance; and (j) marriage.

Microtakaful Best Practices

Conventional microinsurance is more developed than microtakaful. To provide guidance for the development of microtakaful products, table 11.2 shows which products are available in which countries or regions. The first microtakaful scheme was established in 1997 in Lebanon, and nowadays microtakaful is still in its infancy, with a handful of providers, mostly in the countries where operations are described next.[23]

Indonesia

The world's most populous Muslim-majority nation, with tens of thousands of cooperatives involved in Islamic microfinance, is perhaps the most developed in terms of microtakaful. The earliest beginnings can be traced to 2006, when a study on microinsurance in Indonesia was sponsored by the United Nations Development Program.[24] This survey gave origin to two initiatives.

Table 11.2   Availability of Conventional Microinsurance Products, by Country or Region

Product	Country or region
Life and endowment	India, Bangladesh, Sri Lanka, Nepal, Vietnam, Pakistan, Indonesia, Lao PDR; East Africa, South Africa, West Africa; Colombia, Guatemala, Mexico, Nicaragua
Health and critical illness	India, Bangladesh, the Philippines, Cambodia, China; East Africa, South Africa, West Africa; Colombia, Mexico; Georgia, the Russian Federation
Crop and weather	India; East Africa, North Africa; Mexico, Nicaragua
Property, asset, livestock	India, Nepal, Bangladesh; East Africa; Albania
Funeral	East Africa, South Africa, West Africa; Colombia, Mexico
Integrated package	India
Rural insurance	India
Group personal accident	West Africa
Unemployment	East Africa
Flood	China

In late 2006, Takaful Indonesia started to collaborate under the partner-agent model with Peramu, and in January 2007 they launched Takaful Micro Sakinah, a shariah-compliant credit life program.[25] Earlier, Peramu had set up the Takmin Working Group to run the microtakaful program as a pilot project in Bogor, with technical assistance provided by the Microinsurance Association of Netherlands. Introduced in response to a request by an Islamic microfinance apex organization, the program seeks to provide risk mitigation based on mutual assistance and solidarity. The insurance term offered matches the financing period, which is usually between six months and one year, and is offered through Peramu, which serves as an intermediary to the market, as a mandatory group policy for sharia microfinance institutions.[26] These institutions are well-established players in the local microfinance business, are close to the target group, and are generally well perceived by the poor. Premiums are calculated monthly on the individual balance outstanding and paid with each installment.[27] The product does not involve additional riders. The benefit package is small and easy to understand, and 80 percent of the claims are settled within seven days. Takaful Indonesia distributes its product through Islamic *and* conventional microfinance institutions, as it has opted to cooperate with the latter to raise awareness of the concept of sharia-compliant microinsurance.[28] The product is based on a *wakala bil ujra* contract (which is mandatory for sharia-approved insurance in Indonesia), whereas the operator receives a *wakala* fee (*ujra*) as well as a share of investment and underwriting surpluses. A very interesting development is that Takaful Indonesia has used part of its *zakat* obligations to introduce and promote its microproducts. Finally, last year, Takaful Indonesia partnered with the National Alms Board (Baznas) to develop a microtakaful scheme for alms receivers. The policies will pay out benefits for death resulting from natural causes or from accidents.

The second initiative was the introduction by Germany's Allianz of a micro version of the takaful policies it had been underwriting in Indonesia, through a dedicated window, since 2006.[29] After a 16-month-long pilot phase, a credit life program, Payung Keluarga (meaning Family Umbrella) was introduced in January 2007, featuring several benefit options. First, Islamic microfinance institutions can choose to cover either the outstanding balance or the initial amount. Second, the Islamic microfinance institutions can opt for an additional benefit. In that case, heirs would receive twice the original amount.[30] Third, microfinance institutions can choose to receive a payout if the spouse of the debtor dies.[31] The insurance term matches the credit period, which averages 20 months. Through this scheme, Allianz has insured more than 42,000 microcredits, covering debtors of seven partner IMFIs[32] against natural and accidental death for an average premium of US$0.66.[33] It has also provided extra payouts to families. Moreover, the IMFIs can adapt the amount of extra payouts to the needs of their customers. To keep premiums low, Payung Keluarga is a compulsory product, and, to reduce complexity, the IMFIs centrally decide on the product benefits. The IMFIs also collect premiums, which are deducted at the time of the disbursement of financing. In general, coverage is directly approved by the Islamic microfinance institution,[34] and administrative processes are minimized. Underwriting is outsourced up to Rp 50 million.[35]

Malaysia

Microtakaful schemes are slowly increasing in one of the world's most advanced takaful markets. In April 2007, Takaful Ikhlas launched a microtakaful scheme in conjunction with the Farmers Welfare Federation of Malaysia, a nongovernmental organization (NGO) looking after the needs of destitute farmers. The compulsory scheme, funded by the government, provides immediate death expenses of RM 500 (US$140) for a premium of RM 1.80 and covers 100,000 members. A voluntary personal accident death and disability scheme provides capital protection of RM 10,000. Takaful Ikhlas has signed an agreement with the Selangor Zakat Centre—which has 10 representing agencies, such as the Malaysian Post and the Malaysian Commercial Bank, that collect *zakat*—to create the Collective and Intensive Takaful Fund. The fund makes a deduction from monthly payments to the poor, and benefits include death, disability, critical illness, funeral, and hospitalization, as discussed above.

Bangladesh

This Muslim-majority country traces the beginning of its microinsurance industry to more than 20 years ago, although its development was pursued more vigorously in the last 10 years or so. In fact, the growth of the life insurance industry is due largely to the microinsurance schemes now offered by all private sector life companies. Bangladesh's first micro-insurance product, Grameen Bima or village insurance, was launched by Delta Life in 1988. Subsequently, it introduced an urban microinsurance scheme, Gono Bima, that offered a similar endowment product. Microinsurance schemes in Bangladesh are aimed not only at providing risk cover, but also at pooling the savings of the poor. Hence, such plans provide cash, whereas plans in other countries mostly offer renewable term insurance plans covering death and disability risks only.

Jordan

In 2007, Microfund for Women, an organization that funds women entre-preneurs in Jordan, launched a loan insurance product covering death and total or partial disability through a compulsory premium of 0.11 percent on all disbursed loans. This scheme is offered in partnership with Jordan Insurance.

Lebanon

Established in 1997, the Agricultural Mutual Fund provides microtakaful for health coverage and meets costs not covered by the Government Social Security Fund, which usually covers 85 percent of hospital fees. The fund covers more than 5,000 families (23,000 beneficiaries), the premium per family is US$10 per month, and those who cannot afford the premiums are sponsored by local villagers or other policyholders. It is open to all sects and religions. The fund has preferential agreements with health care providers, which give discounts of up to 50 percent. The fund operates in 180 villages in southern Lebanon, and the target population is the economically weak. In addition to health protection products, the fund provides scholarships to schools.

Morocco

Microfinance activities emerged in Morocco at the beginning of 1990s to finance microenterprises and serve those who had been excluded from the traditional banking system. Al-Amana, the largest microfinance institution in the country based on its portfolio of outstanding loans, aims to serve half a million clients in urban and rural areas by providing access to an array of financial services and products, including insurance.

Sri Lanka

Amana Takaful Insurance runs a microtakaful scheme called Navodaya. Participants can obtain a policy as a group, and if at the end of the policy year no claim has been made by the insured group, Amana Takaful Insurance will sponsor a special event for the group and refund the surplus. Benefits include cover against death, disability, and funeral expenses, as well as education.

Pakistan

Kashf offers life and accident insurance tied to financing in cooperation with a national insurer, New Jubilee Insurance Company. Kashf acts as the agent, and purchase of insurance is compulsory for all clients who obtain financing.

Trinidad and Tobago

Takaful Trinidad and Tobago, founded in 1999 by the Muslim Credit Union Cooperative Society (7,000 members), provides funeral benefit schemes and runs an Islamic investment fund. Members pay an annual membership fee of US$20 (US$5 for persons under 16).

Somalia

In Somalia, the financial sector has been affected by civil war, and banking is based largely on informal and unregulated arrangements that depend on trust. The country is set to have its first microtakaful services if a pilot study being conducted by the U.S. Agency for International Development and global microinsurance company MicroEnsure is successful. MicroEnsure, which designs microinsurance products and provides back office services, will be the underwriter on this project.

Microtakaful as a Key Element of a Poverty Alleviation Strategy

Poverty is the outcome of the deprivation of land and assets, access to education, remunerative occupations, and opportunities to diversify income sources. To alleviate poverty, distributive measures are necessary, but not sufficient, because raising productivity appears to be the key factor. For this reason, effective conventional microcredit programs aiming to distribute capital resources and create opportunities for self-employment and wage employment have been implemented for a while, not only to lift the poor out of their condition but also to help them to cope with natural or social catastrophes and protect them from downward mobility. It is time to progress further and focus on the requirements of the sharia-compliant markets.

That said, a thorough strategy with action at the macro level (legislation, regulation, and supervision),[36] meso level (support services and infrastructure), and micro level (financial services for low-income households) is certainly required. A successful poverty alleviation process in the Islamic world needs to involve both public and private parties, such as the following:

- The government (sometimes in the form of *bayt al-mal*), as the institution responsible for pooling and distributing public funds such as *zakat*, *infàq* (donation), *sadaqah*, and *waqf*. With regard to microtakaful, the use of *zakat* funds to pay premiums should be thoroughly investigated.
- The IMFIs, as commercial players offering financial services, such as financing and investments.
- The providers of microtakaful policies, as the means to offer benefits to the IMFIs by securing their revolving fund and to the insured by securing the payment to the IMFIs in case of disability and death as well as providing additional benefits to the family of the deceased. In addition, the provider of microtakaful could offer the poor additional products to make their life more secure, such as education and pensions.

As microcredit is receiving more priority than any other tools for alleviating poverty, various other financial services need to be introduced, including microinsurance products. Indeed, many potential borrowers of microcredit have been financially ruined by a single accident. A single comprehensive microinsurance package for both risks to life and property can be of great help to the poor and small entrepreneurs. In this perspective, economic security becomes part of total welfare.

Insurance in itself is an essential service that a modern state should ensure is available to its people, especially the working poor. Specially designed insurance products should be made available to rural areas and to the socially and economically backward classes, with a view to reaching all insurable persons in the country and providing them with adequate financial protection against death and loss of property by different perils.

Providing financial and social security to the economically weaker segments of society is a major social responsibility.

An alternative to conventional and commercial insurance and a complement to takaful,[37] a microtakaful proposition should be made available to both the IMFIs and the poor. Its mutuality features should be stressed and enhanced,[38] and they should be used to the advantage of the poor[39] and in the holistic development of local clusters. In a full Islamic developmental perspective, microtakaful is not the sole solution to poverty, but rather a key component of any poverty alleviation strategy.[40] Without protection against losses and natural perils, many individuals will remain in or fall into poverty. Microtakaful can provide the safety net for communities to achieve a sustainable development of their standard of living, providing the basis for families to look to the future with a sense of security and giving much-needed dignity to individuals.

Notes

1. Such as Indonesia (207 million), Pakistan (160 million), India (151 million), and Bangladesh (132 million). The Muslim population is set to increase more than 30 percent by 2050 compared with only 9 percent for populations in the industrial countries (United Nations Population Fund 2010).

2. Only five Muslim countries score high on the Human Development Index of the United Nations, the Arab world has the highest unemployment among developing regions, and the majority of Muslims, especially females, are illiterate and lag far behind populations in other parts of the world (World Bank 2007).

3. This unique situation was the focus of the session on "Finance and Philanthropy" at the Fourth World Congress of Muslim Philanthropists, "Defining the Roadmap for the Next Decade," held in Dubai on March 23–24, 2011. See, especially, the following contributions to that conference: Ahmed (2011); Brugnoni (2011); Buttigieg (2011); Chalikuzhi (2011); Umar (2011). The need for a comprehensive approach to lift people out of poverty will also be investigated at the Fifth World Congress of Muslim Philanthropists in 2012. For a three-pronged approach to local development based on *bayt al-mal* (*zakat* and *qard al hasan*), see Haryadi (2007).

4. The sharia version of microinsurance is a risk protection tool for low-income people based on the same actuarial and economic principles as conventional microinsurance; as such, it is a business proposition, not a charitable activity.

5. Also known as the triple bottom line (3BL), these paradigms capture an expanded spectrum of economic, ecological, and social values and criteria for measuring organizational and societal effectiveness. With the ratification in

early 2007 of 3BL standards for urban and community accounting of the United Nations (UN) and the Local Governments for Sustainability, they have become the dominant approach to public sector full-cost accounting. Similar UN standards—such as the eco-budget standard for reporting ecological footprint—apply to natural and human capital measurement to assist in measurements required by 3BL. In the private sector, a commitment to corporate social responsibility implies a commitment to some form of 3BL reporting.

6. Islamic finance has grown continuously in the past few years, with sharia-compliant assets crossing the US$1 trillion mark, and total takaful contributions reaching close to US$12 billion.

7. However, conventional microfinance and, to a certain extent, conventional microinsurance have been active even in the Muslim world.

8. All figures are from Karim, Tarazi, and Reille (2008). The situation in 2010 has shown no notable improvement.

9. This situation is not unique to the Muslim world, as, according to the latest data available, 88 percent of insurance premiums are collected in developed countries, which include only 1.4 billion inhabitants, whereas the rest of the world's 5.3 billion inhabitants account for a mere 12 percent of insurance activities. It is of significance that these ratios were roughly the same 20 years ago.

10. As an example, only 3 percent of poor lives are insured in India and China, and only 0.3 percent of the poor are insured in Africa (figures from the Microinsurance Centre).

11. According to Bhatty (2011), "Takaful is all about social beneficence: it brings solidarity through mutual assistance and co-operation amongst groups of people. It is the ideal way of appealing to those sections of society who normally can't afford financial protection."

12. Differences between insurance and microinsurance include (a) microinsurance targets low-income people who are living slightly above the poverty line and usually work in the informal sector and, as such, are neither part of the social security system nor recognized as insurable by conventional insurance companies; (b) premium payments and insured amounts are relatively small; (c) products offer basic coverage; (d) design, documentation, and processing are simple and easy to understand, as financial literacy is almost nonexistent. An additional difference is that microinsurance frequently focuses on credit life insurance.

13. Those strategies heavily affect the possession and accumulation of assets as well as future income flows, as people might fall back under the poverty line forever if they are hit by a loss or damage.

14. In India, for instance, every company is required to allocate a percentage of its insurance portfolio to persons in the "rural and social sectors." According

to Bhatty (2010), "Companies such as AIG, Allianz, and Tokio Marine have been very active in microinsurance, especially in India. Tokio Marine's IFFCO-Tokio company in India has the world's largest single microinsurance policy covering 49.53 million lives, with a total premium of some $17 million. The policy has $90 of personal accident cover and $45 of disability cover automatically effective for the purchaser of 50kg fertilizer bag from the company's recognized outlets, subject to maximum cover of $2,222. The policy document is simply the purchase receipt or credit memo from the company's co-operative society."

15. We are indebted for this section to several talks held in Dubai and London with Ajmal Bhatty, chief executive officer and president of Tokio-Marine Retakaful.

16. The partner-agent relationship between a microtakaful insurer and a microfinance institution is, of course, possible only if the latter provides sharia-compliant products (in case of non-Islamic institutions through a window). Islamic microfinance institutions have limited reach due to the narrow asset base on which they build their activities: this hindrance prevents them from operating widely and replacing conventional microfinance institutions that, at present, are the main conduit to the poor in Muslim countries. The obvious solution would be to use the cash-*waqf* instrument to fund the liabilities side of the balance sheet.

17. As the underwriting goes along with the financing application process, the takaful operator usually relies on the sharia analysis conducted by its partnering microtakaful institutions.

18. Covariant risk events affect a large number of persons or assets at the same time. For example, an earthquake affects all within the region where it occurs, although the degree of the effect is variable. In contrast, random risk events such as traffic accidents affect only one or a few persons when they occur (http://www.microinsurancenetwork.org).

19. The Microtakaful Support Centre provides financial and technical assistance; it is managed by the International Cooperative and Mutual Insurance Federation (ICMIF) secretariat. The most important players in the takaful industry participate. The center also provides sharia advice and lobbying at the regulatory level.

20. From a practical point of view, it is the duty of an Islamic state to collect *zakat* from every Muslim who meets the requirements for paying it. In the past, when there were legally constituted Islamic governments, *zakat* was collected through official channels, and its distribution was the function of a special department of the government. Now, especially in non-Muslim countries, giving *zakat* is an obligation for which each eligible Muslim adult must take responsibility. In most Muslim countries (such as in Bahrain, Bangladesh, Jordan, Kuwait, and Lebanon), *zakat* is collected through a decentralized and

voluntary system: *zakat* committees are established and tasked with the collection and distribution of *zakat* funds. In a handful of Muslim countries, such as Pakistan and Saudi Arabia, the *zakat* is obligatory and is collected in a centralized manner by the state. Taxes paid to the government are never included in *zakat*. *Zakat* may be distributed directly to the individuals or to Islamic organizations, and the contributor should use his best possible judgment in finding the most deserving beneficiaries. Finally, *zakat* should not be confused with *sadaqah* (charity), which is a voluntary contribution.

21. They are the poor, the needy, the *zakat* collectors, converts, people who are not free, debtors, wayfarers and travelers, and all activities performed in the cause of God. *Zakat* cannot be paid to relatives.

22. The use of *zakat* proceeds is, with the exploitation of *waqfs*, a key issue for the proper implementation of the (micro)takaful and Islamic finance propositions.

23. Some of the information discussed in this section was provided by Sabbir Patel, senior vice president of the ICMIF.

24. The survey revealed that low-income people in Indonesia rely on informal risk management strategies. Insurance, neither conventional nor sharia-compliant, is available, and formal insurers are reluctant to enter the market. Sharia-compliant credit life insurance, for example, is not available, and only a few Islamic microfinance institutions opt to insure with a conventional insurer.

25. Established in February 1994 with the support of the Association of Indonesian Muslim Intellectuals, Takaful Indonesia was the first takaful company to operate in Indonesia. Its founding fathers were the Abdi Nations Foundation, Bank Muamalat Indonesia, PT Tugu Mandiri Life Insurance, the Department of Financial Affairs, as well as some Indonesian Muslim businessmen. It operates as a subsidiary of Syarikat Takaful Malaysia Berhad through two subsidiaries: PT Asuransi Takaful Family and General Takaful Insurance Company, the first offering life insurance products and the second focusing on general insurance. The introduction of sharia-compliant credit life microinsurance in cooperation with a local nongovernmental organization (NGO) has been its first experience accessing the low-income segment. Peramu is an NGO that had been closely involved in the Indonesia government's Baytul Maal Bogor/Trust Fund and had set up IMFIs such as the Islamic Rural Bank/BPRS and Baytul Maal wa Tamwil Cooperative/KBMT in Bogor.

26. Which means that underwriting goes along with the financing application process; if financing is approved, the customer simultaneously receives insurance cover.

27. Therefore, insurance costs are diminishing and spread over a longer period, which further disburdens the households. For premium rates that are 0.5 percent of the monthly amount outstanding and an average loan of

Rp 1 million (€70.32), the premium would amount to Rp 5,000 (€0.35), equal to the price of one can of soda. Pricing is identical for all microfinance institutions that are associated with the NGO, but varies for microfinance institutions that are linked directly to the insurance provider. See Erlbeck, Altuntas, and Berry-Stölzle (2011).

28. Although it does not train the staff of the microfinance institutions or conduct awareness campaigns for the general public. These tasks are delegated to Peramu, which runs informational presentations during which the benefits of Mikro Sakinah and microinsurance in general are explained to the partner microfinance institutions and their staff.

29. Allianz has been present in Indonesia since 1981, and it operates a life and a general subsidiary. The microtakaful product also shares some of the features of a successful conventional credit life microinsurance product introduced in 2006 in partnership with a donor from the field of development cooperation.

30. This additional benefit is intended to support dependents if the breadwinner of the family dies by helping them to pay for productive assets, educational expenses, or consumption needs.

31. Because many microbusinesses in Indonesia are jointly run by spouses, several IMFI partners that finance these businesses have requested such joint-life coverage.

32. These are rather large and well-established microfinance institutions, requiring a minimum annual premium of Rp 40 million (€2,812.56) for one group policy.

33. Pricing is based on the insured group. Depending on the choice of benefits package, the premium is calculated and varies between 0.24 and 0.70 percent a year. Premium payments are also adapted to the irregular cash flows of the policyholders.

34. Only financing above Rp 50 million (€3,515.70), which exceeds national microcredit standards, needs approval by the insurer.

35. Collected premiums are transferred once a month to the insurer, along with up-to-date information about current policyholders. If claims have to be settled in between, the IMFI can deduct the claim amounts from the collected premiums (up to Rp 50 million) and transfer the remaining balance.

36. Given the positive causal relationship between insurance penetration and economic growth, Muslim emerging countries can facilitate economic growth by creating incentives for international insurers to offer microtakaful products in their own markets.

37. All takaful products, such as financing, education, fire, and pension, can be delivered to the poor with some modification to allow the collection of low premiums on a periodic basis.

38. An issue in itself is the limited access to capital markets and a relative lack of management accountability as well as a sectoral approach, as some mutual insurance companies operate, for example, only in a given type or class of insurance such as farm property.

39. Mutual insurance is owned by the policyholders who share the profits. In reality, there are no profits as such, since any excess income is either returnable to the policyholder-owner as dividends or is used to reduce premiums. A natural advantage of mutual ownership is the ability to mitigate potential conflicts between the policyholders and owners of the company.

40. Several empirical studies that investigate the effect on economic growth of the insurance sector as a provider of risk transfer find a positive relationship in this regard, and some studies provide evidence for non-life insurance.

References

Ahmed, Habib. 2011. "Waqf as Sustainable Social Enterprise: Organizational Architecture and Prospects." Paper presented at the Fourth World Congress of Muslim Philanthropists, Dubai, March 23–24.

Bhatty, Ajmal. 2010. "Protecting the Forgotten through Microtakaful." *Middle East Insurance Review* (July): 60–61. http://www.meinsurancereview.com.

———. 2011. "Microtakaful: The True Essence of Co-operation." *Premium*, August 23, 16–19.

Brugnoni, Alberto G. 2011. "Islamic Finance: A Necessary Tool to Unlock Muslim Philanthropy." Paper presented at the Fourth World Congress of Muslim Philanthropists, Dubai, March 23–24.

Buttigieg, Reuben M. 2011. "Modern Challenges in Establishing Trusts and Foundations." Paper presented at the Fourth World Congress of Muslim Philanthropists, Dubai, March 23–24.

Chalikuzhi, Azad. 2011. "Problems and Prospects of Contemporary Zakat Management." Paper presented at the Fourth World Congress of Muslim Philanthropists, Dubai, March 23–24.

Erlbeck, Anja, Muhammed Altuntas, and Thomas R. Berry-Stölzle. 2011. "Microtakaful: Field Study Evidence and Conceptual Issues." Department of Risk Management and Insurance, University of Cologne; Terry College of Business, University of Georgia, February. http://www.rug.nl/gsg/Research/Conferences/EUmicrofinconf2011/Papers/13.Erlbeck-Altuntas-BerryStolzle.pdf.

Haryadi, Agus. 2006. "Developing Microtakaful in Indonesia." Paper presented at the Second International Convention on Takaful and Retakaful, Kuala Lumpur, November 23.

————. 2007. "Reaching Out to the Poor with Microtakaful." *Middle East Insurance Review* (July): 62–63.

Karim, Nimrah, Michael Tarazi, and Xavier Reille. 2008. "Islamic Microfinance: An Emerging Market Niche." Consultative Group to Assist the Poor, Washington, DC.

Umar, Sohaib. 2011. "The Zakat Opportunity and a Proposed Model for Its More Effective Use." Paper presented at the Fourth World Congress of Muslim Philanthropists, Dubai, March 23–24.

United Nations Population Fund (UNFPA). 2010. *State of World Population 2010: From Conflict and Crisis to Renewal; Generations of Change.* Geneva: UNFPA.

World Bank. 2007. *World Development Report 2008: Agriculture for Development.* Washington, DC: World Bank.

CHAPTER 12

Retakaful

Ismail Mahbob

There is no such word as "retakaful" in either Arabic or English. The term was coined by the takaful and insurance fraternity in their efforts to Islamicise or Arabicise terminology for components of the industry's sharia-compliant supply chain. Retakaful is a derivative of the takaful industry. Replicating the concept of reinsurance as being "insurance for insurance companies," retakaful is thus viewed as "takaful for takaful companies."

In global Islamic finance, retakaful is relatively young. The first fully dedicated operator was Asean Retakaful International, which was incorporated in 1997 in the Malaysian tax haven of Labuan and initiated by the first Malaysian takaful operator, Syarikat Takaful Malaysia Berhad. Activities heightened after 2005, when major regional and global reinsurance companies started to show interest in the idea. The concept is still in the experimental stage, with issues being tackled by individual operators and cohesive industrywide efforts still not apparent. The industry is very much in its formative stage and thus highly evolutionary. Investors are reluctant to commit resources fully for fear of uncertainties, such as insufficient business and profit to guarantee long-term sustainability. This is evident in the nature of retakaful operations, which often come in the form of a "window" or a dedicated division within a conventional reinsurance company, a branch, or a stand-alone subsidiary or entity.

Capital commitment varies, usually guided by regulatory requirements and the promoter's business plans. Taking Malaysia as an example, paid-up capital of RM 100 million (US$33.3 million) is the minimum required for a stand-alone entity and RM 20 million (US$6.7 million) for a branch.[1] The onshore jurisdiction in Kuala Lumpur does not allow for window operations, although its offshore counterpart in the Labuan Island does, with minimum capital of RM 1 million (US$333,300). For a stand-alone entity, Labuan imposes a minimum capital requirement of RM 7.5 million (US$2.5 million) for both reinsurance and retakaful.

Retakaful has a big role to play in the success of any retail takaful market and is indeed an important component in the supply and value chain of Islamic finance. Due importance needs to be accorded to it, especially to takaful, which is becoming increasingly commercialized. Retakaful arose to support the retail takaful sector, which, as a propriety business, is focused on realizing a profit.

To understand the importance of retakaful, it is useful to trace the evolution of the primary market's understanding of takaful as a concept and as a commercial and economic instrument.

Evolution of Takaful

The first formal takaful operations were established in Sudan and Malaysia in the late 1970s and early 1980s as subsidiaries of Islamic banks. The Sudanese Islamic Insurance Company was formed in 1979 by Faisal Islamic Bank of Sudan, while Syarikat Takaful Malaysia Berhad, which started operations in 1985, is a subsidiary of Bank Islam Malaysia Berhad. They served to complement the financing activities of their parent banks. These takaful companies provided protection for the underlying assets that were financed by the banks against losses or damages arising from both natural and man-made perils such as fire, explosion, storm, flood, and earthquake and the minor perils of burglary and accidents. They also provided bank clients with cover on loss of life or disability. For all intents and purposes, the terms in takaful contracts were mostly copied from those of their conventional insurance counterparts.

What Is Retakaful?

The Accounting and Auditing Organization for Islamic Financial Institutions (AAOIFI) defines retakaful as "a contractual arrangement under which the reinsurer will be liable for part or all of the risks that the insurer has insured. The insured legal right will not be affected by the reinsurance arrangement and the insurer is liable to the insured for paying claims as per the insurance policy terms and conditions."

The Malaysian Takaful Act 1984 does not define the term per se but imposes a requirement that "an operator shall have arrangements consistent with sound takaful principles for retakaful of liabilities in respect of risks undertaken or to be undertaken by the operator in the course of his carrying on takaful business" Act 312.

Attempts to define retakaful have used the jargon and terminology of conventional reinsurance. There is nothing wrong with this, as both retakaful and reinsurance are both mechanisms for managing risks. A point of concern is the overuse of conventional references, which could be confusing for someone trying to comprehend the retakaful concept from the Islamic finance perspective.

Role of Retakaful in the Growth and Development of the Takaful Industry

There is a clear need to ensure sharia compliance in all Islamic finance transactions. Retakaful plays this role by extending the supply chain of the takaful industry. Figure 12.1 shows various components of the industry's supply and value chain.

From the technical perspective, retakaful helps retail takaful operators to spread risk and underwrite more risks, large and small. Three principles need elaboration: the principle of pooling, the law of large numbers, and

Figure 12.1   Supply Chain of the Takaful and Retakaful Industry

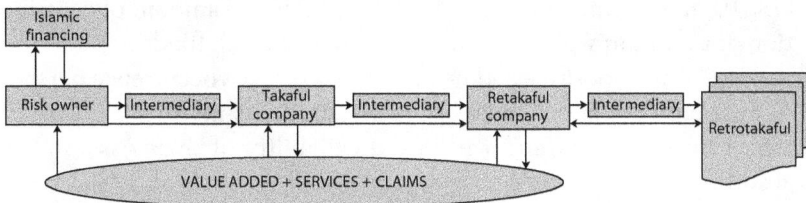

Note: Takaful coverage of underlying assets that are financed via sharia-compliant instruments is placed directly with takaful operators or through intermediaries. In anticipation that the value of some of the assets may be too high for the operator's risk fund, the retail takaful operator arranges a retakaful protection program on an automatic or ad hoc basis with the wholesale retakaful market. Likewise, the retakaful operator approaches the upstream retakaful market in order to protect its own pool, if necessary, a process commonly termed retrotakaful. Apart from the financial transactions involving contributions received and claims paid, the operator also provides value added elements to its respective "clients" in the form of staff training, risk improvement surveys, and the like.

the principle of large loss. The operation of these principles enables retakaful to assist in making takaful operators more efficient.

- *Principle of pooling.* Every participant in a retakaful pool shares in the portfolio of risks written by other participants. Although homogeneous risks are ideal for a pool, a standard industrywide basis for the definition of "homogeneity" is yet to be formulated. The pool in its simplest form can be divided into *general* and *family* retakaful pools. Both pools can be subdivided along their lines of business: proportional treaty, nonproportional treaty, and facultative retakaful. In an ideal situation, separate subpools can be created for various retakaful classes under business lines such as fire, marine, motor, and casualty. The same is true of the family sector, where separate pools can be created for classes under medical, mortgage-reducing schemes, investment-linked schemes, and endowment schemes. The homogeneity of risks making up a pool is left to each retakaful operator to decide. There is no established rule on this. An operator may select business based on portfolios per territory, per business lines, and per product lines to suit its business strategy.

- *Law of large numbers.* The greater the number of specimens, exposures, or risks taken into consideration, the more accurate the prediction with regard to the deviation of actual from expected losses. This mathematical law provides a "statistical expectation of loss" and enables operators to understand the "pure risks" that could trigger losses and to calculate the right premium or contribution to impose on the retakaful protection program of each participant. For example, if a retakaful operator expects the number of losses to be 500 and the amount of losses to be US$10 million, the calculation in determining the amount of contribution or premium will factor these in so that the risk funds or pools they manage remain positive and healthy. From the loss occurrence perspective, operators expect more frequent incidents involving individual losses that are small and within the capability of their risk funds to absorb.

- *Principle of large loss.* This is almost opposite to the law of large numbers. It is a concept of low frequency, but high severity. Large losses seldom happen, but their occurrence could be extensive and catastrophic in nature, both physically and financially. Examples are losses and damages resulting from earthquakes, tsunamis, hurricanes, windstorms, and major industrial explosions. Retakaful operators provide protection to cover part or all of such losses, so that the pools of retail takaful operators are not severely affected.

The workings of these three principles afford many advantages for takaful operators. The following are the most notable:

- *Additional underwriting capacity.* The larger spread provided by retakaful enables takaful companies to write more risks for building up their respective risk funds. Translated to financials, retakaful enables takaful companies to enlarge the pools they manage.
- *Coverage against catastrophic losses.* The burden of catastrophic losses that can cripple a takaful risk fund or pool and also the operator's financial position is offloaded, as most of these losses are shared or transferred to the retakaful sector.
- *Entry into new markets.* New markets could be in the form of new territories, new market segments, new product lines, or even a new business strategy. Many uncertainties are associated with anything new. From the takaful perspective, uncertainty tends to be associated with potential losses in occurrence and amount. Retakaful helps the company to absorb and reduce such potential losses and provides "sleep easy" protection.
- *Value added services and expertise.* Retakaful companies are expected to have deeper technical resources and reach. The experience in operating and writing business internationally in diverse markets has continually enhanced their market knowledge, product knowledge, and technical expertise, which could be applied to benefit takaful operators in human capital and product development, pricing, and marketing.
- *Contingent asset.* Retakaful is a "contingent asset" that the takaful operator can deploy at times of large claims.

A healthy takaful industry is essential for the success of the Islamic finance industry.

Differences with Conventional Reinsurance: Elements of Sharia Compliance

Many voices have loudly proclaimed that retakaful is no different from and is, in fact, akin to a "cut and paste" version of conventional reinsurance. This perception is reinforced by how the concept is being put into practice. Part of this misconception is attributable to the limited knowledge of Islamic finance among practitioners, regulators, investors, and interested parties and partly due to the failure of propagators to present the concept in its proper light. There is no underlying technical difference between takaful-retakaful and insurance-reinsurance. Both manage risk by using the pooling concept to enable the fortunate many to help the unfortunate few and the law of large numbers to price risk.

The structural difference between retakaful and reinsurance operations pertains to the structure and mechanism for ensuring that activities are in line with and do not contravene the sharia. The three elements that differentiate retakaful from reinsurance are that retakaful requires a sharia governance structure, separates the shareholders' fund from the risk fund, and limits investment activities to sharia-compliant instruments. Another notable difference is the role of operator as risk and fund manager, with the expected or imposed responsibility to extend *qard*, a benevolent or interest-free loan from the operator (shareholders' fund) to cover a deficit in the risk fund or to meet claims obligations.

In terms of operation, practices vary between regions, jurisdictions, and companies. Efforts toward standardization made by standard-setting and research institutions such as AAOIFI, the Islamic Financial Services Board (IFSB), the International Islamic Fiqh Academy, and the International Shariah Research Academy for Islamic Finance so far are limited to principles and policies. The same is true with regard to guidelines issued by the regulatory authorities: operational details are left to each individual company to define. The most popular operational models worldwide are based on the *wakala* (agency) transaction principle. Hybrid models are also adopted that introduce a *mudharaba* or profit-sharing element. In the hybrid model, the operator shares the profits from investment activities with the risk fund or pool at a preagreed ratio.

Challenges: Preoperational Issues

Three main issues need to be addressed at the preoperation stage. Basic as it may sound, the first issue is ownership of the retakaful operator. What qualification should be attached to it? Currently, most operators are majority owned by insurance or reinsurance corporations, as shown in table 12.1.

The issue of Muslim or non-Muslim ownership does not arise. Current owner-propagators are reputable organizations and have extensive experience in insurance and reinsurance activities. Standard-setting or sharia bodies need to establish guidelines disallowing ownership by corporations

Table 12.1   Ownership of Major Retakaful Operators

Retakaful operator	Incorporated	Jurisdiction	Majority owner	Owner's core trade
Takaful Re	2005	Dubai	Arab Insurance Group, Bahrain	Reinsurance
Hannover Retakaful	2005	Bahrain	Hannover Reinsurance, Germany	Reinsurance
MNRB Retakaful Berhad	2007	Malaysia	MNRB Holdings Berhad	Insurance, reinsurance
Munich Re Retakaful	2007	Malaysia	Munich Reinsurance, Germany	Reinsurance
Swiss Re Retakaful	2008	Malaysia	Swiss Reinsurance	Reinsurance
ACR Retakaful SEA	2008	Malaysia	Khazanah Nasional[a]	Sovereign wealth fund
ACR Retakaful Bahrain	2008	Bahrain	Best Re Holding Limited	Insurance
Best Re (L) Ltd.[b]	2010	Malaysia	Best Re Holding Limited	Insurance

a. Khazanah Nasional is not a reinsurance group, but its shareholdings in the two companies are significant.
b. The company was originally incorporated in 1985 in Tunisia as BEST RE and relocated to Malaysia in 2010.

when their core activities are in contravention to the teachings of Islam. Examples of such activities are liquor and gaming.

The second issue is that sharia advocacy has to be conspicuous and embedded in the operator's corporate and sharia governance structure. Relevant organs and mechanisms have to be in place. The board of directors and the sharia advisory board (SAB) are the main organs, although some would prefer to expand the functions of relevant board committees to include oversight on sharia risk management and sharia audit. Many jurisdictions tend to focus only on fulfilling the requirement for an SAB. It is felt that the governance mechanisms should include a sharia secretariat to serve as a liaison between management and the SAB, a sharia compliance manual to guide daily operations, and a sharia officer to monitor compliance. Separation of funds between the shareholders' fund of the operator and the retakaful risk fund helps to define ownership of these funds and to ensure that proper accounting treatment is accorded to transactions involving them. The secondary investment activity on both the shareholders and risk funds would be directed only toward sharia-approved instruments to ensure that the fund is healthy and in line with the tenets of Islamic finance.

Retrotakaful protection is the third issue. The retrotakaful or retrocession protection program of an operator has to be in place for it to underwrite any business. Although most jurisdictions do not impose this requirement, it is prudent and expected of management. The retrotakaful market is nonexistent at the moment, and operators have resorted to the conventional reinsurance market. Such capacity becomes even scarcer when the financial strength rating of the retrotakaful operators is factored in. The sharia-compliant supply chain of the industry has not yet been extended to the retrotakaful sector and probably will not be for quite some time. On the grounds of *dharura* (utmost necessity), the SABs are expected to allow capacity to be sourced from non-sharia-compliant conventional suppliers. Debate on the validity of applying the *dharura* principle has been ongoing for a long while in the retakaful market, as many retail operators have cited valid reasons for not using the capacity and services of retakaful companies.[2]

Stand-alone regional operators usually face difficulty in obtaining retrotakaful capacity from the open market due to limited supply and relatively higher cost. However, it is a smaller problem for branch and window operations, as capacity could be obtained from their parent company or be combined with the parent's retrocession protection program. SABs usually provide guidelines with regard to first exhausting the available capacity provided by the retrotakaful market. However, this is weakly observed, as factors such as pricing, financial strength rating, and value added capabilities are major economic and technical considerations.

Prior to underwriting any risks, retakaful operators have to ensure that their own retrotakaful protection is in place. This is out of prudence or regulatory requirement. An automatic capacity in the form of a retrotakaful treaty program has to be arranged. The cost of protection is paid from the retakaful fund, which at that moment in time is still empty, as contributions to the fund have not yet been collected from business transacted (it is common practice for the initial contribution on proportional retakaful treaty business to be received about six months after the transaction date and for nonproportional treaty business to be received within about a week to a month). Operators thus have to use their own shareholders' fund by granting *qard* or a loan to the retakaful fund to pay the cost of retrotakaful. A point to note, the cost of retrotakaful is usually paid immediately after the transaction date, with little margin for the credit period. The operator can only recover the principal loan amount when the retakaful risk fund is in surplus.

Challenges: Operational Issues

The operating model popularly adopted is based on the *wakala* transaction principle, whereby the operator acts as risk and fund manager for the retakaful pool. The operator charges a *wakala* fee for the underwriting

services rendered to the fund. Core activities include seeking new participants in order to build up the fund, arranging a retrotakaful facility, processing and paying claims, and maintaining technical reserves as required
by the authorities and as determined by actuarial experts. Investment of
idle retakaful funds is one way of strengthening the retakaful pool. For
this secondary service, operators either opt for a *wakala* fee that is
charged on the investible fund or take a share of the investment profits
made. The latter arrangement is a popular variation that combines the
wakala and *mudharaba* (profit-sharing) principles. In some models,
operators may also charge a performance fee on the underwriting surplus
prior to distributing the surplus to pool participants. Not all regulators are
agreeable with operators charging a performance fee. The level of fees
and profit-sharing ratios differ between companies and markets.
Table 12.2 shows operators' possible revenue streams under the pure
wakala and the hybrid models. Figure 12.2 presents a specimen model
showing the financial flows of the models.

Sources of Business

Retakaful operators as wholesalers in the supply chain are expected to
transact business only with retail takaful operators. The underlying logic
is to ensure that every risk covered in the pool via treaty and facultative
transaction is *halal* (permissible) and does not contravene sharia.
The operator is expected to screen every risk on offer. A *treaty* retakaful
transaction is an automatic arrangement that provides cover to a takaful
operator for all risks falling within the terms and conditions of the treaty
contract. A portfolio of risks underwritten by the operator is pooled
together with the portfolios of other operators to make up a larger retakaful pool. The takaful operator is obliged to offer and the retakaful
operator is obliged to accept every risk falling within the contract terms.
A *facultative* transaction, in contrast, is an ad hoc arrangement,
not automatic in nature, whereby the takaful operator has the option to
offer and the retakaful operator has the option to accept or decline such
risk. Each risk is considered based on its own merits.

There is a difference in opinion over transacting treaty business with
conventional insurance companies. It lies in the possibility that some risks

Table 12.2   Possible Revenue Streams, by Model

Model	Underwriting services	Investment activities	Fee on underwriting surplus
Pure *wakala*	*Wakala* fee	*Wakala* fee	Nil
Hybrid (1)	*Wakala* fee	Share of investment profits	Nil
Hybrid (2)	*Wakala* fee	Share of investment profits	Performance fee

Figure 12.2   Financial Flows in the Pure *Wakala* and Hybrid Models

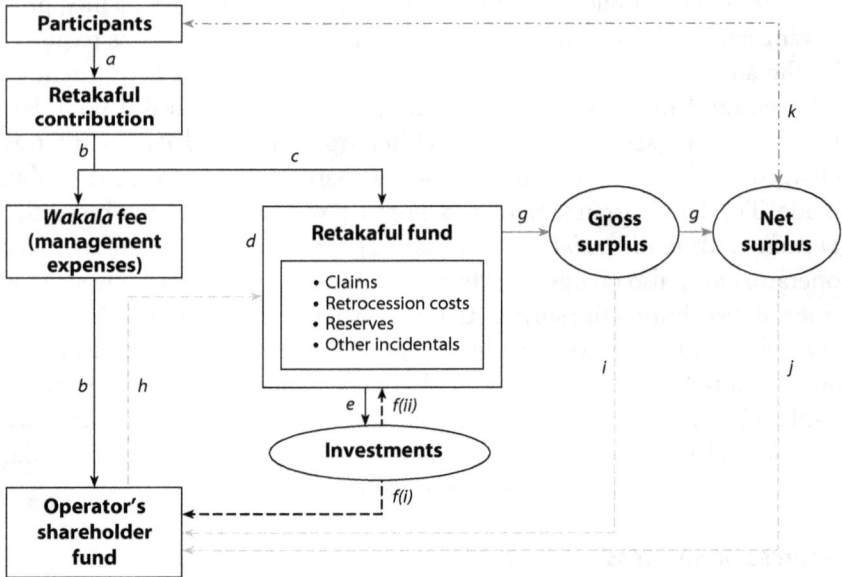

Note: The model is initially applied to the general or non-life proportional and nonproportional retakaful product lines. a = participants' pay contribution; b = *wakala* fees for retakaful operator (shareholders' fund) for services rendered in managing the underwriting activities of the retakaful fund; c = allocation to retakaful fund net of *wakala* fee; d = management of retakaful fund that includes retrocession costs, claims settlement, reserves (claims that are outstanding or incurred but not reported), incidental costs such as exchange rate differentials, credit control and bad debts, receipt of profits from investment of funds, and calls for *qard al hasan* (if applicable); e = investment of investible retakaful fund; $f(i)$ = *wakala* fees on investible fund of the retakaful fund or share of investment profits (*mudharaba*) under hybrid; $f(ii)$ = investment profits returned to retakaful fund; g = surplus in retakaful fund; h = *qard* to the retakaful fund, if necessary, from shareholders' funds of retakaful operator; i = recovery of *qard* in part or in full by retakaful operator from the surplus (where applicable); j = performance fee charged to net surplus (where applicable); and k = surplus distributed to participants, where applicable. Under k, surpluses may not be returned to participants and instead flow back to the retakaful fund to strengthen the reserves and integrity of the fund. This is due to the high volatility of the two product lines.

in the portfolio are not *halal* in their core activities and, in fact, may contravene sharia. Examples of such risks are gaming premises and liquor outlets. Retakaful operators are not in a position to know all of the risks included in the portfolio. The absence of a sharia governance mechanism in the conventional setup to ensure that the risks written are sharia compliant only makes the argument stronger. With regard to the ad hoc facultative transaction, a retakaful operator is in a position to verify the *halal* status of each risk offered. The disagreement comes when the up-front contract issued by the conventional insurer is not sharia compliant in nature. Some operators, with the agreement of their SAB, have covered *halal* risks from conventional sources by imposing certain subjectivity in their acceptance contract. Such acceptance is usually limited to faculta-tive transactions, where every risk is considered on its own merits. This stance helps to uphold the *maslaha umma* (general good of the public), especially in countries with a significant Muslim-minority population, but no takaful companies. It accommodates the wishes of the insured (Muslim community) to use a component of the sharia-compliant chain for the reinsurance of their properties, religious or otherwise. Declining is tantamount to abandoning the needs of the Muslim community and fail-ing to propagate the good takaful-retakaful concept; accepting it is tanta-mount to encouraging dealing with questionable sources. This may appear as a judgment call for the operator's SAB, but it is an issue the sharia fraternity needs to address at the global level, especially in coun-tries such as China, France, Germany, India, and the United Kingdom, which have a significant Muslim-minority community and no takaful operators. Similar considerations need to be looked into for life or family retakaful, whereby the risk insured—the life of a human—belongs to Allah and thus the *halal*-ness is built into it. Some regulators have allowed retakaful operators to conduct such transactions.

The *qard al hassan* (benevolent loan or interest-free loan) is a unique concept being practiced by the retakaful industry. It is an organized mechanism, either due to regulatory requirement or out of practicality. Mutuality, the underlying concept in takaful-retakaful operations, implies that losses incurred by any participants of a taka-ful-retakaful pool will be compensated from the pool; in cases where there are insufficient funds in the pool, participants are required to make good on the shortfall, and retakaful operators will collect cash on behalf of the pool. This may not be practical due to the large number of participants residing in multiple jurisdictions. Other impediments may come into play as well, and this makes the collection of additional or top-up contribution very difficult. Such difficulties affect the effi-ciency with which retakaful operators service claims.

The challenge is to establish the amount that would trigger the demand for *qard*. Should it be based on actual deficit (actual claims exceed the risk fund) in the retakaful fund or based on a technical deficit arising from the need to create or maintain reserves for outstanding claims, claims incurred but not reported, and so forth? If viewed from the perspective of conventional insurance, it should be based on a technical deficit, while from the takaful angle, it should be based on an actual deficit. Another issue is whether a certain amount of shareholder funds should be put aside or assigned as reserves, thus allowing the operator to enjoy the investment profit accruing to it, or whether it should be an outright transfer in which the amount needed to cover the deficit is immediately transferred to the retakaful fund. By virtue of fund separation, the accrued investment profit will stay in the retakaful fund and not be available to the operators. This leads to the issue of probable impairment in case of nonrecovery of *qard* (due to a continuous technical deficit). Under the sharia environment, the loan was granted and has to be repaid, regardless of duration.

Surplus Distribution

Under the takaful-retakaful concept, the pool participants are owners of the risk fund, while the operator is the risk and fund manager of the pool. Being owners, participants are entitled to a share of the underwriting surplus if they are available for distribution. Technically, all participants, regardless of performance of the business they bring to the pool, are entitled to the surplus in proportion to their contribution. Some argue that distribution to all is unfair to participants that have produced better results. Retakaful operators differ in their philosophy toward surplus and thus have their own ways of "developing" fairness to participants and the pools they manage. For example, some operators may plow any surplus back into the pool to build up reserves in the risk fund. Some may only distribute surplus to participants with positive results and apply the "loss carry forward" approach to participants with negative results until such time as their surplus can cover the previous losses.

Retakaful Contract Terms

Contract terms vary among operators and markets, which gives rise to gaps or overlaps in the interpretation of terms. As the terms and conditions are based on conventional reinsurance contracts, two main issues need to be addressed. The first is the issue of ex gratia claims: claims that, for whatever reason, are outside the scope of cover. A conventional insurer settles such claims on commercial grounds when the affected clients are considered important to them. It is a unilateral decision, and there should be no controversy, as the funds belong to them. Under retakaful, the operator may need to seek permission of all participants with regard to the treatment or settlement of nonadmitted claims. To ensure that claims are handled smoothly and that retakaful is on par with conventional reinsurance, contract terms should allow operators to exercise their own good judgment.

Delayed Remittance of Premium or Contribution

Under a proportional treaty arrangement, retakaful provides back-to-back cover as per its shared proportion throughout duration of the contract. In line with conventional practice, the retakaful premium or contribution is remitted by the takaful operator between five to six months after treaty inception, although the operators concerned have already collected the amount from their retail participants at the inception of cover. Such an arrangement is intended to simplify administration of the treaty program. The retakaful operator is then at a financial disadvantage. During the period (six months), it cannot collect the *wakala* fee. Despite having no fund to manage during that period, the shareholders' fund is used as *qard* to pay for the retrotakaful costs and to pay up-front cash calls on large claims. This is in addition to the management expenses it has to incur. The retakaful operator therefore loses investment opportunities both from the contribution that it should have received and from the amount of the shareholders' fund that it has extended as *qard*. The arrangement favors the takaful operator, which usually has collected the contribution and *wakala* fee and earned investment income. At the same time, any large claims incurred are funded largely by the retakaful operator. It is suggested that a more balanced arrangement using certain forms of deposit payable within a shorter time frame be promoted to assist the retakaful operator. The sharia transaction principle that can be considered is that of *urbun* (advance deposit), whereby a certain percentage of expected contributions is paid up-front and reconciled later, when the actual figures are known.

There are opposing views in the nonproportional or excess-of-loss treaty transactions. On the one hand, they are considered a risk-sharing concept; on the other, they are considered a contract of exchange in the form of a sale and purchase transaction. Proponents of risk sharing are of the view that the pooling of various nonproportional treaties is actually the sharing of similar portfolios under one retakaful pool. Believers in the contract of exchange view it as a series of individual transactions. Under this interpretation, contributions and claims are not shared proportionally as practiced under the proportional retakaful arrangement. In effect, the retakaful operator sells the cover to the takaful operator in consideration of the contribution or premium. The cover and premium are uncertain, as the actual amounts of both are tied to the occurrence of uncertain events (peril or hazard). The sharia fraternity needs to deliberate and provide a ruling, as nonproportional treaty arrangements are cost-effective and efficient mechanisms for managing risk and strengthening and protecting the operator's pool.

The *qard* mechanism, while helping to smooth a retakaful operation, also creates a potential financial burden for the retakaful operator, as more *qard* will be required to cover any deficit in the pool arising from regulatory requirements, especially with regard to capital adequacy, solvency margin, and technical reserves. In case of a continuous deficit, there is no certainty that the operator will recover the *qard*. One option is to write off the *qard* amount completely if it remains unrecoverable for a defined period. However, this may undermine the risk-sharing concept of retakaful, as writing off *qard* is tantamount to a transfer of risk, a concept similar to conventional reinsurance.

Other operational issues external to the operation are worth mentioning. As retakaful is similar to the insurance industry, it is more often subjected to regulations similar to those imposed on insurance and reinsurance companies. This is to make sure that the management and financial positions of takaful operators remain in good condition and that their obligations to customers are honored accordingly. Additional costs are also incurred to ensure that the sharia governance structure and mechanisms are in place. Due to the industry's young age, competition in the marketplace is high. Operators need to look beyond religious and ethical appeal if they are to penetrate the market, which is already crowded with conventional players. Like reinsurance, retakaful is an international business. It is common for local authorities to require operators under their jurisdiction to obtain retakaful capacity only from securities with an "A" rating for financial strength. For example, the regulatory authority of an important emerging takaful market requires A-category securities and limits B-rated ones to a maximum 20 percent of an operator's treaty program. This erects an entry barrier for non-A-rated retakaful companies, which could stifle their growth. As many operators are new start-ups with short trading histories, it is unlikely that rating agencies will give them high ratings. These companies are thus relegated to a follower position and have to use the terms, conditions, and pricing developed by the A-rated leaders to suit their own business agenda, which stifles the intellectual development of the non-A-rated companies.

Critical mass is important for takaful and retakaful operators. The law of large numbers and sufficient retrotakaful protection would ensure that losses remain sustainable by the retakaful fund. Without a reasonable critical mass, the fund is subject to volatile results, swinging from marginal surplus to significant deficits. Surplus is marginal, as previous years' positive performance is usually rewarded with lower contribution rates being charged on renewal, which technically means "higher exposure at lower capability." Losses can easily occur even to good risks for reasons beyond the comprehension of underwriters. The 2004 Indian Ocean tsunami and the 2011 Thailand flood are good examples. Previous tsunamis were localized, while the 2004 event crossed many countries from Southeast Asia to Africa. From an insurance underwriting perspective, Thailand is not a natural catastrophe market, but the 2011 incident incurred heavy losses to the reinsurance and retakaful industries worldwide.

Prospects

The growth and future of retakaful depend on three factors: (a) demand for its capacity and services by retail takaful companies, allowing the attainment of critical mass; (b) commitment of practitioners of Islamic finance to ensure that the supply chain of the industry remains as sharia compliant as possible; and (c) the financial performance of the operating models (*wakala* or hybrid models) used by operators.

In general, retail operators have managed to reach the stage where takaful is considered a viable alternative to conventional insurance. The profile of risks underwritten by companies (stage one to four) is characterized by low insured value and simple trade activities. The retakaful protection programs that are required for such a risk profile will be in accordance with the business plan of individual retail operators. The demand for retakaful will be limited to underwriting of such risks, with priority placed on the organic growth in volume of top-line contributions.

After the subprime crisis that shook the conventional finance sector, Islamic finance has grown in stature, and many Western economies are looking into Islamic finance as an alternative. Many infrastructure and industrial projects are financed via Islamic financial instruments. The airline industry is using *ijara* (leasing) to finance aircrafts. Many corporations and governments issue *sukuks* (Islamic bonds). Ideally, to complete the sharia-compliance chain, the underlying assets should be insured by takaful and reinsured by retakaful operators. If takaful operations are not prepared to underwrite such risks, there will be leakage back to the conventional market, and the retakaful industry will be deprived of another potential channel for growth. The sharia advisory boards of Islamic financial institutions, which are responsible for these instruments, should make it mandatory to observe the sharia-compliant supply chain as much and as long as possible.

These two factors are external to the retakaful operation. Currently, the mind-set and hence the approaches of regulators, professional bodies, and standard-setting organizations are strongly conventional in nature. Retakaful operators are obliged to observe the requirements set, although some may have negative impacts on an operator's financial performance. One area of concern is the compulsory giving of *qard* or loan to cover technical deficits in the retakaful fund. Such deficits include outstanding claim provisions, reserves for claims insured but not reported, and unearned contribution reserves. There is a high degree of uncertainty in the calculation of these provisions. Logically, *qard* should be given only for actual deficits (when the risk fund is insufficient to meet actual claims). Such a mandatory requirement puts pressure on the shareholders' fund of retakaful operators. If the deficit prolongs, there will be strain on shareholders and no surplus to distribute to participants. In addition, shareholder value will erode. Retakaful thus will lose its attractiveness for potential investors and its value (in the form of surplus distribution) for participants.

Relevant parties need to address this predicament, as it has both sharia and commercial implications.

Conclusion

Elements of sharia compliance are the main factors differentiating between a retakaful and a conventional reinsurance operation. Sharia advocacy should remain paramount among industry stakeholders ahead of commercial returns. Islamic financial institutions must seek to enhance knowledge of Islamic finance so as to stimulate a proper approach to the enhancement and development of products and services. A lack of such knowledge stunts the intellectual and operational development of the industry, as some sharia issues could be side-stepped. Failure to emphasize the need for knowledge of Islamic finance will see practitioners falling back to conventional practices. This would not be good for the future of retakaful or Islamic finance and economics.

Notes

1. US$1 = RM 3.00. Malaysia's currency is the ringgit.
2. The sharia maxim with regard to *dharura*—"Necessities justify that which may be unlawful"—is often interpreted to mean situations that pose considerable danger to one's life, intellect, or wealth.

CHAPTER 13

Regulatory Framework

Serap O. Gönülal

This chapter discusses the regulation of takaful. Regulations have as their primary goal protecting the interests of participants and ensuring their equitable treatment. Regulations alone cannot ensure that this is achieved, and, as such, regulators normally require that insurers and takaful companies have a strong focus on corporate governance. Regulations also promote reliability, solvency, and technical soundness of takaful operators as well as competitive markets (Odierno 2010). This chapter begins with a discussion of the unique aspects of takaful that regulators need to consider. This is followed by consideration of the need for regulations to look at substance over form when comparing takaful to conventional insurance. The challenge of setting solvency standards is elaborated, as well as the reasonable expectations of shareholders and participants and ancillary concerns. Finally, regulations in Malaysia and Bahrain are compared and contrasted.

Unique Aspects of Takaful

Takaful presents a unique challenge to insurance regulators, not least because of its "hybrid" nature (figure 13.1).

As shown in figure 13.1, takaful is both a proprietary setup, driven by shareholders' desires to maximize their return on capital, and a risk-pooling

Figure 13.1   Hybrid Nature of Takaful

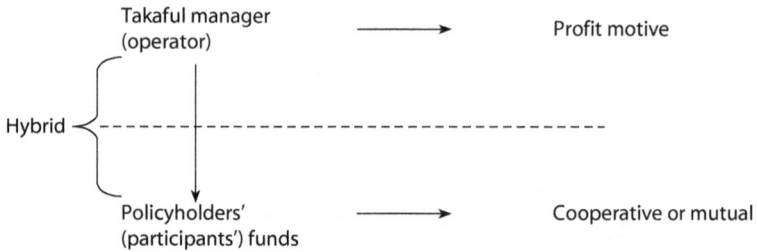

policyholders' fund (policyholders are called "participants" to recognize their "membership" in the fund). This hybrid nature is what makes regulating takaful and ensuring proper corporate governance so challenging. Regulators need to determine the extent to which takaful should be regulated, as for any other proprietary setup, and the extent to which it should be required to incorporate specific cooperative or mutual practices, such as giving participants a say in how the operations are run. Considering the unique nature of takaful, there may be a need for a participants' advocate to ensure that the rights of participants are being met. Alternatively, the regulator may need to take on this role as part of its mandate.

Another challenge is the need to satisfy two "regulators": the insurance regulator and sharia law. However, the sharia law applicable to takaful is general in nature—that is, the same laws apply to dealings and transactions in all business matters (termed *muamalat*), while insurance regulations are specifically for the conduct of insurance and insurance-like businesses. What makes resolving this challenge all the more important is that insurance is one of the few businesses where contributions (premiums) are paid before services (claims) are rendered; regulations are required to ensure that insurers will honor their obligations.

With the unique setup of takaful, the issue of fairness also has unique elements and considerations. Takaful is built on fairness and transparency. Regulators play an important role in determining whether the sharia advisory board (SAB) of the takaful company has the responsibility to ensure fairness in all aspects of its operations. This is perhaps an unfair expectation, even if the SAB has the ability to do so, which is very unlikely considering the myriad technical aspects in takaful and the complexity of managing a takaful company. Perhaps the regulator should exercise this responsibility through regulatory guidelines. In any case, this is an important consideration in takaful and one the regulator will need to consider carefully.

Fairness also comes into play in determining who is entitled to any surplus arising in the participants' funds. This will determine whether surplus should be shared with the operator, the participants, or both and what surplus-sharing regulations are necessary. Related to this are issues such as whether differing risks should be allowed to be held in the same risk fund, such as motor and fire risks, as the expected claims volatility (and therefore surplus experience) of these risks is likely to be very different. The sharing of unexpected losses is a key feature of takaful, whereas subsidization of one group of participants by another is not (Odierno 2007).

Another complication is that takaful coexists with conventional insurance in most jurisdictions. Furthermore, it is not unusual to find that a conventional insurer has a takaful operation within its group. Where these two coexist in a particular jurisdiction, the regulator could grant insurers an option to choose one of them. Under free-market conditions, consumers should have the option to choose among the various instruments available. Adequate information for potential consumers is desirable, especially where there is a need to promote takaful. Any preferential treatment is risky, as regulatory arbitrage within a group with both takaful and conventional insurance could have unintended consequences. Also, due to the complicated nature of insurance in general and takaful in particular, even if balanced treatment is desired, this is easier said than done.

Reference should be made to the International Association of Insurance Supervisors set of Insurance Core Principles (ICPs) and how these apply to regulating takaful. ICP1 states that the principal objectives of insurance supervision should be clearly defined. Thus, when regulating takaful, the regulator has to decide if it will be signing off on the sharia compliance of a takaful operator. In jurisdictions where the regulator provides explicit regulations for takaful, the implication is that the regulator has taken on this role. However, in jurisdictions where takaful is expected to follow conventional insurance regulations, ensuring sharia compliance is not an objective.

ICP5 on the suitability of persons notes that the significant owners, board members, senior management, and key persons in control functions of an insurer are fit and proper to fulfill their roles. Does this extend to knowledge of the sharia? The Accounting and Auditing Organization for Islamic Financial Institutions (AAOIFI) has ruled that compliance with the sharia is the responsibility of management (AAOIFI 2004). If management of a takaful operation is not familiar with the sharia, does this imply noncompliance with ICP5?

ICP7 on corporate governance notes that the corporate governance framework recognizes and protects the rights of all interested parties. The supervisory authority requires compliance with all applicable corporate governance standards. This can be complicated in takaful, as the corporate governance of technical and sharia issues can be intertwined in many cases. Here, there is the risk that issues will be mistakenly considered purely technical and not brought before the sharia board for consideration. Alternatively, potential technical complications may be overlooked before sharia decisions are made. Ultimately, though, given the range of interpretation in some aspects of sharia law, decisions of the takaful operators' SAB should not be allowed to override the regulations in a country. Where there is a conflict, the takaful regulator should refer to its own sharia advisers, where this is provided for in the regulations.

ICP8 on internal control states that the supervisory authority should require insurers to have in place internal controls that are adequate for the nature and scale of the business. The oversight and reporting systems allow the board and management to monitor and control the operations. This needs to be extended to sharia controls and audits.

ICP18 on intermediaries states that the supervisory authority should set and enforce requirements, directly or through the supervision of insurers, to ensure that intermediaries conduct business in a professional and transparent manner. This includes the need for intermediaries to have a basic knowledge of the sharia as it applies to takaful (Odierno 2010).

Substance over Form

At the outset, it is important to define takaful clearly and distinctly over conventional insurance. If separate regulations are to apply, there is the risk of "false labeling," where in form they are supposed to differ, but in substance they are the same.

The important consideration is whether the regulations of the country should allow takaful "windows," which are a means through which conventional insurance companies can sell or distribute takaful products. These are notional takaful products, meaning that they can work when the company is ongoing, but will likely fail to conform to sharia should the company wind up. The advantage of takaful windows is that they allow takaful products to be launched quickly and at minimal cost. The takaful window rides on the existing infrastructure of the conventional insurance company and can ensure that the venture will be profitable to shareholders from day one. Allowing takaful windows is one way to fast-track the introduction and development of takaful.

Ultimately, though, regulations will need to manage through substance rather than form. When a product is called "takaful," it is not necessarily an arrangement where all risks are only pooled among participants. The takaful operator usually also takes on risk, so the question is, what are these risks, which party is ultimately responsible for them, and to what extent are they responsible? Where takaful contracts are seen to transfer some risks to the shareholders, the appropriate solvency capital from the shareholders will need to be in place, even if, from the perspective of takaful, the insurance risk is minimal.

The Challenge of Setting Solvency Standards for Takaful

Very few new cooperative or mutual insurers are being set up in the world today. This has a lot to do with the regulators' need for solvency capital at the outset of the operation. Those mutual insurers that currently exist in Europe face an uncertain future with the imminent introduction of Solvency II, which has no separate provisions for them. By definition, the capital of a mutual insurer comes from its policyholders' undistributed profits. A brand new setup has no such retained profits.

In takaful, the shareholders are expected to provide the initial capital to finance the business (capital is used to meet the initial expense over-runs and the necessary initial regulatory capital and solvency margin), but ultimately the participants (that is, policyholders) are expected to build up the necessary solvency capital. This raises interesting dilemmas with regard to participants' reasonable expectations and intergenerational equity among participants.

The International Financial Services Board (IFSB) has a standard in place with regard to solvency requirements for takaful (IFSB 2010). It draws heavily on Solvency II in terms of how the basic solvency structure is determined. The standard envisages separate ring-fenced shareholders' and policyholders' funds, where each fund would need to have sufficient assets to meet its solvency obligations, but with an assumption that the shareholders would be obliged to extend a loan to the policyholders' fund should it experience a shortfall. Over time, this means that surpluses would be accumulated in the policyholders' account. For this to happen, the takaful policies would need to be priced at more than "best estimate." As demonstrated in an earlier chapter, under a best-estimate scenario, no surplus can be expected to accumulate, and financial support is likely be required in any given year. The standard is silent on how takaful products will be priced and how equitability among generations of policyholders will be assured; for example, when surpluses are retained to build up the solvency margin rather than returned to policyholders, the contributing policyholders will be effectively financing future policyholders.

Any solvency standard must be explicit. The solvency capital required should be clearly defined for each risk. This has to do with the need to define which stakeholder(s) is responsible for the risk so that the solvency capital can be allocated appropriately. How liability is actuarially determined must also be clearly specified so that free surplus can be determined on a consistent basis. These decisions are especially important in takaful, as "surplus" can be distributable to participants (and sometimes to shareholders as well) on a regular basis.

Regulating solvency in takaful will likely be heavily debated for quite some time. There is the potential here for the regulator to introduce creative solutions to these issues. For instance, participants could be asked to pay an additional contribution to cover their own portion of the solvency margin. Once the participants leave the fund, this contribution can be returned to them (with accruing investment income) when the actuary signs off that it is prudent to do so. This would allow takaful to avoid having the operator hold solvency margins related to the risk fund, as, by right, the operator is managing, rather than taking on, risk.

Shareholders' and Participants' Reasonable Expectations

The success of modern takaful depends on the presence of shareholders with capital willing to invest in the venture. Implementing takaful as a pure mutual, though aesthetically desirable from the sharia perspective, is probably not feasible under the modern regulatory framework, as shareholders would be allowed to earn a fair return on capital. Nevertheless, regulations could encourage the growth of takaful by allow-ing a pure mutual to grow (initially) without the burden of regulatory capital, either through a temporary operator (shareholders) or through government assistance. This would likely be a low-cost operation, as there would be no need to satisfy shareholders' profit requirements; thus, it would be able to provide coverage in underserved areas such as microfinance (microtakaful).

Unnecessary and punitive capital requirements can either discourage investment in takaful or result in the takaful operator "short-changing" the participants. Ultimately, the challenge is to ensure that the interests of shareholders and participants are aligned. The alternative is a strong regulatory framework. Such a framework may be effective in the short term, but probably not in the long term for the industry as a whole unless accompanied by steps to incentivize managers to strive for the long-term sustainability of the business.

Managing participants' expectations is fundamental to managing takaful. There are two extremes to this. In some jurisdictions, takaful management tends to be very lenient when handling claims. This could be the result of weak internal controls and a perception by some in management that takaful is akin to a charity. The point that has been missed with this approach is that, by being lenient on claims, participants who do not make a claim and are usually in the majority will be disadvantaged. The other extreme is where a takaful operator is driven to underprice the risk (resulting in claims that exceed the risk contribution or premium) on the misguided assumption that participants alone bear the claims risk. This can be the result of management's literal interpretation of the contract between the operator and the participants. Under certain takaful contracts, the operator collects a fee based on a percentage of contributions (premiums). Thus the higher the volume of premiums, the higher the total fees collected and the more "profits" the shareholders make. In some instances, the fee is set too high as a percentage of contributions collected. The problem, then, is that the remaining contributions net of fees are insufficient to cover claims, resulting in perpetual deficits in the takaful funds. Given that surplus is usually distributed to participants to promote takaful, participants are likely to be disappointed, as no surplus will be forthcoming and their future claims will be imperiled due to creeping insolvency. Regulations are required to manage this risk. The risk is highest for property and casualty takaful and, in particular, for personal lines, where competition among takaful and insurers can be intense.

Claims volatility is part and parcel of insurance, and takaful is not spared such volatility. The level of volatility varies by type of risk insured and can be due to either volatility in claims frequency or volatility in claims severity. Although retakaful (sharia-compliant reinsurance) can assist greatly in managing claims volatility, the possibility of a deficit in a takaful fund cannot be ruled out. The question is, how should such deficits be funded?

The practice in the more regulated jurisdictions is to require the takaful operator to extend a temporary loan (termed *qard*) to the takaful fund when there are deficits in it. This loan would be a first charge on future surplus until it has been fully repaid. Regulations would need to be in place to mandate such funding and ensure participants' expectations that claims submitted will be honored. The treatment of such *qard* from the accounting perspective has been subject to much debate, especially with regard to the ability of a "loan" to eliminate deficits. Regulations need to tread carefully here, as unintended consequences of regulations on *qard* could include a takaful operator selling unprofitable business, collecting its fees, and simply providing a loan for the resulting deficits. The takaful operator will appear profitable, masking the underlying problems of the fund (Odierno 2009).

Ancillary Considerations

Takaful does not exist in a vacuum. Issues apart from regulations also have to be considered. There are accounting standards to adhere to, tax to pay, and a lack of diversity of sharia-compliant asset classes to address.

Accounting for takaful is an important consideration as accounting principles require the recognition of surplus or deficit in a manner that represents the interests of the shareholders and participants present during the accounting period. Regulators need to understand the implications of regulations and accounting standards for how assets are valued and how surplus and profits are computed and distributed.

Tax is also an important consideration. The Muslim tithe (called *zakat*) may also be payable, so how shareholders and participants are taxed needs to be considered when regulations on valuation of actuarial liabilities are decided. Participants and shareholders of takaful companies should not be disadvantaged due to the hybrid nature of takaful. Tax as it applies to sharia-compliant asset classes is also important. This is especially true when considering the asset-backed nature of *sukuks* (sharia-compliant bonds), where additional stamp duty and taxes can apply simply because of how such instruments are structured relative to conventional bonds.

As mentioned earlier, in takaful, just like insurance, premiums are due before service is rendered. This means that premiums need to be invested in suitable sharia-compliant assets. For contingent benefits where claims can happen at any time, investing in volatile assets like equities is not advisable. Investment in equities would be appropriate for the savings portion of any family (life) takaful product, where the duration of the policy is long term. Thus, it is important that investment risk—in particular, how the value of assets interact with how contingent liabilities are valued—should be considered when setting solvency requirements. Unfortunately, there is a dearth of sharia-compliant asset classes. In particular, other than in Malaysia, *sukuks* with adequate spread (for diversification) and depth (for liquidity) are not available.

Contrast in Regulating Takaful

When regulating takaful is discussed, the route that Malaysia has taken will certainly take prominence. Takaful's growth in Malaysia is only one part of the general growth of Islamic finance in the country. Malaysia has a vibrant Islamic banking and capital market, with by far the largest *sukuk* market anywhere in the world. It also has a large (but not large enough) base of human capital trained in Islamic finance, including takaful. Thus, using Malaysia as a standard as to how takaful should be regulated may not be appropriate for a country only now venturing into takaful. The human capital engaged in takaful has been drawn heavily from people who had experience managing conventional insurance before coming into takaful. Furthermore, the development of Islamic finance, including takaful, had the strong backing of government. This means that Islamic finance in general has benefited from the patronage of the government and the public sector.

From the outset, Malaysia has had a separate law regulating takaful. This has meant that takaful windows have never been allowed. Businesses, including takaful, in Malaysia are regulated by secular law, largely modeled from the laws put in place by the last colonial power before independence in 1957. Furthermore, Malaysia's regulation of takaful has taken place in an environment where the regulation of conventional insurance has gradually been upgraded to a risk-based approach.

Initially, like many developing countries, insurance regulation was "rules based." Rules covered how insurance contingent liabilities should be valued and how much could be invested in which asset classes. Solvency capital was calculated simply as a percentage of premium or liabilities. The insurance industry adapted slowly to the introduction of risk-based solvency capital by changing its product mix and increasing its capital base.

In order to keep up with developments in conventional insurance, takaful has had to "grow up" quickly. The transition from rules-based to risk-based conventional insurance took more than 10 years. Takaful is going through that same process in about a third of the time. Recently, many takaful operators have had to change their operating model, as the sharing of fees and surplus between operators and participants changed with the introduction of a takaful operating framework for the industry (Bank Negara Malaysia 2012b). The number of takaful operators has also grown, from only one in 1984 to 12 currently.

Takaful regulations are only one part of the "law" governing takaful. Equally important is that takaful must be sharia complaint. It is not unusual to have differences of opinion among scholars. What must be avoided is confusion among the public as to what is and is not sharia compliant. Recognizing the diversity in the implementation of sharia law, Malaysia also introduced the concept of a supreme sharia advisory board at the regulators' level, which by law has the last say in terms of sharia matters involving Islamic banking and takaful (Bank Negara Malaysia 2012c).

In contrast to Malaysia, Bahrain's conventional and takaful industry remains rules based. Regulations are set out in rulebooks that provide guidance as to how insurance and takaful liabilities should be valued (Central Bank of Bahrain 2011). There is built-in flexibility, though, as other methodologies can be acceptable, if justified. As in Malaysia, takaful windows are not allowed. However, the regulation says that only the *wakala* (agency) contract can be used in takaful, with a subsidiary *mudharaba* contract for assets being invested. This is currently under review by the regulators. In Bahrain, there is no explicit guidance as to how takaful products should be priced. Thus, operators are free to set their fee under the *wakala* contract, and this has been exploited by some takaful companies, with little consideration for whether the premium net of *wakala* fees is sufficient to pay claims. This has led to deficits in takaful funds, while the operator is profitable. Intense competition among takaful companies (and with conventional insurers) has also led to underpricing, which has not helped the long-term viability of the takaful industry.

Table 13.1 summarizes the approach to regulation by general themes. Regulating insurance and takaful is a complicated subject and very dependent on the stage of development of the industry in the country. Where insurance products are simple, a simplified basis of regulation can be sufficient and cost-effective. Unfortunately, takaful is anything but simple, and its hybrid nature usually requires greater thought as to what should apply. Even Malaysia, with its relatively advanced regulatory environment, is still struggling with the question of how solvency capital should be structured in a takaful setup.

Table 13.1 Structure of Takaful in Malaysia and Bahrain

Regulation	Malaysia	Bahrain
Standardized takaful model or contracts	There is no restriction on the takaful models to be applied, but any "non-standard" contract requires approval of the regulators (Bank Negara Malaysia 2012a). In addition, a takaful operating framework sets the maximum fees and charges that the operator is allowed to charge the participants and the maximum share of surplus the operator can take for itself. The framework also states that all takaful companies in Malaysia must use retakaful instead of reinsurance.	Yes. *Wakala* is the standard takaful model. All takaful firms licensed in Bahrain must organize and operate their business according to the *wakala* model. Specifically, in exchange for the provision of management services, the shareholders of the takaful firm are allowed to charge a specific consideration (a *wakala* fee). For the insurance assets invested on behalf of takaful funds, the takaful operator can use the *mudaraba* model and, under this contract, receive a set percentage of the profits generated from the investment portfolio. In early 2012 Central Bank of Bahrain was reportedly in the process of changing the standard takaful model.
Regulatory requirement to treat customers fairly	Yes. The board of directors is responsible for ensuring that its products are appropriate for its targeted market.	Yes. The insurance code of practice is made up of overarching principles applied throughout the customer relationship.
Requirement for certification of pricing of family (life) takaful products by an actuary	Yes. This requirement ensures that the product is priced correctly before it is sold to the public. Those operators who are deemed to be sufficiently prepared are allowed to practice "Launch and File," meaning that there is no need to wait for regulatory approval before launching.	No. However, with a requirement for an annual actuarial valuation, any insufficiency in pricing results in actuarial deficits. Indirectly this means that family takaful products require actuarial certification.

(continued next page)

Table 13.1 *(continued)*

Regulation	Malaysia	Bahrain
Requirement for a sharia certification on its operation	Yes. Every takaful company must have a sharia board consisting of at least five members, at least three of which must be qualified to advise on sharia matters. In addition, a supreme sharia board at the regulators' level has the power to overrule the decisions made by the takaful operator's sharia board.	Yes. Bahrain requires that takaful operators in its jurisdiction adhere to the sharia standards issued by the AAOIFI, which is based in Bahrain.
Solvency requirements	Yes. A risk-based solvency requirement has been proposed and is awaiting finalization. The initial proposal sees a significant proportion of the solvency capital being required of the operator.	Yes. Primarily formula-driven basis. A requirement that solvency capital has to be maintained in the takaful fund has contributed to difficulty in distributing any surplus to participants.
Regulation for the payment of a *qard* in case of a deficit in the takaful fund	Yes. In case of a deficit in the takaful fund, whether due to insufficient money to pay claims or a technical valuation strain, the operator is obliged to pay a *qard* to the takaful fund.	Yes. Even for solvency capital, as it is mandated that solvency capital has to be maintained in the takaful fund. There is an exemption from this requirement in the first year of a takaful operation in the Rule Book, which we understand has been extended to the initial five years of the takaful operation.

Conclusion

Regulating takaful is different from regulating insurance. This stems from the hybrid nature of its setup. A risk-based approach to regulating takaful is desirable, but a well-thought-out, rules-based regulation may suffice initially. An important early decision for the regulators is whether to allow takaful windows. Sharia is flexible on this only if regulations preclude the setup of stand-alone takaful companies.

To avoid confusion among the Muslim population, there should be a consensus among sharia scholars in the country as to how takaful is implemented. While in Malaysia, the majority of Muslims are happy for the government to decide what sharia-compliant means, in other jurisdictions this may not be possible and an early consensus among local scholars on how takaful is structured is important.

The message that regulating takaful should look at substance over form is important, as ultimately if risks are similar, then "branding" should not be a consideration when determining solvency capital requirements. Regulators should look for arbitrage opportunities between takaful and the insurance industry. For example, a similar product could require lower solvency capital if it were sold as takaful than if it were sold as a conventional product. Such arbitrage may harm the takaful industry over the long term if such lower solvency capital is not justified.

As takaful is new, there may be strategic reasons why regulations should initially favor it over conventional insurance. However, the associated risks that come with such a decision should be clearly understood and will require frequent reassessment.

References

AAOIFI (Accounting and Auditing Organization for Islamic Financial Institutions). 2004. "Governance Standard for Islamic Financial Institutions No. 1: Shari'a Supervisory Board; Appointment, Composition, and Report." In *Accounting, Auditing, and Governance Standards for Islamic Financial Institutions*. Manama: AAOIFI.

Bank Negara Malaysia. 2012a. "Guidelines on Introduction of New Products for Insurance Companies and Takaful Operators." Publication BNM/RH/GL 010-14, Prudential Financial Policy Department, Bank Negara Malaysia, February 13. http://www.bnm.gov.my.

———. 2012b. "Guidelines on Takaful Operational Framework." BNM/RH/GL 004-22. Islamic Banking and Takaful Department, Bank Negara Malaysia, February 13. http://www.bnm.gov.my.

————. 2012c. "Shariah Governance Framework for Islamic Financial Institutions." BNM/RH/GL_012_3, Islamic Banking and Takaful Department, Bank Negara Malaysia, February 13. http://www.bnm.gov.my.

Central Bank of Bahrain. 2011. "TA Takaful / Retakaful." In *Central Bank of Bahrain*. Vol. 3, *Insurance*. Central Bank of Bahrain, October 1. http://cbb.complinet.com/cbb/display/display.html?rbid=1822&element_id=2.

IFSB (Islamic Financial Services Board). 2010. "IFSB-11-Standard on Solvency Requirements for Takaful (Islamic Insurance) Undertakings." IFSB, December. http://www.ifsb.org.

Odierno, Hassan Scott P. 2007. "Achieving Common Standards in Takaful Regulations." *Middle East Insurance Review* (January): 71–72.

————. 2009. "Corporate Governance in Takaful." *Takaful Articles* 19 (November).

————. 2010. "Regulating Takaful." *Islamic Finance News*, April 21. http://www.islamicfinancenews.com.

www.ingramcontent.com/pod-product-compliance
Lightning Source LLC
Chambersburg PA
CBHW070309200326
41518CB00010B/1952

* 9 780821 397244 *